Welcome to My World

❖

By Charlie Vincent

Detroit Free Press

Edited by Tom Panzenhagen, with Bob Ellis and the Free Press sports copy desk.

Special thanks to Bill Collison, Jim Dwight, Andrew J. Hartley, Ken Kraemer, Tim Marcinkoski, Gene Myers and Steve Schrader.

Cover photo by Tony Spina

Illustrations by Keith Webb

Overall design by Wayne Kamidoi

Coordinator: Dave Robinson

Printed in USA on recycled paper

Detroit Free Press Inc. 1994
321 W. Lafayette Blvd.
Detroit, Michigan 48226

ISBN 0-937247-62-6

❖

To Lisa, Dixie, Chuck, Jack and Suzie.

Finally an answer to those years of asking:
"Where's Daddy?"

FOREWORD

THEY SAY a guy named Vincent cut off an ear for his art. I'm not sure what Charlie Vincent would cut off.

Got rid off that mustache, I know that much.

Charlie Vincent has a lot to give. He is so much better than that clown the Free Press used to have. I have nothing but good things to say about Charlie. People ask me all the time how Charlie compares to the best sports columnists in the country, and I always give the same answer: "Taller." He is one of the very best writers working in Detroit today, and, unlike Bob Talbert, he almost never writes about what he eats.

Charlie came north from Texas, where everyone called him Chorly. It was not his nickname. That's the way they talk down there. (It took me months to understand that when Charlie said he couldn't find a place to "pork my core," he meant park his car.) Anyhow, his coming to Detroit was a lucky break for Detroit. I forget how he got there. Possibly Wells Fargo.

I first met Charlie when he was covering the Pistons. This was back when somebody should have been covering the Pistons with six feet of dirt. Charlie got through this period in his life with, I believe, tact, wit and a flask of booze. The Pistons were bad back then. They weren't the Bad Boys. They weren't good enough to be bad. They were the worse boys.

Both Charlie and the Pistons survived and eventually became great at what they did.

Too bad only Charlie stayed that way.

For as long as I can remember, Charlie Vincent has been at the top of his game. He had so many areas of expertise. Baseball, for example. Charlie always knew when to bunt, when to steal and when to think Jack Morris was a jerk, which was usually. I guess Sparky Anderson said it best when he said: "I ain't never got nothing negative to say about Charlie Vincent, and I don't ain't never won't."

Charlie also was an authority on motor sports. (Hey, good town for it.) Me, I didn't know a Grand Prix from a LeSabre. I thought NASCAR was the astronauts. Charlie, he knew everything, from what the A.J. in A.J. Foyt stood for (I suspected Apple Juice) to what the latest improvements were for Renault and Ferrari, while I presumed each was still trying to get the letters of transit away from Humphrey Bogart. My first week in Detroit, Charlie asked if I cared to accompany him to Brooklyn to see the Michigan 500. I said: "Sure thing, pal, and maybe later we can go to the Bronx for the Ohio 500."

Working with Charlie Vincent was one of my greatest pleasures, which will give you some idea of the sheltered life I've led.

Charlie is smart, works hard and cares about people — in other words, not your average sports writer. He's a little bit bats and has plenty of balls. That makes a good columnist in my book, and also in his book, the one you are about to read. Reading Charlie Vincent on a regular basis is one of the things I miss most about living in Michigan — that and a great-looking woman who lives in Grosse Pointe.

I intend to read every word in this book, then negotiate the movie rights, with Harrison Ford as Charlie and little or no nudity.

There are many things to enjoy about Charlie Vincent: his common sense, his sense of humor, that really nice turtleneck he wears and that he almost never writes about college hockey. He has given you glorious accounts of the Tiger, Piston and Wolverine championships of the 1980s, just as he will give you an equally glorious account of the Lions' first Super Bowl championship in the mid- to late-21st century. Charlie can be charming, Charlie can leave you chortling, and Charlie can be the hardest-hitting individual in Detroit sports since that creep hired by Jeff Gillooly.

Enjoy the book. It's just like "the Bridges of Madison County," except without the bridges.

Mike Downey,
Los Angeles, California

TABLE OF CONTENTS

Slightly personal

CHAPTER 1

CHARLIE VINCENT

Garbage days

July 21, 1985

S ometimes home is an impossible place to grow up in.

In the place where you took your first faltering steps as an adult, there are those who will forever and always look upon you as someone just beyond puberty, an awkward bundle of arms and legs, long on dreams and short on common sense. At home you're more apt to be remembered for all the foolishness of your youth — things like getting the family car stuck in mud, then trying to tow it out by attaching a chain to the tail-pipe clamp — than for the accomplishments of your adult years.

I spent most of July deep in the heart of Texas, where I grew up, and where my parents still enjoy the sunshine of their autumn years, my dad on the golf course, my mom visiting neighbors of 40 years' standing.

I could hardly wait to tell them about my new job as a columnist — a challenge I had wanted for years.

"So," said my 80-year-old father on the day of arrival, "tell me about it. How often will you write?"

"Three times a week, Sunday for sure and probably Tuesday and Friday."

"Garbage days," he said.

"What?"

"Garbage days — our garbage is picked up on Tuesdays and Fridays. It'll make it easy to remember what days you're writing."

Unintentionally, with two words, my father had reduced my dream to rubbish.

Garbage days.

I'll never be able to sit before the blank screen of this computer without wondering if, in Victoria, Texas, my dad is thinking of my work as he carries out the garbage.

Respect is often hard to earn at home. Often we have to leave to earn acknowledgement. But just as often, we have to leave home to appreciate that it is a very special place. ❖

Gambling will get you

October 30, 1985

I know this guy, just an ordinary sort. But he likes to spice up his nights by trying to outguess a pal of his.

His pal is an athletic mathematician. A bookie.

His pal has a bundle of what used to be other people's money in his pocket this morning.

Some of it used to belong to my friend.

When I saw my friend the other morning, he was frowning.

"Those are the biggest bunch of choke artists I've ever seen," he said without bothering with "Hello."

"Geez, I don't know why they even bothered to take bats to the plate with them. The only guy on the team that had any life was Joaquin Andujar. He had more life than those other 23 slugs combined. What a bunch of deadbeats. I can't believe the way they played. Cripes sakes!"

My friend, it seems, had put a few bucks on the St. Louis Cardinals.

He was not happy with them.

"They're the biggest bunch of chokers in the history of baseball," he said. He didn't say it more than 12 or 15 times, though.

He was not happy with Don Denkinger, either. Denkinger is the umpire who missed a call at first base in the ninth inning Saturday night, keeping Kansas City's World Series hopes alive. He's the same guy who threw Andujar and Cardinals manager Whitey Herzog out of the game Sunday.

"Did you see that call he made Saturday?" my friend blustered, waving his arms and frowning.

"Hey, guys make mistakes. Even umpires," he was reminded.

"Not in the World Series, they don't. They're not supposed to. Geez!"

About that time a mutual friend showed up, smiling and cheerful.

"How about those Lions?" he said, pulling up a chair. "Weren't they something Sunday?"

"Hah!" said my friend, who had gone tap city over the weekend. "They're a bunch of fakers. They'll get theirs in Minnesota, just watch."

Seems he had put a few bucks on the Miami Dolphins, too. I sympathize with him.

I know what he's going through.

I don't deal with athletic mathematicians anymore, but I used to.

Long ago and far away, I made $150 a week and used it to house, clothe and feed a wife and four children. I used it for that until I was introduced to a neat guy named George. George took bets. Because I was weak, he took my money. That was his job. My family didn't eat as well as it had. They weren't dressed as well, either. A lot of nights, I'd toss around in bed worrying about how I'd pay bills.

I got to be well-known in a lot of loan company offices.

I couldn't pick a winner. It got so bad, I'd pick all the teams I was sure would win, then I'd bet against them. That didn't work, either. I still lost.

Betting is like drinking. Most people can handle it, keep it in perspective, use it as a diversion and nothing more. For most people it's a lark, a little light entertainment.

Some folks can't handle a drink.

Some can't handle a bet. That was me.

My game was football. I'd start the weekend betting on the University of Miami game because the Hurricanes always played on Friday nights. Then I'd bet a half-dozen or so games on Saturday. Sundays I'd pick one pro game and bet as much as I needed to catch up because it seemed I was always stuck by then. One Sunday, when I was making $150 a week, I bet $330 on the Dallas Cowboys. I won that bet — and $20 for the weekend. If the Cowboys had lost, I'd have had to come up with $610 for my bookie the next afternoon.

It was agonizing and it was gorgeous because I was one of those who cared only for the "sweat," the rush I got from putting more on the line than I could afford. Winning was a bonus. It didn't happen often.

That's why I don't bet anymore.

I was a loser. Like my pal, I blamed the players.

Why did they do this to me?

Why couldn't they catch the ball? Why couldn't they tackle?

How could the officials be so bad?

A long time ago, I somehow found the strength to stop gambling. I realized it was to me what alcohol is to some people: an addiction. If I made one bet, I would make another. If I lost, I'd have to try to catch up. If I won, I'd have to try to win more.

I was fortunate enough to quit without help.

Some people want to and can't. For them, help can start with a phone call.

Call Gamblers Anonymous. ❖

Christmas 1985

December 24, 1985

I never met Amy Yeast, but I've thought about her a lot the last couple of days.

Amy Yeast's parents buried her Monday afternoon in Battle Creek. She was 21.

Friday night, five days before Christmas, she was selling programs at the NCAA women's volleyball semifinals in Kalamazoo. Saturday morning, Kayla Skelly, her roommate, found her sprawled across her bed, struggling to breathe. Skelly, who has been accepted into Wayne State University's medical school and is trained in cardiopulmonary resuscitation, tried to revive her friend after calling paramedics. But a couple of hours later, Yeast was pronounced dead at Bronson Methodist Hospital.

A spokesman for the Kalamazoo County sheriff's department said there was no apparent cause of death. And after a preliminary autopsy, a hospital spokeswoman said: "Cardiac arrest is all we could come up with."

I know only one person who knew Amy Yeast.

John Beatty is the sports information director at Western Michigan University, where Amy Yeast was a senior. He knew her for four years. He knew her as the best woman tennis player in the Mid-American Conference. And as a lot more.

He knew her as a bright, talented, caring young woman with a career and a lifetime ahead of her.

"I talked to her at the volleyball match," Beatty said. "She was helping out because a lot of students are gone for Christmas break. This was a total shock. She was very conscious of her health. She worked on conditioning. That's what makes this so hard to take."

Amy Yeast was the captain of WMU's women's tennis team, the only woman ever to win back-to-back No. 1 singles titles in the MAC. She was invited to the 1984 Olympic tennis tryouts. She was a B student. She was active in the Big Brothers and Big Sisters program. She was engaged to be married next summer to Todd Billingsley, a distance runner on Western's track team, and she hoped to test herself on the pro tennis tour, playing the likes of Martina Navratilova and Chris Evert Lloyd.

Instead she died, leaving dreams unfulfilled.

And I can't get her out of my mind.

Today and tomorrow are days we're taught from childhood to treasure. Christmas is bright ribbons and gaily colored paper and gifts from Mom and Dad and the grandparents. It's teddy bears and bicycles and clothes from Esprit and Guess and Calvin Klein. Swatches and LeSportsac. And checks from the in-laws.

It's one more sale at Highland Appliance. And a competing one at Fretter.

A glut of gifts. An orgy of the material.

And in this land of plenty, it seems, we're always left wanting more.

Always there's the temptation to overlook what we have and point to what we haven't.

Tom Brookens wants more than the $350,000 a year the Tigers are offering him. Kirk Gibson wants $1.5 million. Michigan's football team wishes it were going to the Rose Bowl instead of the Fiesta. We wish we were younger and richer and had two-car garages with electric door openers.

None of us is exempt.

I know I'm not.

Presents are heaped beneath our family's tree, and I suspect when we open them most of what I've asked for will be there. But I was prepared to feel a little sorry for myself anyway.

Four of my children — daughters 24 and 23, and sons 21 and 19 — are in Texas and won't be here to share the opening of Christmas presents and the warmth of the fireplace and the holiday.

I'm going to call them.

And when I do, I'm not going to be able to keep Amy Yeast out of my thoughts.

I'm going to thank God for what I've got.

Merry Christmas. ❖

Flight 255

August 18, 1987

Darkness had just begun to envelop the airplane carrying the Detroit Tigers home from Kansas City and, looking at his watch, Jack Morris knew it was about time to begin the descent into Metro Airport.

When you spend as much time in airplanes as professional athletes do, you develop a special perception. You get to know what a proper takeoff feels like, when a descent is steeper than normal, when a flight attendant looks uneasy and when a pilot isn't telling you everything he knows.

You get to know what is ordinary in the air and what is extraordinary.

So Jack Morris was not fooled when the pilot of the TWA charter got on the intercom and told the Tigers that their flight was being diverted to Toledo because "there's been a problem in Detroit."

"Gibby and I figured it out real quick," Morris said, "because there was no weather problem."

Below, as they veered from Detroit, lay the burning wreckage of Northwest Flight 255 and the bodies of as many as 158 men, women and children.

"We pretty much figured out what had happened," Morris said. "We were all aware of it when we were landing."

Flying and the accompanying risks, though, go with the territory if you are a professional athlete.

"It's a way of life for us," Morris said. "There's no other way we can do our job. When something like that happens, it definitely makes you think a lot…. I've descended fast a couple of times, and it gives you an idea of what might happen. It's scary. There are times you think about it. But you can't think about it all the time or you couldn't do your job."

Darryl Rogers was home when he heard what happened.

When he quit as head coach at Michigan State, he became head coach at Arizona State. And when he left Arizona State, he became head coach of the Lions.

He can't count the times he has flown between Detroit and Phoenix.

Goose bumps rose when he heard the flight number.

"Two-fifty-five kind of rung a bell," he said. "We take that flight all the time."

Among the casualties was one professional athlete: Nick Vanos, a center for the NBA's Phoenix Suns. He had been visiting his girlfriend in Plymouth.

Also among the casualties were Nel and Doug Thompson.

They were not athletes.

They were just two people who had endured and eventually beaten the hurdles life puts in our way. At middle age, they had overcome bad marriages and bad habits to find strength and happiness in each other.

They spent most of their lives around Jackson but moved to Scottsdale, Ariz., a few years back. When Doug got homesick for Michigan, he would go to the Phoenix public library and read its copies of the Free Press.

They were the only people to come from out of state when my wife and I were married two years and one day ago.

They spent the night on our sofa bed.

We saw them at the Daytona 500 and at the Fiesta Bowl. We ate with them. We laughed with them. We hugged them and envied them. In their 50s, they held hands and were incredibly in love and content with their lives. They had been among my wife's best friends, and now they were mine, too, because we had so much in common.

We last saw them two months ago when my wife, Karen, was in Phoenix for a seminar. Knowing I had time on my hands, Nel told me where the prettiest mountain drives were, where I could find a preserved cliff dwelling, how to get to a dam that was built 80 years ago with the help of Italian stonemasons who hauled in their materials by mule.

We ate Mexican food and listened to music under clear desert skies. And when we waved good-bye that night, we promised to get together again soon.

About 10 p.m., my dad called from Texas to make sure I was not on the plane that crashed at Metro. "You travel so much," he said. "I just wanted to be sure."

Half an hour later the phone rang again.

"Charlie, this is Paula, Doug's daughter.... We think my dad and Nel were on that plane that went down."

Karen and I spent the rest of the night cradling each other and crying.

And in the morning it was confirmed: Nel and Doug Thompson were among the dead.

Damn! Damn! Damn! ❖

Christmas 1987

December 22, 1987

I t was just a letter from someone I didn't know, an old-timer, and I was in a bit of a rush.

But the letter stopped me in my tracks.

"I hope you can help me," Ken Jones wrote. "In the year 1924, I pitched a couple of innings in my first major league game … played at Fenway Park in Boston. I wonder if you could possibly have this write-up and if you could send me a copy. I am enclosing bits of the write-up to help you.

"I am 85 years old now, and my grandchildren would jump with joy if you could help me."

Accompanying the letter from Simsbury, Conn., were crumbling yellow fragments from a 63-year-old newspaper clipping, carefully placed in a small plastic case.

We tried to piece them together on a desktop, but most of the story was missing. We could tell K. Jones had pitched for Detroit. And we could tell the Tigers had lost to Boston, 9-1. Beyond that, nothing.

We looked up Ken Jones in "995 Tigers," a book that lists everyone who has played for the Tigers. Under his name it read: "Ken pitched in one game, two innings, for the Detroit Tigers in 1924. He had no decisions… . Came back with the Braves in 1930, where he pitched in eight ballgames, did not win a game but lost one."

We looked him up in "The Baseball Encyclopedia" and found that Kenneth Frederick Jones pitched 21⅓ major league innings, with a 5.40 ERA. And we found he was nicknamed "Broadway" — Broadway Ken Jones. Forty years before Joe Namath.

Ken Jones, 85, was intriguing me.

A trip to the Detroit Public Library yielded a roll of microfilmed copies of the Free Press from 1924. And on the screen there soon appeared the information we sought.

Broadway Jones made his major league debut May 19, 1924.

"Kenneth Jones, the recruit pitcher who worked the last two innings … looked good under fire," Harry Bullion wrote in the Free Press the next morning.

Jones, coaxed away from Georgetown University by a $5,000 bonus extended personally by Ty Cobb, "pitched the seventh and eighth in laudatory style."

It was time to call Connecticut.

"Hello?"

"Ken Jones?"

"Yes."

"This is the Detroit Free Press. I'm calling about a letter you wrote."

"Oh, c'mon, you're kidding."

"How would I know you wrote the Free Press, if I wasn't from the Free Press?"

"I guess you're right."

"I've got the clipping here of your first game."

"You're kidding. I can't believe it."

Ken Jones, it turns out, didn't accomplish much as a major league pitcher. He never pitched in Tiger Stadium.

Cobb, who liked him enough to lure him away from college after his sophomore year, sent him to Birmingham, Ala., for seasoning, and eventually he was traded from the Tigers' system.

After his eight games for the Braves in 1930, he knocked around the minors for another nine years before giving up baseball.

He worked for Continental Can Co. for 25 years, then retired to Connecticut, where he works the snack bar at the Golf Club of Avon.

"I think I had the tools," he said, recalling all those years he tried to get to the big leagues and stick. "But I just couldn't get it together…. The Depression years were very, very hard. You couldn't concentrate on what you were doing."

Ken Jones reminded me so much of my father.

Dad is 83 now. He was a minor league infielder in the late '20s after dropping out of the University of Alabama. He worked in a couple of pants factories in Mississippi during the Depression.

He umpired in the minors one year. And until about a year ago, he worked at Riverside Golf Course in Victoria, Texas.

"I have a 12-year-old grandson who lives just down the street from me," Ken Jones said into the telephone while I was thinking of my father. "He's going to be thrilled when he sees those clippings. This is some Christmas present for me. Thank you."

I hadn't done any shopping, but my day was complete. ❖

Slick Vincent

March 28, 1989

The crying has stopped now, and I'm over feeling sorry for myself, and I'd like to share with you — in four or five minutes — 84 years of a man's life.

My father's life.

He died 11 days ago, taken in an instant, when his heart quit and he fell at the feet of the woman he had loved for 50 years.

Probably my dad wasn't special. Probably he was a lot like your dad.

A good man. An honest man.

A golfer you could trust in the rough.

A man who left behind so much love that he will never really die in the hearts of those who knew him.

He was born in Birmingham, Ala., fewer than five years into this century. He was christened Charles Eagar Vincent, but by the time he was a teenager he was called "Slick," a tribute to the things he could do with a basketball. My dad was Southern, the product of a gentility that does not exist today, even in the Deep South. He was "Yes, sir" and "No, ma'am."

He was a rock, too, an athlete who inspired a sports writer in Birmingham 65 years ago to write: "His smashing plunges at the line, his tricky runs at the ends, his accurate passing and fine defensive work set an inspiration for his mates that resulted in victory for Simpson High (13-0)... . But for the play of Slick Vincent, the tally might have been of a zero denomination."

And when he played basketball at the University of Alabama, someone wrote: "Vincent pushed a bounding ball in front of racing feet up and down the court and shot with an eagle's eye and a will to win. It was Vincent who sent the sphere through the netting from center court with 35 seconds left to play, and he, for his team, did what no other club has done this year, defeated the Birmingham Athletic Club Blues."

In high school, he was twice All-South and led Simpson to the National High School Tournament in Chicago in 1923 and '24.

He played professional baseball with Miami in the Florida State League and umpired in Texas in the Valley League and played semipro basketball across the country in the late 1920s and early '30s.

Somewhere along the way, Dad realized he could not make a living playing sports. The Great Depression drove him to work in pants factories in Mississippi and eventually in auto dealerships in Texas, where he and Mom were married on Christmas Eve 1938.

He was 34, she 28. And they eloped.

My earliest vivid memory of my dad is of his taking me on hot, humid, midsummer nights to dimly lit minor league parks, the air thick with cigar smoke and mosquitoes, and as we worked our way through the crowd, he would place his hand on the back of my neck, guiding me through the openings.

Later, he was my manager in a kid league. He taught me how to slide and how the second baseman straddles the bag awaiting the throw from the catcher.

I tried his patience, I know. I was always afraid of a fastball, was never big or tough enough to play football and have never mastered hitting a golf ball into the fairway.

Four years ago, when I got this job, he asked which days I would write.

"Sunday for sure and probably Tuesday and Friday," I told him.

"Garbage days," he replied.

"What?"

"Garbage days — our garbage is picked up on Tuesdays and Fridays. It'll make it easy to remember what days you're writing."

His love was his family. And his golf.

Until his 80th birthday, he worked at Riverside Golf Course in Victoria, Texas, so he could be around the game and the men he loved.

Even after my mother finally talked him into total retirement, several mornings a week he would dress and tell her: "Well, I think I'll go out to the office for a while," and he would be off to the golf course.

He still hit the ball straight, but he couldn't hit it far anymore. Angina forced him to take medication and to ride the golf carts he had ridiculed only a few years before.

We played at Maple Lane in Sterling Heights a few summers ago, and it broke my heart when — after three unsuccessful tries to get the ball over a water hazard in front of a par-three hole — he had to accept that he could no longer hit the ball that far.

That did not keep him from playing, though.

He played golf the day before he died. Then he put his clubs away for the last time.

We cleaned out his locker at the golf course the other day, my youngest brother and I. We had to cut off the combination lock to get to the bag of clubs, the golf shoes, caps, dirty socks and bottle of Scotch.

I took a putter and put it in my bag, then we went to the house where we grew up, consoled Mom the best we could and shared Dad's last bottle of Scotch.

One of my grandchildren, 3-year-old Scott, had begun asking questions about Dad's death.

"How," he asked his mother the other day, "did he get through the ceiling to heaven?"

I don't know.

But I know he did. ❖

Christmas 1990

December 25, 1990

T here is a foot locker under our Christmas tree this morning.

It is dark blue with brass hinges and locks, and in a few days it will carry away the most treasured possessions of my last young love.

She's 20 now, and it is time for her to go off on her own to a different town and a different school, where the first faces she sees each morning will be those of her apartment mates, not her mother's or mine.

She asked for the foot locker a few weeks ago, not long after she laughed when I screamed at her: "Stop it!" Baffled, she asked, "Stop what?" and I replied, "Stop growing up."

The realization hit me, as I sat and watched her and my wife decorate the Christmas tree, that she might never again be here to trek through the lots, discounting one tree because it is too scrawny, another because it has a bare spot, another simply because it is "wimpy."

She might never again be around when the lights are strung and the balls hung and the star placed atop the tree.

There will be school the next few years, and by the time classes are out, the tree will be in its familiar corner of our living room.

And after that there will be work.

And then a family of her own.

I don't really want her to stop growing up, of course. She just seemed to become a woman so quickly.

How could she — the youngest of my five children — grow up without me growing old? Where did all the years go?

Wasn't it yesterday that she was almost homecoming queen? Wasn't it the day before yesterday that she got hit in the head with a water ski the first time she tried the sport? Wasn't it a week or so ago that she played in a peewee softball league, using an old glove of mine?

Could it really have been that many years since she would toddle to the Christmas tree and rip ribbons and bows and paper from presents with 4-year-old glee?

Could it be that this Christmas I am giving her not dolls and toys or little-girl jewelry, but a trunk to fill with clothes for a journey that will change her life?

That might put a lump in my throat and a tear in my eye, but it will make her smile. And that is enough to make this my favorite day of the year.

To be truthful, Thanksgiving leaves me cold. I never have liked turkey much, and I don't relate well to pilgrims and the like.

But Christmas is different.

It is a day to put things into perspective. To understand what is valuable and what is not.

Some people think we've made Christmas too commercial, and maybe we have. But what is wrong with putting a smile on a child's face? What's wrong with giving to someone you love?

Christmas is my day of thanksgiving — for health and happiness and family gathered around, and for the love that gives meaning to the presents beneath the tree.

We don't have as many toys there as we used to, not as many football helmets and T-ball sets. Grandkids are in Texas and Ohio and California, and others in Michigan have to be shared with other grandparents, so presents are mailed weeks in advance.

At Christmastime I want the house full of family and friends. I want little babies underfoot and teenagers hovering over the food and friends raiding the refrigerator.

Their absence, though, gives me an excuse to get sappy, to telephone sons and daughters, brothers and my mother, old but not forgotten friends in all corners of the United States.

You hear people say all the time that we have forgotten the meaning of Christmas, that we have strayed from its beginning and forgotten it is to celebrate the birth of Christ.

I don't agree.

On no other day of the year do we seem to care so much for each other. On no other day of the year does there seem to be so much love in the world.

I was taught somewhere a long time ago that God is love.

That much religion I believe in firmly. And I don't believe Christians have a monopoly on love.

I think this is a season for us all, if we can somehow fall into the spirit of it. If we can stop, for just a little while, wanting what the other guy has, if we can be thankful for what is ours.

And more important, for the people and the love that surrounds us.

I give thanks at Christmas.

I've got a pretty good job.

I have my health and most of my hair.

And I've got a family that has survived all the traumas of modern families, illness and divorce, death and long absences, and remained intact and close.

I looked into our family album the other day. I looked at pictures from Christmases past and at the smiles on the faces, and I realized something that had escaped me all these years:

Nobody deserves to be as happy as I am.

I am blessed, and it is a gift.

I hope your Christmas is as merry as mine. ❖

Shelby Strother

March 4, 1991

A friend of mine died.

Shelby Strother was an original. One of a kind. And just about the best sports writer I've ever known.

With frightful but merciful quickness, cancer took him from his family, his friends and from readers who in less than six years had come to appreciate the things he could do with words.

He was a storyteller.

He was a poet, a man who could string words together in a lyrical way that few can match.

But to me, he was so much more than a writer who worked for the wrong paper. He was human, with human weaknesses and human failings. And from the day we met, we knew we would be friends.

We each started writing a column in this city about the same time. I'd been

with the Free Press since 1970, but Shelby came to the News in 1985 from
Florida, leaving behind St. Petersburg, Denver, Cocoa Beach and Vietnam,
hoping Detroit was the city that was ready for his unique approach to the world.

He was a brilliant writer, never afraid to explore a piece of himself that less
self-assured writers would avoid.

The first time we found ourselves at Tiger Stadium on the same night, he
walked up to me after three or four innings and asked: "Charlie, who threw the
first slider?"

I had no clue and didn't know why it was suddenly important.

Several innings later he came back to me and asked: "Charlie, what's the
fifth planet from the Sun?"

Again, I had to tell him I did not know. But by then I knew his column
would be the first thing I read the next morning.

It was a fanciful piece about taking a spaceman to a baseball game and
explaining the sport to him, a column no one else in this city — or probably any
other — would have attempted.

We both did columns from the Daytona 500 a few years ago and, since he
knew Florida, he led the nightly social excursions. One night we found
ourselves — many beers into the evening — in a motorcycle bar in a tough part
of town. Shelby decided that I, in a polo shirt and slacks, looked more suited
for the golf course than a motorcycle bar, so he bought me a black T-shirt with
the bar's logo on the back and insisted I change shirts there in the bar.

He was persuasive, so I pulled the polo shirt over my head and replaced it
with the T-shirt while a bar full of bikers looked on — confounded, I'm sure, at
the behavior of these two strangers.

When the approval of the Joint Operating Agreement was slow in coming,
Shelby and I decided it was time for employees of the Free Press and News to
do something about it, so we gave a JOA party: "Just On Account" of we
wanted to have a party.

On New Year's Eve 1990, we were together in New Orleans for the Sugar
Bowl the next day.

While thousands elbowed their way down Bourbon Street, we were a
couple of blocks away in a neighborhood Mexican bar where salsa music
blared from the jukebox and the owner served us food at the stroke of midnight
as if we were treasured old friends.

Shelby Strother was an altogether uncommon man with a knack for
stumbling into uncommon events. Always, he found the unique — or it found
him.

We covered a big part of the World Cup soccer championships together in

Italy last summer, but only Shelby managed to be in the middle of a battle between a rowdy group of fans and police on the island of Sardinia. And only he managed to get a billy club in the ribs.

His interests went far beyond sports. He talked of writing a book about people he knew in the Everglades, who lived on boats and wrestled alligators, to whom mainstream America was almost a myth.

When we first met, we talked music a lot. He liked country, Zydeco and folk.

John Prine was one of his favorites. I had never heard of him, but at Shelby's suggestion, I bought "The Best of John Prine." One of the songs on the album is "Souvenirs," a verse of which proclaims:

I hate graveyards and old pawn shops, for they always bring me tears. I can't forgive the way they robbed me of my childhood souvenirs. Memories, they can't be boughten. They can't be why the carnival is free. Well, it took me years to get those souvenirs, and I don't know how they slipped away from me.

The memory of Shelby Strother will always be one of my life's most precious souvenirs.

Being with him was never less than an adventure.

In 44 years, he lived a lot of life. So I don't know if he got shortchanged.

But his family did.

And his friends did. ❖

Thanks

June 17, 1992

Sometimes I think I waste too much time worrying about what is wrong with today instead of what is right with it. So today I have no complaints. Today I'm thankful for:

Springs like this.

Occasionally being able to play bogey golf.

Alan Trammell.

Living in a two-newspaper (most days), all-sports town.

Taxes that actually go toward useful, helpful and humanitarian purposes instead of bomb-building and research on the sex lives of fleas and airfare for junketing politicians.

Two-hour baseball games and four-hour rounds of golf.

Dave Bing.

All those trying to find a way to buy the Tigers from Tom Monaghan at an honest price.

Being able to see Carl Lewis run, Michael Jordan dunk, Cecil Fielder hit and Arnold Palmer attack a golf ball. Being able to walk barefoot in the grass.

Being able to walk barefoot in the sand.

Being able to walk.

I am thankful for the sound of birds singing in the morning.

And for Joe Dumars.

The sound of a golf ball well hit.

Laughter.

The smell of cigar smoke at a ballpark.

Sunsets.

Country music.

Waves crashing on a beach.

Chicken fried steak.

Hal Newhouser.

A baby clutching my finger in its tiny hand.

I am thankful for the Indianapolis 500.

And that in movies and on television we no longer pretend drunkenness is a joke.

I am thankful for AIDS research.

For being able to meet Bob Franklin and Bob LaFave, Lou Gehrig's disease patients whose courage I should remember every day.

For Lowell Lawson's Kardiac Kids softball team, which has enabled scores of heart transplant recipients to discover life can begin long after some expected it would end.

For Tiger Stadium, a lovely antique.

The Palace's modern efficiency.

Ernie Harwell.

The World Cup coming to the Silverdome.

The America's Cup going nowhere for the next four years.

Not having to write about tractor pulls or wrestling or indoor sports that should be played outdoors.

Only 38 days to the Barcelona Olympics; 54 days to vacation.

Golf holes without water hazards.

Ball retrievers.

Daytime baseball.

Fax machines.

Richard Petty.

Chocolate.

Bill Davidson's wise ownership policies that made the Pistons a franchise to be copied on the way up and might make it a model franchise in the art of rebuilding.

I am thankful George Perles and Dr. John DiBiaggio will be on different campuses before the 1992 college football season begins, a separation that should end the disharmony in Michigan State athletics.

And for 260-yard drives (but only the ones that land on the right fairway).

And for athletes who understand what my job is and attempt to make it easier instead of more difficult.

Men such as Baynard Dinkins, who stayed in the inner city when so many others fled, providing three decades of baseball instruction to kids in Detroit's Southeast Little League.

The kindness of strangers, who responded with bats and balls and equipment and money when the Southeast Little League's lack thereof was mentioned in the Free Press last summer.

Technology in television that allows me to watch one pitch from a game in New York, another from a game in Los Angeles and a third from a game in Detroit, all in five seconds.

Jim Abbott.

I am thankful for the Michigan-Michigan State rivalry.

For Jud Heathcote.

Gary Moeller.

And for the Fab Five's success.

And for how well Belle Isle and race cars went together.

For car heaters on cold winter mornings and car air conditioners in June.

The odor of vanilla extract (but not its taste).

All the people who helped along the way as a kid from Victoria, Texas, who always wanted to spell develop with an e on the end, somehow made it to the Detroit Free Press. And has lasted 22 years.

And I am thankful for readers who write to say nice things.

For readers who write to say bad things.

For readers who don't write at all.

For good health.

The Special Olympics for special people.

And for the family: Hers, mine and ours.

Ain't life grand? ❖

Two coaches

September 29, 1992

EAST LANSING — I talked to a couple of football coaches the past two days.

One has a 2-2 record and thinks he will lose his job if his team loses either of its next two games. He will have to look for another job, and he and his wife and two preschool-age children will have to pack and move to another city.

The other coach is 0-3 and probably won't lose his job regardless what happens the rest of the season. "The advice I would give him," George Perles said of the other coach, "is to get a contract."

With his Michigan State Spartans going into Saturday's Big Ten opener against Indiana winless in three games and 3-11 since the beginning of last season, we have Perles to kick around again this fall.

Signs calling for his firing probably will be displayed at Spartan Stadium and boos will cascade down on him at the first MSU mistake. But the circumstances of this season have cost Perles neither his appetite nor his sense of humor.

"I've been 0-3 before," he said. "I don't know if we've ever been 3-0, though."

Perhaps it is easier to joke when you have the security of a long-term contract. Almost certainly, MSU, with a new athletic director and the avowed desire to prove sports is something less than life-and-death in East Lansing, will make no move to buy out his contract regardless what the remainder of this season brings.

And only the most optimistic can think it will bring many good things.

One of the Spartans' problems is that they are outrageously young, with a punter who turned 18 five days before the season opened and three red-shirt freshmen in the starting lineup.

Their leading tackler is a true sophomore, Matt Christensen, and their leader in unassisted tackles is safety Steve Wasylk, which makes you wonder what the defensive line and linebackers are up to.

The problem seems to shake out one of two possibilities: Either Perles' recruiting has been poor the past few seasons, or his coaching has. Either the players are not good enough to compete with the schedule they face, or they are good enough but not well enough prepared.

And Perles is perfectly willing to let you and me draw our own conclusions.

"I don't make excuses," he said. "You've got to come up with them, and I'm not very much help, so you've got to make 'em up for me."

Perles likes the macho image.

He likes to stand between the critics and his team, a target on his stomach, and say shoot me, not them.

And, really, that's the way it should be. He has the title, he has the money, he has the contract and he has the responsibility.

Lately, he hasn't been earning his money. And as much as Perles would like to deflect all the criticism from his squad, it isn't possible.

Christensen, himself the son of a coach, said: "People (around campus) are blowing us off a little. I don't think they know what it's like to get out there and play, but it doesn't bother me too much."

I don't think Perles has suddenly become a bad coach. But I do think he forgot to recruit for a while. And I think his constant flirtation with the pros left a lot of potential Spartans unsure who would be their coach, leading them to decide on other options.

Of Michigan State's 22 starters, 12 went to high school outside Michigan. That's acceptable if you're Notre Dame or Army, but what happened to all the great Michigan high school players? Where did they go?

Perles will not say his players are less talented than others.

"There's talent on this team," he said. "For sure you expect us to win, and when you don't, it looks bad, but I'll never talk about anything negative that will give a player or me an excuse for not doing well."

So there he stands, with the target on his stomach, and you figure some day, like almost everyone who has ever coached, Perles, who never has been fired, will be.

"I've been lucky," he said. "I've never been fired from a coaching job, but I was fired once and that was because of sports. I had a Detroit News paper route, and when I got into high school, the basketball coach recruited me. Well, the first day of practice he told us we couldn't leave until we made six free throws in a row. I never did make six, but he finally let me go, but I was so late getting my papers that day, they fired me.

"Darn newspapers have been a problem for me all my life."

The coach in jeopardy does not have Perles' contract. He does not have Perles' contacts and at the moment does not have Perles' sense of humor. If his school tells him it does not have a place for him to coach next season, he does not have any idea where he will go.

He is just 28, and he is the offensive coordinator at LaGrange High in central Texas, and his contact is year-to-year. Just as Spartans fans expected much of MSU this fall, around LaGrange, much was expected of their football team.

I spoke to that coach on the telephone Sunday.

He told me: "Dad, if we lose either one of those games, I may as well start packing my bags."

Forgive me if today I'm sympathetic toward coaches.

The Spartans lost six of 11 games, yet Perles returned as coach in 1993 and '94. The other coach, Chuck Vincent, returned in '93 but was released at the end of the season. He now coaches at Fort Worth (Texas) Dunbar High. ❖

Pinch me

June 15, 1993

My son, the coach, dips.

He takes a pinch of Copenhagen or Skoal or something like that, sticks it between his lower lip and gum, and every now and then spits a little of it onto the ground or into an empty beer can.

It is disgusting.

He is grown now, 28 years old, so I cannot tell him what to do. But I tell him it is a nasty and dangerous habit that I wish he would quit. He knows I am saying so because I love him, and he reminds me he loved me, too, when he begged me for 15 years or so to give up smoking.

Finally, I did.

He'll quit dipping one day, too, I suspect.

When he does, I hope it is because he has realized it is unhealthy, a decision he has made on his own, with input from his loved ones. A decision made of his own free will.

If he played minor league baseball, he wouldn't have any option.

I got a release from "Major League Baseball, Office of the Commissioner" the other day that said use of all tobacco products by "players, managers, coaches, and other uniformed personnel and umpires" is being banned in the minor leagues, effective today.

I'm not quite sure who issued the release because baseball has been without a commissioner for a while now. Personally, I think baseball should do something about getting a commissioner instead of messing with the individual rights of the people who play its game.

But baseball thinks differently. It thinks it should meddle with the personal habits of its employees. Violators will be dealt with. Players will be fined $100 to $300 if they use tobacco anywhere in a stadium. If they use it on the field, they will be ejected. And so will their manager.

The ban includes not just the players' time at a stadium, but while they are traveling as a team, too.

Dick Wagner of the Major League Baseball Executive Council said the ban is being put in place "to address our concerns for both the health of our baseball personnel and the image they may portray."

The politically correct thing, I suppose, is to applaud the action.

Frankly, I am sick of politically correct.

I worry about personal liberties. Dipping and chewing, though repulsive to most, do not endanger the health of others as do smoking or drunken driving.

I think every time someone or some group tells someone else they cannot do this or that, a little of our freedom is eroded. A little liberty is lost.

Of course, there are always the righteous who insist they are making this a better world by forcing their beliefs down someone else's throat.

Dr. Larry Coughlin said: "On behalf of the Association of Major League Baseball Team Physicians, we are in complete agreement ... in the total ban of all tobacco ... in the minor leagues. As physicians, we are in favor of anything that promotes the well-being of players."

He is president of the Association of Major League Baseball Team Physicians.

Oddly, major league players are not covered by the new rule.

Their players association is probably strong enough to protect individual rights. Minor leaguers are not as organized.

Dr. Peter Greenwald of the National Cancer Institute said: "The association of spit tobacco with our national pastime has always been, for me, a travesty. The minor league ban is certainly a positive step forward."

Those who agree say the minor leaguers can dip at home or in their hotel rooms. That's not an argument — it's a cop-out.

We're not talking morals. We're not talking endangering anyone else's health. We're talking suspending individual liberties.

Dipping is disgusting.

It's nasty.

But so is cursing and profanity. And in the locker rooms and dugouts of the minor leagues, guys will still be saying things they would not say in front of their children or the people in the stands.

Not unless they are Ken Griffey Jr., that is.

So baseball players will go on scratching and cursing, and maybe some will even chase women. But they will not dip or chew around the ballpark, and maybe the majority endorses that.

Maybe it seems to fall in baseball's realm of responsibility to legislate the image and health of its employees.

But what happens if baseball someday has a commissioner who embraces the cause of endangered species and declares that no alligator shoes may be worn to the stadium? Or ostrich boots?

What if baseball, worried about image, decides players could drive only American cars into the park?

Or worried about players' health, it orders them not to eat high-cholesterol foods while at the stadium. Red meat is bad for you. And eggs. And butter. Ban them all.

Silly?

Of course it's silly.

But how far removed is it from telling a grown man he can't take a pinch of tobacco and put it in his mouth? ❖

Isiah

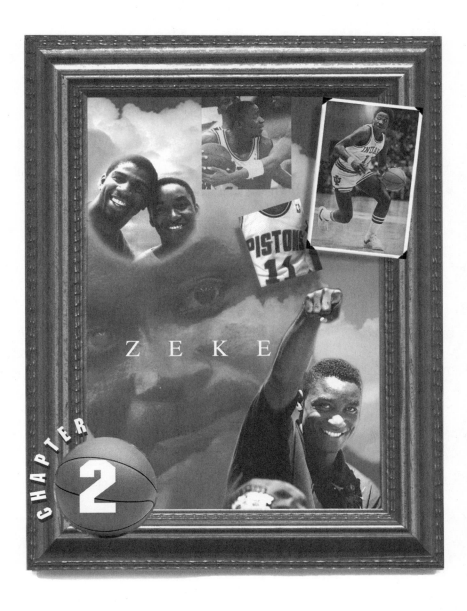

ZEKE

CHAPTER 2

Oh, Isiah

April 30, 1981

Across from the rundown old Hoover Hotel at the corner of Jackson and Homan on Chicago's west side, old men tired of the daily drudgery of doing nothing sit on benches and endure what remains of their days, stocking caps pulled down over their foreheads and a communal bottle of wine at their side.

It is a neighborhood of vacant buildings with all the glass broken out of the windows and the walls leaning precariously at drunken angles.

It is a neighborhood of weed-choked lots filled with abandoned cars and rotting tires where the sharpies lean against lampposts and whisper temptation of sweet but illegal delights to those who will listen.

It is a neighborhood of asphalt basketball courts enclosed by 12-foot-high wire fences.

It is Isiah Thomas' neighborhood in Isiah Thomas' town.

And, after two years of the pastoral life among the tulip trees and meandering streams of Bloomington, Ind., Isiah wants to go home.

Certain to be one of the first three players chosen in the NBA's June 9 draft, Thomas — who celebrates his 20th birthday today — wants to play for the Chicago Bulls.

But it's Detroit and Dallas who will flip a coin to determine who will pick first in the draft. And Pistons general manager Jack McCloskey said it "would be reasonably safe to assume" that he would take Thomas, the 6-foot-1 All-America guard and the outstanding player in the NCAA tournament if Detroit wins the flip.

Thomas, who announced that he is giving up his last two years of college eligibility at Indiana University to turn pro, hopes the Bulls will make a deal that will take him to Chicago.

It's not that he is prejudiced against either Detroit or Dallas. It's just that Chicago is home, and the Bulls have the kind of team he thinks he can help.

"My job is to get the ball to someone who can score. In Detroit, who would I pass to?" Thomas asked, sitting on the arm of a couch in his Bloomington, Ind., apartment.

"My opinion about Detroit — I'm not a general manager or a coach, I'm just a player — but my opinion about Detroit is that it needs somebody to score. Detroit would need a Mark Aguirre, to be perfectly honest with you, somebody who can score at will. I think it would be best for me and best for them to draft someone else."

The Bulls have proven scorers: Artis Gilmore, David Greenwood, Reggie Theus. But there's something more important.

Nobody has to tell Isiah Thomas about roots. Though he has been at Indiana two years, he reads none of the state's newspapers; he subscribes to the Chicago Sun-Times. His soul is so deeply rooted in the west side of Chicago that he admits feeling guilty about leaving the city to play at Indiana University.

"Sometime when I think about it, I feel bad," Thomas said with a maturity and introspection that belied the fact that he is only two years removed from St. Joseph's high school in suburban Chicago.

"All those guys (at DePaul) stayed home and played for the home team. I don't know. If I'd have went to DePaul, with Mark and I on the same team, well, DePaul didn't make it to Philadelphia (where Thomas led Indiana to the NCAA championship last month), but they had one guy for Chicago there."

Seemingly unchanged by the good fortune that has touched him since he left the ghetto, Thomas worries about not staying in the city to provide an example.

"You're talking about kids in the city who have never had a chance," he said of players like Aguirre, who stayed in Chicago after graduating from high school. "Now they have a chance at DePaul to make their mothers proud, to make their family proud and everybody they went to high school with.

"The majority of people in my neighborhood, where I grew up, didn't have many moments to feel good. Most of them don't do well. They survive, but that's all. They just survive.

"Most of them can't afford to go to Catholic schools and get a good education. So you have 50 in a class trying to understand English. I was lucky. I got a scholarship to go to St. Joseph's. I think there were 23 in my class.

"But if I didn't play basketball, I would never be in this situation. Nobody would know about me."

Thomas lifted his kitten, Tiger, and was silent for a moment.

"I think I'm a pretty good person. But there are good people in my neighborhood, too. They just haven't had the opportunities I've had.

"I'd like to play for Chicago, not for my glory but because of the kind of glory and kind of goals I could set for kids growing up.

"You know the old saying: 'There's no place like home.' "

Isiah is the youngest of Mary Thomas' 10 children. His father left home when Isiah was 3, and his mother and seven older brothers and two sisters kept the family together the best they could.

The lure of the streets eventually caught some of his brothers. Two became heroine addicts and one became a pimp. Some of them went to jail. But even the ones who fell into traps looked out for the baby of the family.

Isiah doesn't like to talk about his brothers' problems. He'd rather dwell on what they did for him.

"I understand basketball today because my brothers explained the game to me, because of my high school coach (Gene Pingatore) and because of coach (Bobby) Knight here at Indiana two years. It's just a combination of my background.

"I always had a basketball in my hands. All my brothers played. That was just the thing to do. In my neighborhood we didn't have swimming pools or golf courses or tennis courts.

"The neighborhood was rough, but it was that way only because that's the way you have to be to survive. I had some problems, but I had a lot of brothers and that alleviated some of the problems.

"But I wouldn't trade those times for anything in the world. I didn't always have a new pair of shoes or a new pair of pants or a new shirt, so I learned how to take care of things, to value things, to wear a pair of shoes two years and hope your feet don't grow."

When he decided to submit his name to the NBA for the draft, he insured that all those days would be gone forever.

"You have problems being poor," he said. "And I'm pretty sure rich people have problems, too. But I'd rather have problems with money than without it.

"I can play pro basketball and also go to school, and I don't think that's a bad situation."

A child of the streets, Thomas has never felt completely comfortable in rural Bloomington, surrounded largely by people who could not relate to his background.

"It did take a while for all of us (on the Indiana basketball team) to fit in," he said. "The problems I had some people on the team couldn't relate to, and some of the problems they had I couldn't relate to."

And he found Bloomington stifling.

"I do. I go crazy in Bloomington," he said. "There's two things we can do here. We can go to the movies or we can go to the bars, and I don't drink so the bars are out. And the movies that come here are old and half the good ones never make it to town."

He conveyed the impression that, lying in bed in Bloomington, he could hear not the crickets chirping through the clear night air but the staccato thump

thump thump of a basketball on asphalt — the sound of his Chicago neighborhood.

"Basketball is the best thing I know to do. There's nothing I can do better than basketball. I'm not a better student. I'm not a better speaker. If something bothers me or I just want to get away, I go shoot baskets. It's my hobby."

Nevertheless, he knows there are some unknowns awaiting him.

"I've never lost much, really. I've never had to face losing, and I can honestly tell you I don't know what I'd do with it. I might turn out to be a bad seed if I was losing 50 games a year out of 82. I'd live, but I don't think I'd be happy."

To Thomas, however, winning is only a byproduct of something else, something he feels is more important.

"I just want to be accepted on the team (that drafts him). I want to be liked and I want to get along, that's what it's all about. I'd rather make a friend than win a basketball game. But I think if you get a group of guys who get along and understand each other and like each other, that team won't lose too often." ❖

MVP Mom

February 10, 1986

DALLAS — Isiah Thomas stopped smiling.

He stopped just long enough to drop his head on his mother's right shoulder and sob his eyes out.

They stood in the middle of the floor at Reunion Arena and embraced and cried together.

They cried for joy. They hugged and closed their eyes, and tears ran down their cheeks, and what memories must have tumbled through their minds.

The flashbulbs popped, the shutters clicked. The pens scribbled cryptic notes. But neither the pen nor the camera could record what was in the hearts of Isiah and Mary Thomas.

Only they knew how far he came to get here, to become just the fifth man to be named most valuable player twice in the NBA's All-Star Game.

Bob Cousy did it. And Bob Pettit. And Oscar Robertson and Julius Erving and Isiah Thomas.

No one else. Not Larry Bird. Not Kareem Abdul-Jabbar. Not Wilt Chamberlain.

Think about that.

Then think about the odds of Isiah Lord Thomas III, from a crime-ridden, drug-infested neighborhood of Chicago, ever doing it.

Do you know how bad that neighborhood is? When the Pistons first signed him, the Free Press sent me to Chicago to do a story on his childhood. I took a cab to his neighborhood, and the driver refused to stop. He wouldn't let me out.

"I don't live far from here," he said. "I know this neighborhood. And I ain't letting you out of this cab here."

That's the kind of neighborhood it is.

Think about the odds of somebody from that neighborhood ever playing pro basketball.

Think about the odds of somebody from that neighborhood just surviving to adulthood.

Isiah Thomas has thought about it.

"There are a lot of good people in my neighborhood," he has said. "But a lot of them just didn't have the opportunities I had."

A lot of them died. From drugs. And from guns.

A lot of them are locked up.

It's an old story that some of Isiah's family got caught in those traps. Got busted. Got in trouble. Got on the hustle and tried to shortcut their way through life.

Mary Thomas didn't allow that to happen to her youngest son.

She got him out of the neighborhood, sent him to a private suburban high school, woke him up in the predawn darkness every day so he could make his bus connections and get to class on time.

Mary Thomas has never told her baby boy how old she is. He can only guess. He knows she's used up more than half her lifetime raising him and the children who came before.

"That's what I was thinking when we were hugging," he said later, after the tears had dried and the smile returned.

"I was thinking of the hard times she had and the struggles she had gone through and how great it is for her to be able to come here to Dallas and stay in the Sheraton Hotel and be with the best people and see these things. And then I think about what a relatively short time she has, I mean, she's not going to live another 60 years.

"It was very, very emotional."

It's a special relationship these two have. One every mother would love to have with her son.

Isiah Thomas's first MVP award is in the living room of his mother's house in Chicago. The second will probably go there, too.

Nothing he can give her, he feels, will repay what she gave him. Anything he gets, she feels, will be only what he earned.

When Mary Thomas dried her tears, she had only one explanation for the emotion that spilled out when they embraced.

"He just works so hard. He deserves it. I'm so proud of him."

That, more than his smile and the quicksilver things he does on the court, is the essence of Isiah Thomas. ❖

No Crime Day

September 27, 1986

T he kid wasn't even 10 when he realized crime was not only in his neighborhood, it was in his house.

It slept in his bed.

His streets were mean because his brothers helped make them that way.

There were Gregory and Lord Henry and Larry. They were his big brothers, and every one of them was on cocaine and heroin. And every one of them was, well, what does a kid of 9 call his brothers when he knows in his heart what they are?

They were crooks.

Criminals.

They mugged and stole and robbed and did what they had to do to get what they had to get.

"Drugs touched my family, which allowed crime to be in my family," said Pistons guard Isiah Thomas. "You have to have the money to support a habit. My brothers were addicted to drugs. My mother didn't have enough money to support their habits. They didn't have enough money to support their habits. So they had to do things to support their habits … and that goes from anything to everything."

Those three Thomas brothers all spent time in jail. More recently, they spent time in drug rehabilitation clinics — paid for by their baby brother, the little guy who once slept with them all because he didn't have a bed of his own.

Isiah Thomas — called naive by those who think No Crime Day is the idea of a do-gooder — never has been locked up. But he could have been. Probably should have been.

He was a street punk in Chicago.

By the time he was 11, he was following in his brothers' footsteps. A novice hood. A kid headed for trouble. For jail. For a short life expectancy.

"I never killed anybody," he said. "I never sold drugs. I never took drugs. I never stole a car. I never raped anybody. I never started a fire.

"Everything else, I've done."

He has felt the power of a gun resting in his hand. He has been one shot, one crime, one cop away from jail.

Isiah Thomas is not naive about the ways of the streets. He has stood on their corners and, without luck, might have wound up in their gutters.

"All the friends I grew up with, from the time I was small on up, everybody with the exception of three, are either dead, in prison or strung out on drugs," he said. "And we're talking about a lot of people."

For more than a month, Thomas has been talking to Detroiters about crime, about trying to stop it and about today: No Crime Day.

He has talked to mothers who have lost children to crime. He has talked with teenagers left paralyzed by gunshot wounds. He has stood on the corner of Mack and Gray with young men who can wind up in prison, in a job or in a coffin.

No Crime Day, he knows, is not going to persuade every Detroit hood, drug dealer and stickup man to go straight. What he hopes it will do is get Detroiters to break the code of silence that allows crime to grow.

"The thing I never really understood is the silence," he said. "People see someone get shot or get bombed, and yet they remain silent. That never really made sense to me because I understood if I remained silent, sooner or later the problem would get me. The code of silence is fine in prison. In the free world, it ain't cool at all.

"Let's face it, you don't buy a home, you buy a community. What makes a community strong is everybody looking out for one another, taking care of one another."

Nobody ever did that in his old neighborhood. Everybody was afraid of his brothers and people like them. It was every man for himself, and only the strong — or the ones with the guns — survived.

"Coming from the area I came from, a lot of average people didn't make it, and it wasn't because they were bad people," he said. "A lot of them played by the rules, went to school, came home, did the right thing. But when they turned 17 or 18, parents couldn't afford to send them to college. They couldn't get a scholarship. There weren't any jobs, and so they wound up on the streets."

Thomas would like to turn around at the beginning of today's march at Woodward and I-75 and see 100,000 people behind him. He knows he probably will not.

"If only six show up, that's six more people doing the right thing," he said. "You take me, one guy, I've done a lot. Six people could accomplish a lot more than I could.

"This is a problem either you're for or you're against. You're either all the way right or all the way wrong. And all the people who stand in the middle, I'd like to let them know one day they're going to be on the wrong street and they're going to end up being the innocent bystander because they chose to do nothing." ❖

Killer instinct

May 11, 1987

I t was an emotion the matador must feel when he sinks the sword to the hilt, then watches the bull sink to its knees. A tingle. A surge. An awareness that you are the hunter and the hunted is dead.

It felt so good, Isiah Thomas could not contain himself.

He ran to Rick Mahorn, and they embraced.

He sought out Adrian Dantley and leaped into his arms, wrapping his legs around Dantley's waist.

He looked for Joe Dumars and buried his head on his shoulder.

And all the while there was on his face this look that was both pained and pleased, as if he were so happy he wanted to cry, but as if he were too bad to shed tears in public.

Isiah Thomas had done it again.

His short bank shot over John Battle with one second remaining left the Atlanta Hawks with glazed looks on their faces and very little hope in their hearts as this best-of-seven series returns to Atlanta for Game 5. It gave the Pistons an 89-88 victory and a 3-1 series lead in the Silverdome.

Poor John Battle.

He had begun this series as such a small part of the Atlanta plan that he did not get off the bench in the first game. But his playing time increased in direct proportion to Doc Rivers' declining self-confidence, so he found himself trying to keep up with Thomas in those crucial final seconds.

Trying to stop the wind.

Trying to contain a spirit.

Trying to forestall the inevitable.

It was he whom Thomas put the sword into for the final time.

It was he who had to stand there and bleed while Thomas went into the high-stepping dance around the court that took him first to Mahorn's arms, then to Dantley's and finally to Dumars'.

And it was he who had to sit in the stone-cold silence of the Atlanta locker room and explain in a small, hurt and halting voice what had gone wrong — how in a single stroke Thomas had turned a one-point Atlanta lead into a one-point Detroit victory and pushed the Hawks within one defeat of elimination.

"I pushed him away from the basket," Battle said softly, looking down at the floor. "I tried to push him into the trap, but he just went around and scored.

"I guess he just beat anyone before they got to him."

Thomas has a way of doing that.

There are times when I wonder, don't people want to read more about the others? About Mahorn's defense in the clutch? About Dantley, left standing about in the first half while the Pistons launched a series of unsuccessful long-range missiles that made his presence only ceremonial?

Then Thomas does what he did — performs miracles that challenge his miracles of Game 3 — and you can write about little else.

"He is," said coach Chuck Daly, "something special."

He is special enough to overcome poorly conceived plays. He is special enough to overcome well-conceived defenses. He is special enough to overcome his own failings.

He made just three shots in the first half — when the Pistons' offense consisted not of plays but of 20-foot jump shots. Of their 37 shots in the first half, 24 were jumpers. And of those 24, only six went in.

But by the time the day was over, he had scored 31 points — more than anyone else. And the 31 included the shot that slew the Hawks and a 45-foot fling-and-a-prayer as the third-quarter buzzer sounded. It did not include a basket he made by shooting from behind the backboard — a basket ruled illegal by referee Earl Strom.

And, in the clutch, there could be no question, either in the minds of the Atlanta Hawks or in the minds of the 17,269 on their feet in the Silverdome, about whom Daly would choose to deliver the final blow.

In a flash, there he was, the littlest Piston, taking an inbounds pass from Dantley, cutting through a forest of red shirts and white shirts, as if he were following a dotted line — or one of those Arthur Murray dance courses, where the footprints are marked on the floor — straight to the hoop.

And there is the ball leaving his hand.

And there it is soaring through the air.

And there it is falling, like a feather, through the hoop.

And there he is dancing into Mahorn's arms.

He had delivered the killing stroke.

And he didn't mind admitting it.

"If we're up three games to one, and I can't say we're in control of the series," he said in the chaotic Pistons' locker room, "we're in trouble."

The Pistons had little trouble with Atlanta, winning the series in five games. However, the Celtics defeated Detroit, four games to three, in the Eastern Conference final. ❖

Boys in the 'hood

May 26, 1989

CHICAGO — Michael Moody remembers the sunlit days of childhood.

He remembers walking down the street to Martin Luther King Boys Club one afternoon with the little boy from upstairs.

They were probably 10 or so — Michael Moody and Isiah Thomas — little boys with big eyes and bigger dreams, walking the sidewalks of Chicago, dribbling a basketball.

"I remember him turning to me and saying: 'When we make the pros, we are goin' to turn 'em out!' " Michael Moody said with a laugh.

"We never said 'if.' After that, we always said 'when' we make the pros."

Michael Moody and Isiah Thomas have been pals since they first met, when they were 3 or 4 years old, shoehorned into the same building — Thomas' family living on the top floor, 11 children sharing a few beds; Moody's family on the bottom floor, 14 children in a space meant for fewer than seven.

If their circumstances were deprived, Moody does not remember it that way.

"There was never any trouble finding people to play basketball with," he said, laughing again.

Basketball tied Isiah Thomas and Michael Moody together throughout their youth. Once upon a time, back when basketball was the only important thing in their lives, Moody — not Thomas — was the point guard on the teams at Our Lady of Sorrows School and Martin Luther King Boys Club.

"He could really handle the basketball," Thomas said. "He could do anything with it. He was the point guard, and I was the small forward."

There were other good players around the Boys Club at Washington and Sacramento then. There was Willie Scott, Thomas' cousin. He's playing basketball in South America. There were Bernard Dortch and Jerome Jackson. They're still around the old neighborhood somewhere. There was Linell Copeland. He was shot in the face five times and killed. And there was Michael Moody, the sweet ball-handler who set up the young Isiah Thomas with his passes.

They were good. And they lived for basketball.

When they hosted tournaments, all the players would spend the night in the club. They would eat together and pray. And they'd sing.

"Michael could really sing. I'd just kind of do the 'Ohhhhhhhhh, Ohhhhhhhh' part," Thomas said.

But they were too good to be satisfied with just beating teams in Illinois. So they traveled to Kansas City and Phoenix and beat whoever chose to play them.

High school separated Thomas and Moody. Thomas rode a series of buses to the suburbs to go to St. Joseph's. Moody went to Orr High in the inner city, then — for half of one year — to Mackenzie in Detroit. "I moved there to baby-sit for my sister," he said. "When basketball season was over, I moved back to Chicago."

By then, Thomas was a star, a 6-foot-1 guard courted by some of the nation's best basketball-playing universities. Moody stopped growing at 5-feet-6.

"Five-six-and-a-half," he corrected. "They told me I was too short to play in college, so Isiah said 'bye' and left me."

Thomas went to Indiana University to play basketball for Bobby Knight and to study criminal justice. Moody went to Quincy College in downstate Illinois to study accounting and try out for the basketball team as a walk-on.

He made the team but didn't play much. One day, Sherrill Hanks, the coach, called him into his office.

"He told me: 'Mike, you are too short to consistently start for my team.' So I quit and got my degree in accounting and left."

Only occasionally does Moody play basketball anymore. He has survived without the game, making his way through life, like most of us, with as many downs as ups.

"We had dreams," he said the other day, sitting in Thomas' mother's living room in Chicago's western suburbs.

"When I was a kid, I wanted to play the game like Walt Frazier and Earl Monroe and Curly, that famous dribbler with the Harlem Globetrotters. You worked every day so people would know you, and people knew us very well. We had a lot of respect. A lot. Just like we looked up to Frazier and Monroe, the kids looked up to us."

For Isiah Thomas the dream lived.

For Michael Moody, a 5-6½ ball-handler, it died.

"It was hard," he said, sitting in Mary Thomas' living room. "But life goes on."

Isiah Thomas' mother had sent people into the city to look for Moody earlier this week, when the Free Press asked whether she could find him.

It took a couple of days, but she found him.

"I must have been at work when they were looking for me," he said, laughing.

Isiah Thomas had scored 33 points against the Chicago Bulls the night before, and in the middle of the afternoon, fresh from the city, Moody had just played 15 minutes of one-on-one with Thomas' 17-year-old nephew, Ashanti Burnette, on the backyard court. At 28, he was no match for the high school sophomore.

"Too old," he said. "Too short."

Now he lives his basketball dream through his old buddy, the little guy he walked the streets of Chicago with so long ago.

"My brother, Jerry, lives in Detroit," Moody said. "And he has every Pistons game from the last couple of years on tape. When I go there, I don't have to leave the house to watch Isiah.

"I can watch him all day long.

"He's the best friend I ever had in my life. The love is there. Like family. When I'm with my best friend, it's like I'm still there."

Moody laughs, exulting in the success of his boyhood chum.

They still get together occasionally, when Thomas is in Chicago during the off-season.

It brings back memories of the sunlit days of youth.

"You play the game 'cause you love it," Moody said. "We never fantasized about the money when we were kids. We were just fascinated about being good, about being a pro. The money was never an issue."

Tomorrow, Isiah Thomas will be on the floor at Chicago Stadium, trying to help the Pistons move a step closer to the NBA championship.

Michael Moody will be in the stands.

In his mind, he is back in uniform. In his mind, he once again is Isiah Thomas' teammate.

"I'm out there with Detroit. I'll always be there in my heart.

"He is my friend." ❖

Joe D.

November 2, 1989

J oe Dumars was doubled over, pulling on his sweatsock and only half listening.

We had been in the otherwise deserted Pistons' locker room for an hour, just Isiah Thomas, the man the Pistons have been built around; Dumars, their future; and me.

Perhaps distraction was setting in. Perhaps boredom.

Whichever, Dumars seemed to be listening as much to the rock music playing in the background as to the question when I asked about the relationship between the two and the widely held notion that they do not particularly like one another.

"What are you talking about?" he asked, looking up with an expression that said he was not sure he had heard correctly.

"The impression people have there is a conflict between you two," I said.

"What are you talking about?" he repeated, but this time with a laugh, as if he were certain I was joking.

"Isiah says he knows it's out there," I said.

"Yeah," admitted Thomas, "people have said that to me before."

"What?"

"That you and I don't get along."

"You're lying!"

"And I just laughed."

"You're lying."

"All I could do was laugh."

"C'mon. You never told me about it."

"What, I'm coming over to you and say: 'We don't get along'? "

"No, you never told me nobody told you that."

"Well," I interjected, "a lot of people seem to have the idea Isiah doesn't want to share the glory, that he will get ticked off if you get too good or too much attention."

"Ticked off?!" Thomas roared, his eyes flashing in mock anger. "I'll be furious, man. I'll see you don't get the motion play any more."

Dumars shook his head. "I never heard we didn't get along. Nobody ever said that to me."

When Isiah Thomas was drafted in 1981, the Pistons were the poor relations of the NBA. They were — and there can be no way of saying this gently — the worst team in professional basketball.

When Joe Dumars came to Detroit, four years later, Thomas' presence had ensured the Pistons would be a playoff fixture as long as he wore their uniform. But before Dumars, the Pistons were only one of those teams that fills out the early rounds of the playoffs, somebody for the legitimate title contenders to beat up on.

Last year, the Pistons were the best team in basketball. Tomorrow, they raise their first NBA title banner to the rafters of the Palace, and no one is more responsible than Dumars, the MVP in the NBA Finals.

The World Champions are a team in evolution. Throughout the '80s, they were "Isiah Thomas' team." Some could accept that. Some could not.

It was never a problem for Dumars. In the school's media guide during his senior season at McNeese State, he listed Thomas as his favorite player.

"I watched the way he played, and a lot of times I looked at what he did and I felt I think the same way he does," Dumars said. "I may not do it the same way, but I always felt like we thought the same way. And from day one when I walked in here, I said to myself: 'Given the chance to play together, he and I would make a real good backcourt.' "

The chance to play together, though, was not to come right away.

"It was," said Dumars, who put his pride and parts of his game out of sight when he arrived here, "one of those things where you have to move slowly. You can't just jump in and say: 'Hey, gimme the ball! I come from Louisiana, and I average 28 points a game.' "

Thomas knew what Dumars was doing. "I saw immediately he had an understanding of winning basketball," Thomas said. "We had Vinnie Johnson and John Long who were playing ahead of him, and he worked hard every day at practice — and, sure, at that time he was good enough to play, but he understood his role and didn't try to buck the system. He didn't make waves for Vinnie, and he didn't make waves for John, and things worked themselves out."

Thomas had been told what to expect of Dumars.

"Will Robinson came back from a scouting trip, and he told me: 'Isiah, I have found the one. The Pistons' backcourt will be set for the next 10 years. I saw this guy play just like you.'

"I said, 'Yeah?'

"He said: 'Yeah. You'll meet him. You two will be wonderful together.' "

And despite all the rumors, all the whispers, all the insinuations they do not get along, they have been — both say — wonderful together ever since.

Thomas said: "I consider Joe to be one of the best friends I have. Since the time he came here, we've always had a good relationship. We just hit it off from the first day."

That was before — and after — Adrian Dantley's time here.

No longer does anyone deny Thomas' and Dantley's dislike for each other. And Dumars' friendship with Dantley has been widely noted, too. Whatever their differences about Dantley, they never have interfered with their personal or professional relationship.

"I told Adrian I was always going to be Isiah's friend," Dumars said. "And I told Isiah I was always going to be Adrian's friend. And whatever problem they have is between them.

"The first and foremost thing about the relationship between Isiah and me is respect. We respect each other. And I like him, and he likes me. I think we are both smart enough to realize that together we make a good tandem."

"Joe was in the middle," Thomas said, "and I understood our relationship very well. I just kinda stepped back a little bit because I didn't want, for the sake of our team, total chaos."

The evolution that led the Pistons to their first NBA title included trading Dantley to Dallas for Mark Aguirre. The evolution designed to lead them to their next title began when Rick Mahorn was left exposed to the expansion draft. And Thomas said the next step should be a larger and more vocal leadership role for Dumars.

"Instead of leading by example, he's going to have to get a little more vocal," Thomas said. "What we've got going here, the true test will be if we can pass it on and keep it going. The mark of a true leader is not what he does when he's there, but what he leaves behind for others.

"It has to be a smooth transition. That's tradition."

Thomas, though, is only 28, and Dumars said it is much too early for talk of passing the baton of leadership.

He described Thomas as "the ultimate competitor, the kind of guy you want beside you when you step on the floor." And, he said, despite the improvements made in his supporting cast, "He is still the core.

"That's where people get a misconception about Isiah and about this team. Just because other guys step up doesn't mean this team isn't still built around him. A good foundation is something to build on. You don't change the foundation, and he is the foundation."

The admiration is mutual.

Thomas said Dumars "is a good basketball player because he is a smart basketball player. He's got a very good work ethic. I wouldn't say he is as talented as a lot of people he plays against. But he works harder at his game. I couldn't be as successful without Joe playing alongside me."

He called Dumars "an extremely good friend." Dumars said Thomas "is intelligent and compassionate, and I always listen to what he says, even when he isn't talking to me. There's always something within what he's saying."

As much as they think alike, though, they do not always agree.

"If both of us agree on everything," Dumars said, his eyes twinkling with mischief, "one of us is unnecessary."

Together with Johnson, Thomas and Dumars give the Pistons what is widely regarded as the best backcourt in basketball.

"I'd rank us, if not the best," Dumars said, "as one of the best."

But ask who ranks with them and he tells you: "I don't know."

Ask Thomas the same question, and you get only a quasi-serious answer.

"The best three guards? Well, you could probably say Magic (Johnson) and Byron (Scott), 'cause you can count Magic as two, 'cause he is 6-9."

And the two slap hands again and laugh like friends.

Despite the skeptics who refuse to believe not only what they hear, but what they see, too, Thomas and Dumars insist they are close. They are so close, they said, that communication seldom requires words.

"A lot of time, we just look at each other and we know what the other is thinking," Dumars said. "It clicks. We look at each other kinda funny now when one of us says something on the court."

"Do you think," I asked, "you can communicate with each other that way better even than you can communicate with your wives?"

"For the sake of our marriage: No!" Thomas said, barely finishing before breaking into laughter.

Newlywed Dumars, silent, quiet, reserved, doubles over in laughter. "If you had said 'Yeah,' " he said to Thomas, "I was gonna leave you out there by yourself."

And in that empty locker room — the rock music drowned out by laughter — Thomas and Dumars held their sides, sharing a moment that can only be shared by friends. ❖

Slowing down

March 13, 1993

I was in Florida, and my mind was on baseball when I picked up a newspaper and began reading about the Pistons' loss to Boston.

"Kevin McHale ... hit a short follow shot with 23 seconds left, and the Pistons' Isiah Thomas blew two subsequent chances to tie the score Friday night as Boston defeated Detroit, 105-101," the Associated Press story said.

Blew?

I had just returned when I picked up a Free Press and read that Thomas had demanded to be taken out of a game because he was playing poorly, and coach Ron Rothstein said: "It was good for him to sit down and regroup."

Regroup?

I was at the Palace for the game against the Los Angeles Lakers when, with the Pistons trailing by one, Thomas tried to drive the lane and lost control of the ball, sending it careening across the floor and into the hands of a Laker.

He will be 32 on April 30, and recurring incidents such as those force the question: Is Isiah Thomas near the end of the line — not as a player, but as a force — in the NBA?

So you ask.

And you are not surprised that he does not welcome the question.

At first he said go away, get my facts straight, then come back, otherwise "one of us is going to get pissed off."

But gradually he relented. It was 90 minutes before game time, and he wanted to respond to what he insisted are silly accusations, premature doubts about what he can do.

"Is there anybody who dominates Isiah Thomas?" he asked. "No.

"Am I still dominating some people? Yeah.

"Do I still go by people? Yeah.

"Clearly it takes me longer to come back from injuries. But am I slower or is there something I can't do? No, I don't feel like that.

"Do I shoot the ball good enough? I'll put it to you this way: Get off me and let me shoot, and we'll see."

When this week began, only a handful of NBA players had committed more turnovers than Thomas; his 16.1-point average was the lowest in his career and so was his field goal percentage of .408. And only four players who could honestly be called starters had worse shooting percentages: Negele Knight, Marcus Liberty, Vernon Maxwell and Walter Bond.

Nice company for a Hall of Famer.

In his first season as the Pistons coach, Rothstein is reluctant to criticize what many consider the poorest of Thomas' 12 NBA seasons.

"He's playing extremely hard," Rothstein said. "We're struggling, and sometimes he tries to take too much on himself. And maybe we have put him in a not-too-advantageous position."

There is a fable about an emperor swindled by a tailor. The tailor does no real work and only pretends to fit the emperor a wonderful wardrobe. The emperor, not wanting it to appear that he has missed something, convinces himself he is wearing the nonexistent clothes. His subjects, fearing his wrath, are afraid to tell him he is naked.

Isiah Thomas resembles the emperor in that fable: If his game is beginning to disappear, no one is willing to tell him.

Thomas himself, though, has conceded one thing: This team is no longer built around him.

"This team is built around Joe's abilities," he said of Joe Dumars. "At the end of the game, we go to him. I carried my team where we wanted them to go (during the championship years). Now the role I find myself in is more of a supporting role than a carrying role.

"Before, I carried and I supported. I was the go-to guy, but not only the go-to guy, I was the distributor, too. Now I'm primarily the distributor.

"And you don't go against the flow."

Thomas has taken 233 fewer shots than Dumars, and Rothstein, noting Thomas' shots are down and his assists are up, said: "He's trying to make that adjustment."

"When the ball is in my hands," Thomas said, "it's in my hands to distribute and not to create for me."

Another of Thomas' concessions is to the frailty of his body, scarred and battered by more injuries than he can recount. An enduring image is of him limping on crutches through the Pistons' hotel in Los Angeles, guarding a severely sprained ankle on which he would play the next day, in a futile effort to win Detroit's first NBA title in 1988.

"Now if I get injured, I stop playing," Thomas said. "I can't do that anymore. In the past, in games where I played hurt, I still was normally better than the other guy. Now when I'm hurt, if I'm not on top of my game, he's usually getting the best of me."

Chuck Daly, who coached Thomas through his best years, said: "That body has paid a toll, injuries and a little bit of age, and more important is the mental thing. You can't stay on the cutting edge all your life.

"He's human. But he can still get it up on a given night."

When Daly brought his New Jersey Nets to the Palace for the first time, Thomas scored 21 points and gave out 14 assists.

When Utah came in — with John Stockton, who was named to the Dream Team instead of Thomas — Thomas scored 40 points on him.

And after I finished asking about his diminishing abilities, he scored 33 points and made nine assists in a 112-104 victory over Denver.

There are some points to be made, it seems.

There probably has never been a player with more pride than Thomas. Or with more sense of accomplishment. Asked whether this season has been difficult, he said yes, then maybe "it hasn't been as difficult mentally as it might appear to be. If I was sitting here playing for the Portland Trail Blazers, it would be extremely difficult because they've never won it. But I did what I was supposed to do.

"And if you give me another opportunity, I'll do it again.

"I never had to deal with that 'potential' tag. Not only did I accomplish what we set out to do, but I accomplished more.

"Am I done accomplishing things in this league? No, I don't think so. If I don't have any other major injuries, I can be around for another championship."

What had begun as a confrontation had turned into a 45-minute conversation.

"Just a couple of more questions, then I'll get out of here," I told Thomas.

"No," he said, "I don't want to rush this because I want to make sure we understand each other when we're done."

So we talked on.

And in the end, there was no misunderstanding. He thinks he can do today most of what he could do yesterday or last year or in the '80s. His pride will not allow him to think anything else.

I've always felt the difference between Joe Dumars and Isiah Thomas was this: Dumars is such a professional, he would never do anything to rock the boat; Thomas is such a competitor, he would blow the boat to bits if he thought that was the way to victory.

"At the end of the day, all I'm concerned about is 'my team won and your team lost,' " Thomas said. "I'll try to be nice. If I can't get it done nicely, I'll do it the other way. I'm not going to lose nice."

He has done all there is to do in basketball.

Two NBA titles.

Two MVPs in the All-Star Game.

MVP of the playoffs in 1990.

Third in steals and assists in the history of the NBA.

NCAA championship at Indiana.

Probably, in his prime, he was the best little man ever to play. Quicker, smarter, better than anyone he came up against.

I know a man who still tries to fit a 38-inch waist into 36-inch pants. And some, going bald, let their hair grow and wrap it around vast bare areas of scalp.

Seeing ourselves as we used to be is not a phenomenon exclusive to athletes.

So what's the point?

That Isiah Thomas is not quite the athlete he was at 21? That he can't do all the things he used to do? That he is far closer to the end of his career than to the beginning?

I don't think so.

Unless you believe in fairy tales, all of that is evident.

Daly said: "He's excused. After all he has done, he's excused."

That is the point.

There might be nights when Isiah Thomas blows games, and there might be nights when he needs to regroup. Those, I guess, we need to excuse, and appreciate the rest because we have seen one of the greats. And on rare and wonderful nights, he recaptures some of those moments and we are treated to basketball as it was meant to be played.

And the past is the present again. ❖

Benched

March 12, 1994

A n era ended.

Without fanfare, without an announcement, as silently and as stealthily as possible, the Pistons made Isiah Thomas a benchwarmer.

For the first time in his career, there were five letters behind his name in the final box score: dnp-cd.

Did not play-coach's decision.

For the first time in 13 seasons, a Pistons coach made a conscious decision not to start him — and after that, not to play him.

Thomas didn't know it was going to happen until he read it in his morning Free Press, buried down in the notes, down where Don Chaney said: "My decision is predicated on Lindsey (Hunter) coming off a good game, and I'm thinking of seeing if he starts, if he can put together two good games."

A couple of stitches in his left hand kept Thomas out of a game against New Jersey. Stitches are mostly an annoyance to Thomas, though. Broken bones keep him out a week or so — sprains, oh, maybe two games. In Los Angeles once, he left crutches behind in the locker room to go out and play a championship game. Stitches? Stitches you spit on, rub a little dirt in and yell, "Play ball!"

Thomas could have played. He was ready to start — as he has done 958 times before. Then he read his morning Free Press. And he understood exactly what Chaney was saying.

For Thomas, change did not come silently or stealthily. It hit him in the stomach. It doubled him over. If it did not make him feel old, it made him feel vulnerable. And for a man of his ego, that is an awful feeling.

And for once in his career, he did not know what to do. Argue about the decision? Pout? Go to the press and plead his case? He won't tell you this, and he didn't tell me, but he spent the morning agonizing over the next move, which was clearly his.

He went to the shoot-around at midday and spent 10 minutes in one-on-one conversation with Chaney. The words might have been passionate, but they were not antagonistic. And when they were done, both knew they would say conciliatory things when asked to comment.

"I understand what he's doing," Thomas said. "He's got my support. And so does Lindsey, by the way. I have never caused any problems, and I'm not going to cause one now. I know he's got to find out what he's got here."

If benching his captain — the man who made the Pistons champions, the best player ever to wear a Pistons uniform — was difficult for Chaney, he did not admit it.

"It was a very easy decision," he said. "I want to see Lindsey as a starter one more time. Basically, it's an experiment. If we were in the hunt, Isiah would play and would start, but I've got to see my rookies."

Perhaps Thomas will not start another game.

The Pistons will not be "in the hunt" again this season. And the evidence points more and more toward Thomas retiring before another season begins.

Chaney had said he wanted to try a three-guard rotation with Hunter, Joe Dumars and Allan Houston. But at one point he used Sean Elliott as the second guard with Dumars. And still, the greatest player in the history of this franchise watched from the bench.

There is a time for veterans, old-timers, the players who have done it all, to yield to the kids. To the youngsters who have no clue yet how to do it all. To the kids who might be the future, or the next failures.

Isiah Thomas, whose ego outlasted his greatness, found that out.

He did not want this to happen. For all the great things he did for this ballclub, his ego would not allow him to voluntarily step aside. It would not allow him to say: "Take my place. Take my job."

But on the day that Chaney made the decision for him, Thomas accepted it with the grace of a champion. I am sure it was a facade. I am sure there was a storm of anger inside him, a silent protest that what he had done for this franchise was being trashed.

Still, he made a point to slap hands with his replacement when Hunter was introduced at the beginning of the game. Then he spent 48 minutes sitting at the end of the bench with Marcus Liberty and Mark Macon. But with the outcome in the balance in the final two minutes, he spoke a quiet word to Hunter after a time-out. Then he stood there with his hands in his pockets.

A spectator. Nothing more.

In Los Angeles, when Kareem Abdul-Jabbar was playing long after most of his skills were gone, the Lakers never made a substitute of him. In Boston, after Larry Bird's bad back had robbed him of his greatness, the Celtics never made him someone else's backup.

In Detroit this morning, Isiah Thomas is just that. He is a benchwarmer.

An era has ended. And there is a sadness to it. ❖

A great life

May 12, 1994

A few pictures and framed letters hang on the walls of my office at home.

One is on a Pistons letterhead dated May 16, 1985.

In part, it reads:

"Just wanted to send you a note thanking you for all the coverage during the playoffs and regular season. I think your coverage of me was very honest. I thought your judgment was outstanding, and it was beneficial to both me and my teammates. Since I really do respect your judgment, please feel free to give me advice. Once again, thanks — you truly make this a great sports town."

It is signed Isiah Thomas. And there is a postscript.

"That doesn't necessarily mean I would take the advice."

And he didn't.

Thomas didn't take advice from many, and perhaps that is at least partially responsible for the abrupt end to his 13-year relationship with the Pistons.

He limped out of the Palace on crutches, his final mementos of a career that saved a franchise, gave it character and pride and honor and two NBA championships. And when the rain splashed down on his face, he was something other than a Piston for the first time since he came here as a 19-year-old with the smile of an angel and — though we didn't know it then — the heart of an assassin.

I met him in the early summer of 1981, when the Pistons were one of the NBA's worst teams and he was one of the most coveted players in the draft.

We talked in his Bloomington, Ind., apartment, and he said I was wasting my time. He was certain the Pistons would not draft him because "my job is to get the ball to someone who can score. In Detroit, who would I pass to?"

Dallas, which had the first pick, wanted him, too. But when the kid from Chicago stepped off the plane for a visit, the Mavericks' owner plopped a cowboy hat on his head, and that was the end of that potential relationship.

"I ain't no cowboy," Thomas said, taking off the hat with such conviction that the Mavericks were convinced to draft Mark Aguirre, leaving Thomas for the Pistons.

Though Thomas was a reluctant Piston, he grew more comfortable after

WELCOME TO MY WORLD

Will Robinson told him: "This will be a place for you that you can always call home."

Yesterday, Thomas said: "Will, you told me the truth."

My first vivid memory of him as a pro was his surprise and disgust at learning veteran players did not give 100 percent all the time. He could not understand that they learned shortcuts, that they sometimes coasted. He had never played an 82-game season.

To his new team he brought hope. He brought an arrogance. And he brought a commitment to excellence he admits has been ebbing in recent years.

"I didn't have the energy, the stamina, the rah-rah-rah I had before," Thomas conceded.

We are not friends. He probably didn't care to be mine, and I have never allowed myself the potential conflict of interest of becoming friends with athletes whose work I critique.

We have screamed at each other — once in a training camp locker room in Windsor with a half-dozen rookies watching in disbelief.

But if ours has not been a relationship between friends, it has at least been a friendly relationship, and one that did not always have to do with basketball.

In the mid '80s, when my youngest daughter was in her mid-teens, Thomas and I somehow got into a conversation about music. I mentioned my daughter liked Prince, who at the time had a hit called "Darling Nikki."

I had never been able to understand the words, but Thomas knew the lyrics and enough about me and my relationship with my daughter to sputter, his eyes bulging: "If you could understand the words, you wouldn't like it. Don't you let her listen to that song!"

I found him unique. I found him committed to winning above all else. I always felt when winning was the objective, few rules would stand in his way.

Some found him to be other things. People have told me he is devious. A back-stabber. A sneak.

I once proposed a book about him to a publisher, and after reading one chapter, an editor wrote back: "I never liked the guy, and now I know why. He is not someone we are interested in doing a book about."

Recently I received a letter from a woman who told me to stop "deifying" Thomas. If I ever did, I apologize.

He is not a deity.

He is a human being, and he has made a lot of mistakes in 13 years here, and that makes him all the more palatable to me.

Probably his worst mistake was whatever happened between that infamous news conference a few months ago, when he announced he would be a Piston for life, and yesterday, when he announced: "I won't have a future role in the Pistons' organization."

There was no animosity, he said. No bad blood. No arguments. No disagreements. No misunderstandings. No problem.

"There were no jobs," he said. "All the jobs were full."

And when he said it, he laughed that little boy laugh we all heard when he came here. The laugh we thought said all there was to say about him.

In time we learned there was a lot more to Isiah Thomas.

He is a complex man, given to tender acts of helpfulness as well as acts of revenge. He is the smile and the laugh. He is "Oh, Isiah!" as surely today as he was when he arrived. But he is also the spirit of the Bad Boys. Bill Laimbeer was their elbows. And maybe Joe Dumars was their heart. Thomas was their spirit, their soul.

Together they could be fearsome.

Or they could be playful children, rich because of the game they play but not yet quite grown up.

My youngest son is a television reporter in Corpus Christi, Texas, and about three years ago he called before a Pistons trip to San Antonio and asked whether I thought Thomas and Laimbeer would agree to an interview. Both told me they would, but I had an uneasy feeling about their promise.

The Pistons arrived a day before the game. At the shoot-around that day, a young and obviously nervous TV reporter approached Thomas and was greeted by having a pitcher of water poured over him. Gotcha, Thomas thought, until he discovered the reporter was not my son. When my son showed up the next day, Thomas and Laimbeer were gracious and helpful.

"This has been a great life for me," Thomas said yesterday. "I think I enjoyed myself more than any other player who ever came through the NBA. I love the Detroit Pistons. I will always love this organization and the people here."

And — despite the rift between him and the Pistons' family, which lay steaming just below the surface — Thomas probably meant most of what he said.

It is never easy for a player to pull off the uniform for the final time, to concede that time has stolen his skills and it is time to go to work in long pants.

"You always think, 'I can still play,' " Thomas said. "The most difficult decision is, when do you quit? When do you let go of the thing that has shaped and defined you all your life?"

Normally, I do not dream of basketball players. And I do not make a practice — as some writers do — of keeping a notepad and pen by my bed.

But for some reason I had a pad and pen there two nights ago, and for some reason I sat upright, suddenly wide awake at 4 a.m. I turned on the bed lamp and wrote this:

"He had incredible goals for himself and his team. He was never quite as big as he would like to have been. Never tall enough to do some of the things that the game's two greatest guards, Magic Johnson and Michael Jordan, could do because of their size. Never quite as recognized as he should have been. Never a member of the original Dream Team.

"But the one thing that struck me as I walked into basketball's Hall of Fame in Springfield, Mass., was that in the lobby there are life-size cutouts of Julius Erving and of Isiah Thomas.

"He beat his coach to basketball's most cherished shrine."

One day that cutout will be replaced by a plaque on the walls with the other Hall of Famers. Maybe one day he will realize the dream he spoke of yesterday, to "own and run a basketball team, if that's possible."

And maybe one day the injuries he and others in the Pistons family have inflicted upon each other will heal, and he will again be one of them.

The future is uncertain, but the past is sure. We've seen something in Isiah Thomas on a basketball floor that most of us will never see again.

Thanks for the memories.

Thanks for the laughs. And the tears.

Thanks for showing an entire state, an entire generation, how beautiful the game of basketball can be.

Thanks for your artistry.

For your heart.

For playing sometimes with only one good leg. Or one good hand. Or one good eye.

Thanks for 13 years as a Piston, 13 years that enriched the organization and its fans as much as it enriched Isiah Thomas.

Two weeks later, Thomas, 33, was named part owner and vice president of basketball operations for the Toronto Raptors, who begin play in the NBA in 1995. ❖

Bad Boys

The Worm

April 23, 1987

Last summer, when Dennis Rodman walked into the Pistons' locker room for the first time, a strange feeling of being out of place swept over him.

He had worked in an auto body shop in Dallas and on a farm in Bokchito, Okla., harvesting wheat and peanuts and feeding cattle. And he had played three years of small-college basketball for the Southeastern Oklahoma State Savages in Durant.

He was 25, and the notion he could play professional basketball had come to him only a couple of months before, after his college coaches goaded him into giving it a shot.

"I looked around and looked around at the names, and I thought: 'I can't believe I'm in a pro locker room.' ... I said to myself: 'Somebody else should be here instead of me.'

"I saw (Earl) Cureton's name up there," Rodman said, nodding toward the top of a cubicle, "and I said: 'This is going to be my locker.' It was really a weird feeling."

It took Rodman awhile to get used to the idea that he was a professional. And it took awhile longer to fully understand what that meant.

He was the other rookie on the Pistons this season, along with John Salley.

Salley came from Georgia Tech, not some obscure school in Oklahoma.

Salley was the club's first-round draft pick, a rookie everyone had heard of. He was the one the Pistons were counting on. Dennis Rodman was a gamble, a guy who didn't even play the sport in high school, who for a long while didn't even consider going to college, and, at 25, was old for a rookie.

But he had skills that could not be overlooked, and by the time the season was a month old, it was clear the Pistons would need the contributions of both rookies if they were to realize their considerable potential.

Then came their first western trip, and what Dennis Rodman calls the worst experience of his rookie season.

He grew up in Dallas, so he knows about big cities. But Dallas is not Los Angeles, where the Pistons beat the Clippers on the trip. Or, as Isiah Thomas put it the other day: "Everybody has heard of California, and when you get there, you want to see California."

So Rodman just did what comes naturally. He saw California. He saw the bright lights, and he saw the glamour, and he saw the sunrise.

The only thing he did not see was the inside of his hotel room.

"I couldn't get mad at him," said Thomas, who spent some time counseling the rookie. "I understood."

Though they may not have approved, all Rodman's teammates understood. Most had experienced the same emotions and grappled with the same choices: The boredom of a lonely hotel room versus the action of Hollywood by night.

"Adrian Dantley said it best," Pistons coach Chuck Daly said. " 'You've got to be able to stand four walls.' That's why he (Dantley) has been in the league 11 years. Some guys can't stand being in their rooms 10 minutes, then they're out on the street."

That trip, Rodman said, "was, by far, the toughest part of the season for me. I didn't know how to take care of myself, and I kind of paid for it. I didn't play well. You can have fun, but you've got to pick your spots to have fun."

The Pistons lost four of the five games — to Utah, Sacramento, Phoenix and San Antonio — and the experience underscored this club's need to get major contributions from its bench.

"When the rookies play well," Thomas said, "we go from being a good basketball team to a very good basketball team."

And when the playoffs begin, Rodman knows he will play an important role in the Pistons' success or failure. In a single season, he has become versatile enough for Daly to use at big guard, small forward and power forward. He has become good enough to average 4.3 rebounds and 6.5 points and to make 54.5 percent of his field goals in just 15 minutes of playing time per game.

He has learned to be confident enough to do his job, but humble enough not to offend the veterans he replaces.

And he has done it all with so much enthusiasm that Utah coach Frank Layden — perhaps the NBA's biggest showman — called him a "hot dog."

Thomas said of Rodman: "Over the years, I've learned something about this 'potential' thing. You take a player for what he is and not for what you want him to be. And I like Rodman the way he is."

That, though, is the perspective of a teammate.

Daly sees Rodman differently, full of yet-untapped ability.

"He has worlds of talent, but he has a lot to learn," Daly said. "He does some remarkable things for a rookie — his offensive rebounding and his speed — but he hasn't started utilizing his basketball intelligence."

He is still unpolished.

He is still unsophisticated.

He is still unrefined.

And he is still relying more on instinct than intellect.

But Dennis Rodman doesn't feel out of place in a pro locker room anymore.

He feels right at home. ❖

LA story

June 22, 1988

INGLEWOOD, Calif. — There is a quota on miracles.

One to a customer.

One a day.

The Pistons used up their quota when Isiah Thomas stepped, ever so gingerly, on the Forum's court for the opening tip-off last night.

So there were no miracles left for them when they fell behind the Los Angeles Lakers by 15 points in the fourth quarter of Game 7 of the NBA Finals. There was only the taunt of the fates that allowed them to come within two points of the Lakers with 1:18 left.

There it is.

Reach out.

Touch it.

Grab it.

The title.

Then the fates — and some questionable shot selection — yanked it away from them.

No more miracles.

Isiah Thomas used up the quota, limping into the lineup after three days of therapy on his sprained right ankle, sustained in Game 6.

Ninety minutes before game time, he came into the Forum on crutches, a frown and a bandage on his face, trailing behind him a small troop of cameramen, recording every painful step.

His mind was made up. Despite the odds and despite the skepticism of the doctors, he was going to start.

Any other decision, in the biggest game in the history of this franchise, would have been a surprise.

Isiah Thomas on the bench might have been inspirational to the Pistons.

Win one for the Limper.

But on the bench, he could not score the 10 points he did in the first half. He could not harass the Lakers with four steals. He might be able to find the open man, but he wouldn't have a ball to pass to him.

On the bench, he could only have sat and thought of all the days and all the nights that he worked to get here. All the sweat and all the blood. He could think only of the joy of the sound of his baby boy's cries reaching him over the telephone line. And of the pain throbbing in his ankle.

So Isiah Thomas played.

He played as well as he could. But he could not really set himself on the aching ankle and, dragging the wounded joint behind him, he could not keep up with Byron Scott.

So in the second half, coach Chuck Daly did what he had to do. He kept Thomas on the bench all but nine minutes.

And in the end, when the Pistons had come three points short of their second miracle of the day, Thomas had no complaints, no regrets, no excuses, no tears.

"The ankle really got bad at halftime. I didn't have any injections into it. It bothered me both ways. I couldn't penetrate on offense. I couldn't really cut. And on defense, I wasn't as good.

"The guys who were in there were doing an excellent job. In the end, A.D. (Adrian Dantley) and I were both sitting there praying to win."

That Thomas played was a surprise to few.

There were those who thought he would play because they are believers and those who thought he would play because they are skeptics.

"Sometimes teams use that type of ploy as a psychological trick," Lakers forward James Worthy scoffed before the game. "So until we see him in street clothes ... at game time, we have to believe he is going to play."

Well, James, there he was.

And in Detroit they were crying, "Miracle!" while in Los Angeles they were screaming, "Fraud!"

Either way, what Thomas did and what he tried to do were enough to move Lakers coach Pat Riley to say: "What Isiah Thomas did tonight gives me goose bumps."

Sometimes fact is more captivating than fantasy. More gripping than a Hollywood script.

This time, the pain was real.

And the agony.

And the suffering.

This time, there was no pancake makeup, no ketchup blood, no phony tears. This was real.

Thomas spent 19 hours over three days in the Los Angeles Raiders' training room hooked up to a Jobst Cyro-Temp, a portable cold-compression unit that combines water and ice in a boot to control swelling.

Every now and then, they gave him a jolt of electrical stimulation, too. And in the final stages of the miracle recovery, they added massage.

This was a miracle of science and medicine and technology, though. An incomplete sort of miracle. One that left its beneficiary idle and aching at the very time he would have been most valuable.

To have healed completely in 48 hours, though, Thomas would have needed to go not to the Los Angeles Raiders but to Lourdes.

Too bad.

Fairy tales aren't supposed to end this way.

And neither are miracles.

But in the moments after the Pistons' dream was ended and the Lakers had made good Riley's guarantee of back-to-back championships, Thomas felt neither pain nor disappointment.

"I've been very fortunate," he said.

"I've been a very blessed young man. Though we didn't win the championship, the good far outweighs the bad."

Amen. ❖

Champions

April 19, 1989

RICHFIELD, Ohio — It came not like a shot in the dark, sudden and swift and unexpected.

It came more like a Mack truck, appearing on the horizon as a speck on an endless ribbon of asphalt, then looming larger and larger until it is on top of you, inescapable and lethal, running over you, then rumbling on, giving a couple of toots of its air horn to bid you farewell.

That is how the Detroit Pistons finished off the Cleveland Cavs. That is how the Pistons assured themselves the best record in the NBA.

The Pistons had been heading in that direction for seven weeks, first as that speck in the Cavs' rearview mirror. Lately the outcome was inevitable; only the timing was in doubt.

But the inevitability did not detract from the sweetness. Everybody knows Christmas is coming, too, but the anticipation does not diminish the fun of opening the presents.

The Pistons did not have to win here. They could have accomplished the same thing — almost the same thing — by winning any of their three remaining games at the Palace.

But they wanted to do it here to prove something. How often has Isiah Thomas challenged the opposition to win one in "our house"? This time the Pistons came to the Cavs' house and won one.

A big one.

"It was as good as I thought it would be," acknowledged Joe Dumars, who scored a career-high 42 points. "We wanted to clinch it here, on their court. But we wanted to play it as loose as possible."

The loose part was easy after the Pistons scored the first 12 points.

It was the Cavs who were tight. They had to play catch-up from the opening basket, and not once could they pull even.

When they got close at the beginning of the third quarter, Dumars, the Pistons' quiet man, spoke to them without saying a word.

In your face!

Again! And again!

And again!

Seventeen straight points he scored. Twenty-four in the third quarter. Thirty in the second half.

He buried the ball in the net and the Cavs in their graves, and long before the game was over, the fans who had packed the Coliseum, hoping this would not be the night the Mack truck crushed their team, were streaming to the exits, resigned to what had happened.

These Pistons have come so far — from the bottom of the NBA to the very top, from laughingstock to the team with the best record in professional basketball's best league.

They have come far even in the past seven weeks. When last they were here on Feb. 28, the Cavs routed them, 115-99, and the Pistons trailed in the Central Division by five games.

There was a carnival atmosphere here. The fans who had suffered so long with the Cavs were enjoying the experience.

It was, it seemed, the year of the have-nots.

That was yesterday, though — February, when the Pistons were a speck on the Cavs' horizon.

The Mack truck is upon them now.

They could not help but sense it when the Pistons went ahead, 12-0, in the game's first three minutes and 20 seconds. And by the time the first quarter was half over, Bill Laimbeer was pointing an index finger toward the crowd after making a free throw, and dozens in the disenchanted crowd were pointing back toward him with their middle fingers.

And when Thomas got hot in the fourth quarter, a voice from the stands encouraged the Cavs: "Break his other hand!"

The Pistons, calm and collected and cocky, didn't begin to celebrate until the final 75 seconds of the game, when Chuck Daly sent Dennis Rodman, James Edwards, Fennis Dembo, Michael Williams and John Salley into the game for Dumars, Laimbeer, Thomas, Mark Aguirre and Rick Mahorn.

As they met on the floor, they exchanged high fives.

"It was a good feeling," said Daly, ever the cautious coach. "But I'm aware of what's ahead. Now we wipe the slate clean and start all over again."

True, the most important part, the playoffs, are ahead. But clearly this team is no longer what it used to be: the team everybody else beat up. No longer is it a team with no fans and few players and no tradition and little hope.

No longer are the Detroit Pistons the pantywaists of this league.

They say, sometimes, they regret coming so far. They regret being thought of as thugs and ruffians.

But after the game, in the locker room, they gathered in a circle, their arms extended above their heads, pounding their fists together, and chanted: "Bad boys ... bad boys ... bad boys!"

It was more a rumble, really, than a chant.

It sounded like a Mack truck, rumbling away from the scene of a nasty highway accident.

There was no stopping the Bad Boys, who went on to win their first world championship. ❖

Daly's biggest fan

February 10, 1990

MIAMI — She had gotten up at four in the morning to catch a plane to get here, and she was waiting for him to get off the hotel elevator. She knew she shouldn't talk about him, but she wanted to anyway.

"He's my idol," she said. And although she was somewhat embarrassed by her confession, she was proud of it, too. Proud enough to add: "Really! He is!"

She is 24, and she stood in the lobby of the Omni International Hotel on the edge of Biscayne Bay and waited for her idol: an older man, whose lips form a tight, perturbed line whenever the world is reminded of his age.

His age is to 60 what toes are to the three-point arc: close, real close.

His name is Chuck Daly. Her name is Cydney Daly, his daughter.

"When you don't get to see your dad any more than I do, and you can arrange the time off, you do whatever you can to spend time with him," she said.

So she flew here on a commercial flight while her parents and the rest of the Pistons' party were boarding the team plane in Detroit. And she was standing in the lobby watching one elevator after another come up from the motor lobby and unload Hakeem Olajuwon and Brad Lohaus and John Lucas, then Magic Johnson, James Worthy and A.C. Green to an eager crowd of autograph seekers.

This is a special week for the Dalys, though the coach won't make much of it publicly.

And his wife, Terry, will go only so far as to whisper: "He doesn't like us to talk about things like that with the press. He likes his private, private. He likes you just to see little bits and pieces of him."

Chuck Daly, who will coach the East in the NBA All-Star Game, shows us only what he wants us to see.

We know he cares about grooming. He likes expensive suits and every hair in place. He likes to wear an obviously costly warm-up outfit with the initials CD stitched on the chest. And he likes to let you believe it is personalized for him, until he tugs at the label to show you it is a Christian Dior.

We know he can stamp a mean foot and throw a clipboard with the best of them. We know he does not always see eye-to-eye with officials, or with his players.

There are, though, some subjects that he simply will not address seriously.

Feelings are to be hidden away. Or joked about. They are not to be discussed seriously.

Ask about the distance he has come from his first coaching job at Punxsutawney (Pa.) High, and he will tell you: "I have a little more talent here, except for that groundhog. He could go to his right and get into the hole."

Ask what coaching the All-Star Game means to him and he'll tell you: "For once, the coaches get the same money as the players. For once! Thirty-five hundred for the losers, five thousand for the winners. I guarantee you I won't walk out of the locker room without my check."

He will give you the superficial — some good stories that will brighten America's sports pages this morning.

He described the suit he will wear for the game (double-breasted, dark blue, "because no one can look bad in a dark blue suit"), and he described the tuxedo he would have liked to wear ("eight buttons, Ferree shoulders, but it was $1,500, and I couldn't afford it").

But he will not tell you what his stomach is feeling like this morning.

He will not tell you what emotions he expects when he looks down the bench and sees Isiah Thomas, Joe Dumars and Dennis Rodman sitting there.

He will not tell you how it feels to have covered the miles he and the Pistons have covered together since he showed up in Detroit seven years ago to take over a team that had won one playoff game in the previous seven seasons.

Cydney Daly can't — or won't — speak for him.

But she is proud to speak about him.

He took this job with the Pistons two weeks after she enrolled at Penn State University, and the move left her feeling alone. The daughter of a coach, though, grew up knowing her father would not always be around.

And three years ago, when she graduated from college, the Pistons were embroiled in a playoff struggle with Atlanta, and he told her he probably would not be able to make it for the ceremony.

"I was running around my apartment, late like I always am," she said, standing in that lobby, "when the doorbell rang. When I answered it, he was standing there with this big bunch of balloons in his hand.

"He had chartered a private plane and flew in and had the pilot wait through the ceremony, then he flew back to Detroit."

The man we know only in bits and pieces has won an NBA championship and will coach the best players in the game.

I don't know how you measure success.

But I count a man a success when his daughter, eyes aglow, stands waiting for him in a hotel lobby and is proud to say: "He's my idol." ❖

Rodman's tears

May 8, 1990

U sually, the moisture on Dennis Rodman's body is sweat.

Half his, half someone else's.

Today, it was something else.

Today, he could not help himself. Today, he lost control, and the moisture on his body was the trail of tears that ran down his cheeks as he stood before the hot lights of the cameras at the Palace and talked about what it meant to be named the NBA's defensive player of the year.

If there is one thing Rodman likes to do more than play defense, it is talk. And suddenly he could not talk. The words caught in his throat. The tears drained from his eyes. And he had to walk away from the microphone and around a corner where the cameras could not see him wipe away the salty joy of what he had accomplished.

People talk of basketball being a team game, all-for-one and one-for-all, pulling together and all of that.

What Rodman does, though, is mostly one-on-one. Basketball lambada. Him on Charles Barkley. Him on James Worthy. And this week, him on Patrick Ewing.

And on Charles Oakley.

And Gerald Wilkins.

And Johnny Newman.

"Against New York," he said, with obvious relish, "I'm going to defend just about everybody. If they want me to go out there and defend the coach, I'll do that, too.

"To me, it's easy. It's just bump and grind, bump and grind, bump and grind. It's anticipating. I talk to myself all the time out there."

Rodman is never difficult to pick out on the floor.

He is the one flying through the air.

He is the one falling on the floor.

He is the one with an arm lock on Trent Tucker.

He never holds another player by the trunks, Rodman insisted. But grabbing hold of an arm "just comes natural." He confessed to flopping, too. But his favorite dirty trick is the butt pat.

"I think that's what they hate most," he said after the tears dried and he pointed out the spot on his locker countertop where he will display his award. "I don't know why, but when I pat 'em on the butt, they just hate it."

Some people play quiet, almost invisible basketball and contribute to their teams. Rodman plays the loudest, most visible basketball in the NBA, and today his kamikaze style of defense was honored as the most effective in the league.

He thought he should have won the award a year ago when Utah's Mark Eaton did. Upset, Rodman called Eaton "just a shot-blocker."

"I said some things that I shouldn't have said. That's not unusual," he said, able to laugh at his reputation for speaking first and thinking later.

"To me, though, man-to-man, that's defense. It's a one-on-one thing. If I screw up, people will notice it."

So much is written and said about the athletes who have every chance, yet ruin their lives. More should be written about the Dennis Rodmans of sport.

He had no chance but saved his life anyway.

He is an example of what sports can do for a man.

In Detroit, his story is no secret: lousy high school student; handyman at an auto repair shop; janitor at Dallas-Ft. Worth Airport who was taken in for questioning when he wound up with a pocketful of watches someone else had stolen; a dropout from the first college that took a chance on him before he became a three-time NAIA All-America at Southeastern Oklahoma State; and a high risk when, at 25, the Pistons made him the 27th player drafted in 1986.

His is the kind of story that becomes a three-hour special on TV.

Rodman did not will himself to success. He worked himself to it.

He knows what he is. And he knows how he is seen. And he has come to grips with both.

"I may not be well-liked," he conceded, "but they say: 'He works hard.' People have called me a hot dog. Now people respect me as something."

And you get the feeling that there is no way that he can find the words to tell you how important that is to him.

Dennis Rodman: Somebody.

Dennis Rodman: The best defensive player in the National Basketball Association.

Some might want to take some of the credit. Rodman even tries to share it.

He said Adrian Dantley helped him. And Bill Laimbeer. And Vinnie Johnson. And Isiah Thomas.

"A lot of times, Isiah pumped me up," he said. "I needed motivation, and he'd tell me, 'Go out there and kick some butt!' "

Today, though, is Rodman's day, and Thomas would do nothing to detract from it.

"I gave him some advice," Thomas said. "But nobody but Dennis Rodman can take credit for what he has done. Nobody did it but Dennis Rodman. He made himself a basketball player. He made himself what he is, and nobody should take even a little bit of the credit."

All his teammates left the Pistons' locker room while the press was huddled around Rodman.

Eventually, he found himself all but alone.

And someone wondered whether he knew what his award looked like. Is it a trophy? Or a plaque? Or a certificate?

"I don't know what it looks like," he said.

"But I've got it now. It's mine."

And where there had been tears of joy, there was a smile of pride. Of satisfaction. Of achievement.

Dennis Rodman is the best darn defensive player in the NBA. ❖

Poor losers

May 30, 1991

L ove is blind, so I'm using that as my excuse.

Around here, we've all been in love with the Detroit Pistons the past five years and in love with what they have given this city and state. Others told us they were bad. But we didn't want to believe it.

Did you ever have a teacher call and say your son had misbehaved in school? Or a pal tell you your girlfriend had been seen at a drive-in with another guy?

No! is your first thought. No! I don't believe it.

I don't believe my son is naughty. I don't believe my girlfriend is unfaithful. I don't believe my basketball team is bad.

When the Pistons walked off the Palace floor Monday, with time still remaining on the clock, arrogantly ignoring the Chicago Bulls as they passed the victors' bench, even those of us who loved the Pistons had to admit we had been blind too long.

Pause first, though, for a moment of remembrance and thanks. Do not detract from their time as champions. They were the best team in the game. They deserved everything they got. They fought for it.

Back-to-back champions of the NBA. They have the rings and the banners to prove it.

But they've got a bad name from coast to coast, too, and even here in Detroit it is difficult to defend them.

In Wednesday's New York Times, Ira Berkow called the Pistons' performance "a miserable display of sportsmanship" and "one of the ugliest examples of basketball in memory."

Because of it, he questioned Chuck Daly's qualifications to coach the United States Olympic basketball team next year, writing: "His team disgraced not only itself but the NBA. Next year he will be coaching a team wearing jerseys with 'USA' on them. It is a sobering thought."

But Daly is as defiant as his players.

"People, and that includes the media, accepted all that went along with winning, but never was all of that brought up then," he said Wednesday. "If you're going to accept all that goes along with winning, you've got to take some of the other, too. Go back to the Los Angeles series or the Portland series. I don't remember a lot of people congratulating us. There just isn't much of that anymore. It's very competitive. It's big business."

I can excuse the Pistons' early exit Monday. Teams do that all the time. The Pistons' misfortune was that the clock stopped with 7.9 seconds remaining. Had the clock not stopped, it would have expired before they left the court.

And I can understand their anger at Michael Jordan's statement that "people want to push this kind of basketball out." He neglected to note that the Pistons won their titles with defense, and all the NBA's better teams now play that "kind of basketball."

But I cannot excuse James Edwards for tripping Jordan or Bill Laimbeer for elbowing Scottie Pippen in the the face. And I can only hope Dennis Rodman's letter of apology to Pippen for shoving him out of bounds is sincere.

The Pistons forgot to ask enough of themselves.

When Mark Aguirre arrived in Detroit, Isiah Thomas, Vinnie Johnson and Laimbeer invited him to dinner and told him what it meant to be a Piston.

He said later they scared him.

But when he exaggerated the extent of an injury this season, converting a medically diagnosed strained thumb into a "sprained thumb and sprained wrist," then pseudo-courageously talked of how he would "have to hide it" in game situations because the team needed his services, his teammates overlooked it.

They never told him more was required of a Piston than that. After I wrote that Aguirre was exaggerating the injury, John Salley asked: "Why'd you do that to my man Mark?"

"Because," I said, "it was BS."

"Yeah," Salley said. "But you still shouldn't have done it."

The Pistons lost their title because they were old and tired and they forgot what it meant to be a Piston. They forgot what kind of commitment went into those two championships.

You can't live in this state and love the Celtics, but I remember two incidents that show the Pistons could learn a lot from them.

First was the infamous Rodman-Thomas-Bird incident in 1987, when Rodman said Bird would be considered an ordinary player if he were not white, and Thomas seemed to agree with him.

The media wanted to bury Thomas for that, but Bird went on national TV to say he was certain Thomas was misunderstood. Thomas could have done that for Jordan.

When the Pistons broke the Celtics' physical and mental hold over them and finally won the Eastern Conference championship, Kevin McHale walked over to Thomas, draped his arm around his adversary, congratulated him and wished him well against the Lakers. None of the Pistons, except perhaps Salley, did as much Monday.

Most of the Pistons seemed to have forgotten those lessons.

We were always told the Bad Boys image was only an illusion, the creation of public relations and marketing.

Monday, it seemed painfully real.

They proved to us over the last five years that they knew how to win.

It's a shame they never learned how to lose. ❖

Return of the Spur

November 20, 1993

The fans weren't sure, when Dennis Rodman showed his tattooed body and blond hair on the Palace floor, just how they felt about him.

By the time the night was over, there was no doubt.

Rodman is somebody else's worry now. Somebody else's headache and — some nights — somebody else's star.

When he came onto the floor — 15 minutes after his teammates and only 10 seconds before game time — he was greeted with a mixture of boos and cheers. Hundreds rose to cheer him, and a cynic at courtside guessed "the Pistons probably piped in the boos."

By the time Rodman was ejected from the game with 1:40 left, there was no need to pipe in boos and no ambivalence among the 21,454. They booed Rodman all the way to the locker room, where he ripped a few things apart as a final farewell to his old franchise.

He has not changed, unless you count the new tattoos and his new hair color. He plays the game ugly, just like the Pistons did in the good ol' days, when they won everything in sight. He bumps and grinds and shoves and gets in your face. He was ejected for giving Sean Elliott a shove out of bounds and, for an encore, he chased after the officials as if he wanted to give them not only a piece of his mind but a piece of his fist.

The crowd hated him for it.

It was the same crowd that loved him when he gave Scottie Pippen a much harder shove, back when the word across his chest was not Spurs but Pistons.

Rodman is still the NBA's biggest enigma. He listens to his own drummer, a beat no one else can hear or understand. But when it is game time, he performs. In defeat, bothered by an infected left eye that was swollen partially shut, he collected 14 rebounds, scored eight points, had two assists and played every second until he was tossed, either for being too physical or for having too many tattoos.

And when he got to the locker room, he pulled a television off a mounting and destroyed it, according to Pistons president Tom Wilson. "I hate to do it, but we'll probably bill him for it," Wilson said.

Rodman's return to the Palace had been awaited with some anticipation, and when the San Antonio bus pulled into the Palace, a group of cameramen jockeyed for position at the bus door.

Lights! Camera! Action!

The door swung open and out stepped the coach, squinting into the bright lights. Out came a reporter. And the trainer and a couple of assistants. Out came all the players. All but the one they were waiting for, the one with the yellow hair and the odd nickname.

Once again, Rodman was operating by his own rules and arriving in his own good time. Instead of staying at the team hotel, he was staying in a home in which he used to live. There's a for sale sign in the front yard.

He arrived an hour before game time — early by the standards he set in his final season with the Pistons — walking in wearing a camouflage cap (backward, of course), a T-shirt, warm-ups and black tennis shoes.

How much did he spend on the wardrobe, I wondered.

"Nothing," he said. "I go to the Salvation Army."

He was kidding. I think. Surely the Salvation Army checks a man's net worth when he comes to the door looking for hand-me-downs. But if Rodman's $2.3 million salary says he doesn't shop there, nothing about his clothes affirms it. He said he doesn't hold any grudges against the guys with whom he used to share a locker room, but that's just political correctness finding its way into the NBA.

He was coming closer to the truth when he admitted: "We're not friends.... . On the court, I don't know them."

On the court he proved that. He and Bill Laimbeer exchanged elbows in the windpipe early on, just to get reacquainted. Laimbeer, the villain just a few days ago when he initiated a skirmish during practice with Isiah Thomas, was the hero in our town when Rodman was the foe.

If Detroit ever was home for Rodman, this proved he could not go home again.

Wouldn't he have liked it to be different? Wouldn't he have preferred to have the people here remember the good times? The part he played in the championships, the rebounding crowns, the award as defensive player of the year?

Wouldn't he have preferred to go away from here with cheers ringing in his ears?

"Why?" he asked. "I ain't gonna kiss nobody's butt. I don't care."

He's still a Bad Boy.

Maybe the last of them. But it just isn't fashionable anymore. ❖

Bad to the end

December 2, 1993

A couple of dozen reporters showed up at the Palace for Bill Laimbeer's farewell announcement.

One or two went to tell him good-bye. The rest went to make sure he left.

That's the kind of relationship Laimbeer had with the media. It is the kind of relationship he had with opposing players. He was the guy you loved to despise. And he made it easy.

He left saying he would always be a Piston and that he loved the organization and the men he had played with these past 13 seasons. And that was a nice sentiment, but it was only partially true. A lot of people who wore the word Pistons across their chests had nothing in common with Laimbeer other than the name on the bottom of their paychecks.

Dennis Rodman said Laimbeer never spoke to him in the locker room.

Laimbeer conceded he had belittled a lot of his teammates, insulted them, intimidated them, tried to goad them into being the kind of player he wanted them to be.

To his enemies, Bill Laimbeer is Hitler. To his family, I suppose, he is St. Francis.

In reality, he is something in between, probably no closer to being one than to being the other.

In the beginning, he was just this big, slow, white stiff who couldn't even get a contract worth signing when he finished his eligibility at Notre Dame. So he went off to Italy for a year to learn to like pasta and miss the United States.

Truth is, he was never very sure of his talents.

In the world you and I live in — where a 6-footer is about normal — it is the little guys who so often have the chips on their shoulders. The Napoleonic complex, it is called. Little guys acting tough and arrogant and belligerent to make up for their lack of size.

In the NBA, size is a given. Talent is what separates people. And Bill Laimbeer, this big, slow, white stiff who had to go to Italy to earn a living, came back with a complex of his own. Maybe someday it will be called the Laimbeerian complex. He made up for his lack of skill by acting tough and arrogant and belligerent.

It made him feel good. It made him feel superior.

And it bugged the hell out of opponents.

In time, he became the most-disliked — not to mention most-fined — man in the league.

At home, he was a father and a husband. Loved, I am sure. In his locker room, he was tolerated for all the things he could do for his team. Everywhere else, Laimbeer was disliked — respected for his competitiveness, but disliked, nonetheless.

He wore the black hat. He didn't seek it. It found him. But once he became the man in the black hat — the bully of the NBA — he accepted wearing it. Often, actually, he seemed to relish wearing it.

"Somebody had to play that role," he said. "And as years went by, I saw it as a tool to help our ballclub. I expanded that role."

Indeed, he did. He shoved and elbowed and hipped and, some say, tripped. And when the fans on the road booed him, he would cup a hand to his ear as if to ask: "Can't you boo any louder?" And they would hate him all the more.

Laimbeer might laugh at being called athletic, but he knew from the first day he played in the NBA that he was an entertainer. His problem was that the whole world was his stage. He didn't know how to get off it when the game was over.

He didn't know how to put away the black hat.

He didn't know how to pat a young kid on the head and smile when he signed his name to a scrap of paper.

Fan mail arrived at his locker in big bags, and he would tear open a letter or two (to make sure there were no checks inside, the cynics claimed), then he would let the rest sit, ignored. He never asked those people to write, he reasoned, so he had no obligation to respond.

So kids in Grand Rapids and Toledo and Lexington watched their mailboxes for days and weeks and finally gave up hope that Bill Laimbeer would ever acknowledge the childish scrawl on their notes.

He was so afraid of showing a weakness that he kept his game face on until he shut his front door behind him and became a father and husband.

I asked whether he had ever wished he could separate the two: Bill Laimbeer on the court and Bill Laimbeer off. Didn't he ever wish he had shown a kinder, more compassionate side to someone other than his family and a few of his closest friends?

"I wondered what it would be like," he admitted. "But it's not gonna happen. It's part of my personality. The person I am — it's difficult to let your guard down around people you don't know."

So when word of his impending retirement spread, only three messages of good wishes came in. Faxes from Chuck Daly and former Pistons assistant Brendan Suhr and a telephone call from former Pistons trainer Mike Abdenour.

"I don't make friends on other clubs," Laimbeer said, shrugging off the lack of communications.

But he didn't hear from Rick Mahorn, either. Or from Ron Rothstein. Or Rodman. He didn't hear from John Salley. Or Scott Hastings. Or James Edwards. All men who once were on his side.

Bill Laimbeer has spent a career being the toughest competitor he knew how to be. To him, that was always worth sacrificing everything else. He didn't need praise, he didn't need the friendships of other players, he didn't need to schmooze up to reporters.

He only needed to compete.

He is quitting, he said, because he was beginning to see in himself all the things he used to despise in other players.

"When we had players who lost their desire to compete and risk it all, I would abuse them," he said. "I have no use for them. When a player broke mentally, I'd ride 'em or dismiss them. They have no business being on the team. And I'm in that position now. I'm one of them. I don't have the desire to compete as a basketball player anymore. I'm tired of talking about the past."

So Bill Laimbeer stepped into the future, writing his own epitaph for his career:

"I did my job," he said. "I was paid to win, and I won. Both at home and on the road, people went away saying: 'Man, that was fun. I got my money's worth.' "

A lot of what Laimbeer did, I hated. I hated seeing him walk past children with a pen and paper and hopeful eyes. I hated the way he would destroy young reporters, long on hope but short on self-assuredness, young men and women who felt about themselves the way Laimbeer once felt about himself.

But I don't think he is Hitler.

I think he made himself a very good basketball player — and a better actor. It was great theater for 48 minutes every night.

I am just sorry he didn't know how to get off the stage when the houselights went down. ❖

Dennis and Madonna

May 5, 1994

I heard the rumors. I wanted the facts.

My inquiring mind wanted to know.

So I picked up the telephone, and I called the man involved. I've known him for eight years or so, and I'm accustomed to finding him on the sports pages of newspapers or in Sports Illustrated or Basketball Digest.

What, I wondered, was he doing on these television news magazine shows? What was he doing being photographed getting into a limo with Madonna? It was just a publicity gimmick for her, right? A photo opportunity. A gag, like Roseanne Arnold and that goofy husband of hers adding a third person to their marriage, then threatening divorce, then making up.

So I called the hotel in Salt Lake City where the San Antonio Spurs were staying.

"Dennis Rodman's room," I said.

"He's not taking calls," I was told.

"Well, let's leave him a message," I responded.

The young lady at the other end of the line tried not to laugh in my ear.

"He's not bothering to pick up his messages," she said. "He's too busy with her."

Omygosh! It was true.

Dennis and Madonna.

I see another tattoo coming.

Maybe her face alongside his daughter's on his left forearm. Maybe a heart with an arrow through it and their names. Maybe she'll pierce her navel as he has and put a matching ring through it. Maybe she already has one of those.

Was this a match made in the fun house or what?

We should have a contest. Name the most bizarre couple you can imagine. Tina Turner and Woody Allen. Dolly Parton and Meat Loaf. Martina Navratilova and Rush Limbaugh.

I sort of suspected some day Dennis would wind up with Tonya Harding.

Tom Wilson, president of the Pistons and Pine Knob, a man who knows sports and entertainment, was, at first, at a loss for what to say about the magical matchup, but once he got over the emotion of receiving the news, he said: "It's nice to see two good-looking blonds get together."

Though I found the coupling bizarre, some of my co-workers thought it was the most natural matchup of all-time. Where else could Rodman find someone who had made more money than he has and at the same time been equally crude and tasteless? Where else could Madonna have found a man with a true appreciation of the variety of her hair colors?

I had to confess to being curious about what they were doing in that hotel room in Salt Lake City. Did they compare hair dyes? Did she let Dennis dress up in her conical bras?

What must they have talked about?

Probably there was a lot of discussion about the elections in South Africa, the fighting in Rwanda and the debate over what Dr. Jack Kevorkian is doing.

Probably they debated the merits of President Bill Clinton's health care package and NAFTA, and they took turns reading to each other from the editorial page of the New York Times.

Not!

I bet she asked Dennis what David Robinson is really like. And he probably asked her to get him an audition with her recording company. I bet they spent the afternoon watching Geraldo and Sally Jessy.

Those are the things I was going to ask when I got Dennis on the phone. What did they do together? What did they talk about? Were they really dating, or is this all a hoax?

I wondered, too, if he recognized the difference between Madonna and most of the other people in the world: Whereas most people collect basketball and baseball cards, Madonna collects the real thing.

For a while, she dated Jose Canseco.

Then it was Mark Messier.

Then Rony Seikaly.

Then Brian Shaw.

Then Dennis Rodman was her man.

She may be going through the alphabet, but I don't want to say she is loose. Let's just call it fickle. Lacking in commitment.

And Dennis?

There is no word to describe him — finally I am convinced of that. We have called him talented. We have called him dedicated. We have called him confused. A dirty player. A child in a man's body. A tattoo parlor's answer to the question: "Where's the rent money coming from?"

He is all that and more. And I have abandoned hope of defining him. Or of understanding him.

I had hoped he would help by returning my call, but the operator was right, of course. Dennis never called back.

So whatever he and Madonna had in mind, I knew I wouldn't get an invitation.

But we'll keep watching for the videos on "A Current Affair." ❖

There were Pistons long before there were Bad Boys. Here are three.

Earl Lloyd

January 14, 1992

On Oct. 31, 1950, one black man wore an NBA uniform.

One in the whole world.

The Boston Celtics had made Chuck Cooper the first black drafted into the NBA that summer and the New York Knicks had made Sweetwater Clifton the first black to sign an NBA contract, but on Oct. 31, 1950, another man became the first black to play in the NBA.

Who was he?

"There's some discrepancy about that," said John Salley, the most Afrocentric of the Pistons. "I always heard it was Sweetwater Clifton, but there was a guy named Cooper, too. I have something about it in my locker."

Joe Dumars wasn't sure, either. "Cooper. Right? I don't remember his first name."

Mark Aguirre at first was completely baffled.

"I don't have any idea. I know Jackie Robinson was the first black to play baseball, but I don't know who the first was in basketball. No, wait a minute, it was Sweetwater somebody."

"There's really no reason they should know me," said the first black man to play in the NBA.

But of course he is wrong.

When the Pistons beat Dallas last night at the Palace, 21 of the 24 players in uniform were black. Before they could be here, Sweetwater Clifton had to be here and Chuck Cooper had to be here.

And Earl Lloyd, the first black to play in the NBA, had to be here, too.

On that October night 41 years ago, he was a forward for the Washington Capitols. Today he is 63 and works for the Detroit Board of Education, and even some of his closest friends don't know his place in sports history.

Several years ago, he was an answer on the television show "Jeopardy!"

and his telephone rang and rang with calls from friends who were surprised at the revelation that he broke the color line in the NBA.

Though hardly anything has been said or written about his contribution, Lloyd said too much is made of it.

"I don't think a scheduling quirk should detract from Cooper," he said. "He played on the first of November, so what's the difference?

"I was just in the right place at the right time; I was lucky all the way. If I had not been a local kid, Washington would not have drafted me, and if they hadn't, nobody else would have because they didn't scout players in black schools."

Lloyd grew up in Alexandria, Va., and played at West Virginia State, and in the summer of 1950, the Capitols drafted him in the ninth round after the Celtics had taken Cooper in the second. Later the Knicks purchased Clifton from the Harlem Globetrotters.

"Sometimes people likened me to Jackie Robinson, but I've always said what I did wasn't even close," Lloyd said. "His own teammates didn't even want to play with him. You've got to remember in 1947, a lot of those baseball players' first pair of shoes were baseball shoes. The people playing in the NBA were college people.

"I had some problems, of course, not as a player, but when I went out looking for an apartment, there wasn't any. Some players probably hit me a little harder than they hit other players, but not one player ever called me a name."

Times were changing, but slowly.

"In Ft. Wayne, I could stay in the team hotel, but they wouldn't serve me in the restaurant. I was shocked when they let me sleep there," he said.

"I called for room service and ate in my room, and my coach, Bones McKinney, a North Carolinian, came up to my room, and we had dinner together. He knew and I knew we weren't going to change things immediately, and it was important to know he was in my corner."

Lloyd's NBA statistics were modest — in his best season he averaged 10.2 points and grabbed 553 rebounds — but Dolph Schayes, a teammate on the Syracuse Nationals, said: "He got the poor end of the stick as far as playing was concerned. He was always doing the dirty work. He helped me a great deal because, with him in there, I was free to rebound and get a lot of glory since his game was to guard the other team's offensive ace."

Lloyd played 10 seasons — with Washington, Syracuse and the Pistons — and for portions of two seasons in the early '70s, he coached the Pistons, winning 22 games and losing 55.

Then he slipped back into anonymity, without regrets.

"I can't count up to $5 million," he said, "but it makes me feel good to know that I was part of contributing something to enable young black kids to make big money.

"A lot of people say: 'I didn't know you were the first black to play in the NBA.' Well, if I went around with a sign on my back, I'd look like a fool and people still wouldn't believe me."

Earl Lloyd?

"I never heard of him," Isiah Thomas said. "But tell him I said 'Thanks for the opportunity.' " ❖

Dave Bing

February 12, 1991

F or most athletes, the cheering stops the day they strip off the uniform the final time.

They hang up the jock, shower with the guys one last time, dress and walk into the darkness. Alone with only memories and a past.

Too many have no future.

Too many know just jump shots or home runs, post patterns or slap shots. Too many sell us their athletic skills for a decade or so and have nothing else to offer. They slip off into a lifetime of anonymous regret when the spotlight no longer shines on them.

The exceptions are so rare and precious we dare not let them escape us.

Dave Bing is one of those. He heard the cheers again last night.

At the "Dave Bing Salute" to benefit the International Afro-American Sports Hall of Fame and Gallery, fans cheered and told him he was appreciated as a basketball player in the dim long, long ago of the 1960s and '70s. But the hundreds who turned out at Cobo Center to salute the former Pistons guard honored him more for what he has done wearing a suit in a corporate office than for what he did in gym shorts on a basketball court.

"Do I know him?" asked Tigers President Bo Schembechler. "No, not really. But I admire him because, of all the pro athletes around here, he has probably put more back into the community than anyone else and has been the best role model."

Ask Dave Bing of what he is most proud, and he will tell you something like that.

"I am proudest of what I mean to this community and what the community means to me," he said. "I can't do any more as an athlete, but for the rest of my life I can do something for this community as an activist — just an interested citizen or in politics. And I plan to make this a better place to live. I've learned that giving makes you feel good."

For almost a decade, the word politics has invariably been linked with Bing's name. He was almost named coach of the Pistons 11 years ago, but when that fell through as a result of premature publicity, Bing never looked at the game seriously again.

"It's best it didn't happen," he said, "because if it had, I would always have wondered what I could accomplish out of basketball.... . Politics is never far from my mind because it gets mentioned so often. You think about it, but my job now is all-encompassing. In the two businesses (Bing Steel and Superb Manufacturing), I have a payroll of about $3 million and employ close to 200 people, so I've got some responsibilities to the folks who are here. And if I start thinking about politics now, I may become unfocused and won't succeed here.

"I've got to make sure I've got the management team in here. That's really an objective of mine, and that's happening."

He doesn't say he would like to be mayor of Detroit.

But he does say, after living in Southfield for 20 years: "For a long time, I've wanted to build a home in Detroit. That is what I want to do."

And once that happens, it is likely he will take a serious look at running for mayor.

Don Adams, who roomed with Bing for more than two years when they were Pistons teammates, could not say he ever thought in those days of his roommate being honored with a "day" and having his name passed around as a mayoral candidate. But, he added: "We don't know the future. We do know, though, that successful people are going to be successful, and he always will be. He never was what the media would call a typical jock.

"This day is 20 years late."

He is wrong, of course. After his career ended in 1978, we could have honored Bing only for being the NBA rookie of the year in 1967, for averaging 20.3 points throughout his career, for being named the All-Star Game MVP one season, for dishing out 5,397 career assists.

Last night, Bing — a 47-year-old who can no longer hit the jumper while hanging in the air, can no longer leave a defender frozen to the floor as he fakes and drives around him, can no longer play in the NBA old-timers' game without being sore for a week — was honored because he has given far more since he left the sport.

Because he is creating jobs in Detroit and offering options to life on the street, on unemployment, on welfare. Because he is an example to star athletes and to those who watch from the sidelines, to kids black and white and brown and red and yellow.

He learned something as a teenager that he never forgot.

"I earned a bricklayer's apprenticeship," he recalled. "I learned how real people lived. With a lunch box every day. With 10 or 15 minutes to wolf down their meal without washing their hands and then have to go home filthy. That gave me a work ethic. That helps me a lot today. Those people respected authority and responsibility and did whatever it took to get the job done."

It is a lesson he is trying to pass along.

Earl Lloyd, Bing's first Pistons coach, said: "The time comes when nobody remembers how many points you scored, but people remember what kind of person you are, and Dave Bing is as great a human being as there is."

Before the 1966 NBA draft, the Pistons and New York Knicks flipped a coin for the first choice. Dave Bing was one of the best players available. Cazzie Russell was the other.

The Knicks won the flip and picked Russell.

Ed Coil, the Pistons' general manager at the time, recalled the moment just before last night's banquet. "We lost the flip," he said.

I don't think so.

The Pistons won that flip.

Detroit won.

Michigan won.

And we're still cheering. ❖

Bob Lanier

November 1, 1983

There is a certain nobility about an ancient warrior, though gnarled and grizzled, rising for one more effort.

The gunfighter, his eyes clouded by time, slapping leather against a younger, quicker adversary. The old pirate, a patch and a hook where an eye and a hand used to be, sailing once more against the armada. The last gladiator, streaked with dirt and blood and tears of frustration, squinting into the sun as he hears the screams of the crowd one more time.

There is nobility in refusing to acknowledge the effect of time and age. But there is foolishness in it, too. And sadness at seeing a man once the stalker now the prey. A man who once lived by his strength and muscle, surviving on cunning and instinct, straining against the objections of his body to re-create the feats of his youth.

Sport is filled with men and women like that.

Gordie Howe was one. And Y.A. Tittle. And Gaylord Perry.

Pete Rose is one. And Billie Jean King. And Kenny Stabler.

And Bob Lanier, whose scarred knees will carry his aging body into the Silverdome tonight when the Milwaukee Bucks visit the Pistons.

There was a time when Bob Lanier was a terror in the NBA. An awesome man to be feared as well as respected. Nearly 7 feet and 270 pounds of desire, determination and ability. He was not to be bullied, and most centers learned the lesson quickly. He did not often fight on the court, but when he did, there was seldom a need for an official to render judgment. An Atlanta center named Bob Christian took a punch at him in Cobo Arena 10 years ago. With one punch, Lanier put him down for the count.

He warred with Wilt Chamberlain and Willis Reed and Lew Alcindor, later Kareem Abdul-Jabbar — and he won as many as he lost.

But Bob Lanier turned 35 last month, and his fists are in retirement. For one more winter, though, he has coaxed his knees onto the court, promising them he never will ask again.

That's what he said last year, too. But it was a promise he could not keep, though he hardly resembles the Bob Lanier who was the heart and the hope of the Detroit franchise through the '70s.

He has not averaged 20 points since 1979. He has not had 500 rebounds in a season since 1980. And last year, his aching body allowed him to play only 39 regular-season games and, for the first time in his career, he failed to make at least 50 percent of his field goal attempts.

Nothing comes easily any longer. The surgeon's knife has left his knees looking like carved slabs of meat. Time and age have dulled his once-great skills, and tonight he will look into the eyes of a man who is what he once was.

Bill Laimbeer is big and strong and jealous of the space under the basket. A scrapper and a fighter, he has made himself one of the NBA's very best rebounders. And he is nine years younger.

On the day the Pistons made Bob Lanier their first draft choice in 1970, Bill Laimbeer was a 13-year-old schoolboy in California. So were Eric Hipple and Alan Trammell. And nine-year-old Isiah Thomas was learning survival in Chicago.

By the standards of the game, Lanier is an old man. But in 13 years, the championship has eluded him, and every now and then there is a hint of what used to be, just enough to bring him back for one more try. It was not coincidence that Milwaukee, with Lanier at center, was the only team to win a playoff game from Moses Malone and the Philadelphia 76ers last spring.

And it was not charity that prompted the Bucks to sign Lanier to another contract after the one presumed to be his last expired last summer.

Occasionally he still can summon, from deep inside, remnants of what used to be. Sometimes you see it, if you look quickly. For an instant, he is the Bob Lanier of old: the intimidator, the strong man, the one not to be messed with. But just as quickly, time reasserts itself.

Like the old gunfighter maneuvering his stalker so the sun shines in his eyes, Lanier must rely on all the tricks he has learned in 13 years. The wit and the will are there, but the body seldom responds to the urgency of the situation.

His mere presence is testimony to his desire.

There is nobility to it.

And sadness. ❖

Baseball

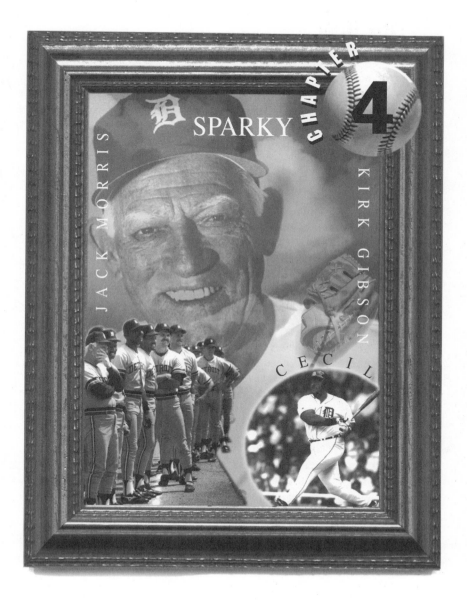

CHAPTER **4**

SPARKY

JACK MORRIS

KIRK GIBSON

CECIL

Strike one

August 5, 1981

I t will never be the same.

Sometime during the summer, the little boy died.

It was probably time. He was 41 and still believed in fairy tales and the Great American Pastime. To him, summer was hot dog vendors and the aroma of cheap cigars wafting through the still night air. Lou Costello in a baggy coat, his hands resting on overly ample hips, glaring at Bud Abbott and demanding to know: "Who's on first?"

Summer was for the game we all learned to play as kids, on a diamond carved out of a small dusty park in south Texas; on chalk-lined asphalt in the heart of Manhattan; with an old broken bat, salvaged from a minor league park someplace and held together with black electrical tape; with a glove our parents bought from Sears, with Ted Williams' real autograph on it.

Baseball stadiums were special places, where the little boy, like millions before him, went through the ritual of growing up when his father left the rest of the family at home and just the two of them — father and son — went to the game.

They'd go early, the little boy and the father, so they could watch batting practice while the old man pointed out how this player stood in the batter's box and how the second baseman straddled the bag while taking the throw from the catcher. Even on nights the home team lost, the little boy never left the ballpark feeling sad.

It was a magic place, an island apart from all that was wrong with life. It was a place little boys could forget the heartache inflicted by little girls in pigtails and braces, where the menu consisted of great, mustardy hot dogs and giant plastic cups of Coke instead of Mom's peas and liver and milk. It was a place where nothing mattered but the wonderful manly ballet taking place on the floodlit expanse of green just beyond the wire meshing.

Going to a baseball game wasn't like watching men at work. The little boy's father never took him to the garage to watch a mechanic knock dents out of a car, or to the department store to watch a man sell shoes.

There was no way to quite put it in words, but no one had to tell the little boy that the game of baseball was different. Different even from football or basketball. Certainly different from hockey or soccer.

Baseball just seemed to belong to everybody.

America's game.

He should have realized long ago that he was living a fantasy, for while he was remaining a little boy, baseball had grown up.

Major league baseball, he should have realized, has for a long, long time been a game in name only. In reality, it is a business. It did not belong to the little boy. It belonged to conglomerates who judge success in dollars and cents or, at the very least, in tax write-offs. What little boy can stand and cheer for General Motors or Bendix, or even Knight-Ridder Newspapers?

No longer, the little boy realized this summer, is there any truth in the saying: "It's not whether you win or lose, but how you play the game." In the real world of major league baseball, the things that matter are net earnings and tax shelters and compensation and arbitration and deferred payments and free agency.

The little boy couldn't find those categories in his box score. All he knew about was RBIs and ERAs, homers and saves and stolen bases. He had clung to a simpler time far, far too long. A time when baseball was played for fun, and even the grown men in their flannel uniforms with the numbers on the back seemed to feel as he did: that they were — deep in their hearts — little boys, too.

Sometime during the summer, the little boy died, killed by the realization that baseball had outgrown his belief in it.

In his place is a full-grown man — a little wiser, but a lot sadder.

Damn! ❖

Ron LeFlore

July 21, 1982

Ron LeFlore spent the first few hours of his suspension by the Chicago White Sox at Hoot Robinson's Bar, while just across the street — in Tiger Stadium — his teammates were breaking a five-game losing streak and seeming to miss him not at all.

Ernie Harwell, his voice flowing through the radio behind the bar, told the story: "And it's a home run by Harold Baines, halfway up into the upper deck in rightfield. And the White Sox lead, four to nothing."

Ron LeFlore wasn't listening. He'd watched the first two innings from a seat behind the White Sox dugout, "because I feel it's my duty to be behind 'em 100 percent," he said.

With a couple of old pals on neighboring stools, Ron LeFlore was doing one of the things Ron LeFlore does best. He was weaving a web of words that portrayed him as meek, humble and very sorry if he caused anyone any trouble.

Some people call it "a way with words." Some call it a con job. Some call it bull, and then a little more.

Under any name, they loved it at Hoot Robinson's.

The snappily dressed lawyer hovered over LeFlore's shoulder, hanging on every word, awaiting an opportunity to add his collaborating testimony to whatever was said.

The peanut vendor from the corner of Michigan and Trumbull — pointing out he understood athletes because he used to be a boxer — sympathized, too.

Autograph this scrap of paper, Ronnie. Put your name on this bag of peanuts, Mr. LeFlore.

I've known Ronnie LeFlore for 10 years, never as a young man, when he was growing up in a neighborhood littered with the carcasses of cannibalized automobiles; nor the LeFlore with the gun in his hand who landed in Jackson Prison.

I met him shortly after Billy Martin and the Detroit Tigers gave him the opportunity to rebuild his life. And I liked him immediately. I could never picture him pointing a gun at somebody and saying: "Stick 'em up or I'll blow your brains out," or anything like that.

He looks you in the eye when he talks. He is glib, smooth. He doesn't blink or flinch.

So why do I doubt him?

There was not a sign of arrogance about him. No anger. No indignation. Ron LeFlore was humble and contrite. He said he was at fault, and he said he was very, very sorry for causing such a fuss.

He couldn't say it often enough.

He said so in the prepared statement he handed manager Tony La Russa earlier in the day. Now he was saying it over and over again as Harwell continued to document the Tigers' demise.

"I want people to look at me as a person who has acknowledged his wrongs.

"I think it (the three-day suspension) was a little harsh, but I'm able to accept whatever measures are necessary.

"I think I'm a responsible person, but I'm a human. Everybody can be in error at times. This time I was.

"I'm with a group of people who can win, and I want to be a part of it.... . That's part of the burden on me for letting them down. I want you to know how bad I feel. I feel worse than anybody because I feel I've let down myself, and that's something I don't want to do.

"Nobody can say nothing will ever happen again. Human beings are always able to make a mistake.... . I'm concerned, but I'm still human."

It was a litany that seemed to require a response of "All is forgiven" after every admission of guilt.

But LeFlore's reputation and indiscretions have followed him from Detroit to Montreal and to Chicago. Sparky Anderson became so disenchanted that he traded LeFlore for Dan Schatzeder.

The track record is the reason managers and fans, the media and teammates might have some trouble believing what Ronnie says. He has always talked a good game. He is running out of time to back it up with actions.

"Maybe this will awaken me," he said, sounding almost like a child thanking his mother for a spanking.

"I've been treated like a gentleman in Chicago. Tony La Russa, as far as I'm concerned, is a super human and a super man.

"I know what position I'm in. It's triple the pressure on me to be punctual."

Forgetting to be punctual is costing him an estimated $3,200 a day. But he promises he'll try to be better.

No bull. No con.

"OK, it's time to go," LeFlore said suddenly, rounding up his friends, pumping hands all around and heading out the front door just as the White Sox completed their 6-0 win over Detroit.

"Hey," the barmaid said to me as the door swung shut behind LeFlore. "Are you paying his tab?" ❖

Gibby

February 24, 1984

L AKELAND, Fla. — Around and around rain-soaked Marchant Stadium they ran, kicking up geysers of water with each footfall. Alan Trammell, in full baseball uniform, cleats and all; Kirk Gibson, in a T-shirt, baseball pants and stockinged feet.

Kirk Gibson, the perennial hope of spring. Kirk Gibson, whose body has always been filled with unrealized promise. Kirk Gibson, the guy they tell all those stories about: playboy, carouser, jerk, arrogant unfeeling snob who insults little kids asking for autographs.

The opening of spring training signals the opening of Kirk Gibson-watching season. As if the gray skies over Lakeland had opened just enough to allow a single shaft of sunshine to catch him in its rays, he stands once again in the spotlight.

Six positions on the Tigers are spoken for — all but third base, where Glenn Wilson and Barbaro Garbey lead the pack, and rightfield, where Gibson gets first crack.

You do remember Gibson in rightfield? Opening Day at Tiger Stadium a year ago, when Sparky Anderson pointed him in that direction — without the benefit of spring training preparation — and Gibson nearly sacrificed his life in mortal combat with the uncatchable batted ball.

It was not a pretty sight. And it set the tone for Gibson's most disappointing season: a .227 average, 96 strikeouts, reams of bad publicity.

"I know everything that's written about me," he said, swiping strands of wet golden hair from his forehead after his run was completed. "I took every boo, every cheap shot. It would bother anybody, but why feel guilty when you know the truth?"

All most baseball fans want from Kirk Gibson is a .300 season, a couple of dozen home runs and maybe 80 RBIs.

But for those who want more — the ones who have been waiting for an admission of some sort of guilt on his part — Gibson offers a confession.

"I might have taken things a little lax," he said, a droplet of rain-diluted sweat dripping off his nose. "But I'm human, and I'm going to learn by it. I've stopped going to bars because I can't be just another guy in a bar. I've hurt myself in the past. I've made mistakes, and I'm not afraid to admit it. I was rude to a lot of people.

"But everybody has to learn for himself. If somebody were to come in here and tell me not to do something because it's bad for me, I'm going to find out for myself."

To some, that might seem hardheaded, like challenging pneumonia by running through the slush in stockinged feet because the new shoes aren't broken in. To Gibson, it is part of growing up.

That process sometimes seems frustratingly slow to the Tigers organization, impatiently waiting for talents that always seem on the verge of blossoming.

He's almost 27, entering his fifth season with the Tigers, and it is time for Gibson to produce.

He said he knows that. He said his winter revolved around a training program, a couple of hours a day, five days a week, in a health club, "making the joints that are stressed most stronger."

He said he has matured. He said past mistakes will not be duplicated and that never again will he allow — as he did last season — his mind to become cluttered with concern about what is being said and written about him.

"I got caught up in concentrating on everything but baseball, and that was my fault," he said. "There's been a lot of changes in my life, but that's my business. It's been tough, but last year might be one of the best in my life because it's a lesson learned."

The mental hurdle, he believes, is cleared. All that remains is the physical.

Anderson has said the rightfield job is Gibson's to win or lose. And Hall of Famer Al Kaline is in Lakeland to help with that, showing Gibson the ropes, what to look for when the ball comes off the bat, how to anticipate, how to conquer the position that crushed him a year ago.

In the end, though, neither Kaline nor Anderson is going to be able to do the work for him.

"Sparky's not going to have to make the play on the line — I am," Gibson said. "He's not going to have to hit lefties — I am."

So, once again, the promise is there.

Once again, the spotlight is on Kirk Gibson.

Once again, we can only wait and hope.

Gibson belted 27 homers, with 91 RBIs and 29 stolen bases in 1984, and the Tigers won their first World Series in 16 years. ❖

Dave Rozema

May 7, 1986

A RLINGTON, Texas — Baseball was patient with Dave Rozema.

It gave him almost 30 years to grow up. And when he finally did, he couldn't pitch anymore.

Sparky Anderson gave up on him two years ago, letting him rot in the bullpen while the Tigers won their first world championship since 1968. Through three American League playoff games against Kansas City and five World Series games against San Diego, he was allowed to sit. He had one of the best seats in the house. But he'd rather have been standing — on the mound. Instead, he only watched and basked in the residual glow of the wonderful series his buddy, Kirk Gibson, had.

Now the Texas Rangers have given up on him, too. Manager Bobby Valentine called him into his office after the Tigers' 10-3 victory and told Rozema the club was releasing him. They didn't let him go because he'd been in any barroom brawls. Or because he'd missed curfew or judged a wet T-shirt contest or started a food fight in the locker room.

They let him go because Rozema — a few months short of his 30th birthday — could no longer get anyone out.

He came to Texas after the Tigers' 1984 World Series triumph as part of a new Rangers experiment: free agency.

He came for a two-year deal at $370,000 a season. In a little more than one season, he won three games and lost seven. And this year, batters hit .404 against him. He made six relief appearances in Texas' first 22 games and allowed five of the seven runners he inherited to score. His totals: a 5.91 ERA in 10⅓ innings.

"He just never did the job for us," Valentine said. "He did everything we asked. He lost weight, and he came to camp with a renewed attitude. But at this juncture, we have to go with the younger guys."

And with a maturity Detroiters might find hard to believe, Rozema did not argue with that assessment.

"I might have to go fishing with Gibby," he said, reflecting on his future. "I just wasn't doing the job. That's what it comes down to…. I wasn't throwing the ball that well, and they have to stick with the young guys so they'll get that confidence."

When Rozema was a young guy, he threw the ball hard and straight and with confidence. He threw it well enough to be named the American League's rookie pitcher of the year in 1977.

And he played as hard as he worked.

His name was always in the gossip columns. His face was always on television. A beer, it seemed, was always in hand.

He was more playful than harmful, but it was not an image the straight-laced Tigers organization appreciated.

As Gibson, Rozema's constant companion, approached superstardom, the club grudgingly accepted his idiosyncrasies.

But Rozema's progress suddenly stopped. He won 10 straight decisions from September 1981 through July 1983, despite a long layoff after surgery on his left knee. The knee was damaged when he took his infamous Kung Fu kick at Minnesota's John Castino in a bench-clearing brawl in 1982.

He was 9-9 through the rest of 1983 and '84. The club grew weary of his pranks and gladly accepted his free agency after the World Series.

He came to Texas seeking acceptance and a rejuvenated career. He found neither. Now he hopes to find them elsewhere. But if it weren't for bad luck …

"I can't go beat anybody up," he said, battling the frustration. "I'd get thrown in jail, the way my luck goes. I'm just going to go home and see what comes up.

"You know, this could be one of the better things to ever happen to me. I wasn't real comfortable here."

Rozema was always more comfortable as a Tiger. As a Michigander.

In the early morning hours yesterday, he and his wife, Sandy, stuck their heads into the bar at the Sheraton CentrePark, the hotel just beyond Arlington Stadium's leftfield fence, where the Tigers are staying.

He didn't order a round of drinks. He didn't pull the chair out from under anyone. He didn't do any of those things that gained him renown in Detroit. He was just looking for old Tigers teammates for a few minutes' reminiscing.

He talked quietly with Alan Trammell and Dan Petry.

Then he wandered out into the night.

Poor Dave Rozema.

He got old too soon and smart too late.

Rozema did not catch on with another team; his playing days were over. ❖

Paul Richards

May 8, 1986

W AXAHACHIE, Texas — They put Paul Richards in the ground yesterday morning.

It was his ground.

Texas ground.

And like him, it was hard and dry and without much about it in the way of humor.

It was the ground from which he sprung 77 years ago, on a piece of land not far from his final resting place.

The first time I met him, I was about 15. My uncle worked for him, and I remember thinking what a hard job he must have, working for this lean, leathery, stern-looking man.

Paul Richards' smiles were infrequent and always seemed labored, as if the best he could manage was the slightest upturn of the corners of his mouth.

He has been called a baseball genius, the Wizard of Waxahachie. An innovator in a game chained to the past.

He managed the Chicago White Sox for five seasons and the Baltimore Orioles for seven. He invented the tactic of moving a starting pitcher to another position to bring in a reliever to face one batter, then returning the starter to the mound. He listened one day in Baltimore when my uncle — Al Vincent — proposed that the Orioles give Gus Triandos a larger glove with which to catch Hoyt Wilhelm's elusive knuckleball, then he went out and had such a glove designed.

He was admired and respected for what he knew about the game — and for what he gave to it.

But few people ever got close to him.

"I went to his home for dinner many times," recalled Dick Butler, the American League's supervisor of umpires. "But we never laughed, and I don't know anybody else who he laughed with. He was no bundle of laughter."

That does not mean there was never humor around him, though. Often those near him made attempts at humor to soothe his anger.

Clint (Scrap Iron) Courtney, Richards' longtime protege, sidekick and golfing partner, once told me about hitting his golf ball into the rough, then trying to kick it to a more favorable position without being noticed by Richards.

"But when I looked up, there he was, standing right behind me and glaring," Courtney said. "So I picked up my ball and said, 'You caught me fair and square, Skip. Let's go to the next hole.' "

Richards, a catcher, played parts of eight major league seasons, including four in Detroit from 1943 to '46. He reached the zenith of his career on Oct. 10, 1945, when he drove in four runs in the Tigers' World Series-clinching victory over the Chicago Cubs.

He was never a great player, but he mercilessly drove others to be better.

Tigers broadcaster Ernie Harwell recalled a time in Buffalo "when a shortstop made three errors in the first game of a doubleheader, and Paul made the poor guy come out between games and batted him ground balls while the crowd looked on."

And Bobby Bragan, who managed against Richards in the minor leagues, remembered a similar story: "When he was managing in Seattle in the Pacific Coast League, he asked a player named Tony York to bunt.... Well, York didn't get the bunt down, and he flied out.

"After the game he told a coach, Roger Cramer, to get a bag of balls and pitch to York so he could practice bunting. While they were out on the field, Richards and the team got on a plane and flew back to Seattle."

He was a man of opinions as much as ideas. In the mid-'60s, he proposed that all players become free agents in their eighth season and every year thereafter, a proposal that would have curtailed long-term contracts. And when the players union, under Marvin Miller, began gaining strength, he proposed shutting down major league baseball for five years.

"He never minced words," Butler said. "If he didn't like something, you knew it."

Richards might have been the only manager who did not go to spring training but brought spring training to him, setting up Buffalo's camp in Waxahachie one year.

Every spring he left the town of 14,000 in the scrubby hills south of Dallas for Buffalo or Brooklyn or Detroit. For Baltimore or Atlanta or Houston or Chicago.

Every fall he returned.

In the final years of his life, he had both his loves: baseball and Waxahachie, living at home and helping the Texas Rangers any way he could.

Last Sunday, after 18 holes of golf at Waxahachie Country Club, he collapsed and died.

Wednesday morning at Hillcrest Burial Park on the highway between Waxahachie and Midlothian, Butler and Bragan and Harwell and George Kell and Sparky Anderson and Bobby Valentine stood with leathery-faced men in straw cowboy hats and with men who recalled when Richards helped Waxahachie High win the 1925 state baseball championship, pitching the first game left- handed and the second right-handed.

And Clyde Verheyden, who grew up with Richards, read a few words from a prayer book, then told his stories of his lifelong friend.

"In 1945, I was a chaplain in the army in Europe, staying behind with some of the boys who were too badly hurt to transport home," he told the gathering at graveside.

"That was the year Detroit won the World Series, and Paul was their catcher... . The day after they won the World Series, I got a big box in the mail from him... . Seven dozen baseballs autographed by every member of the team.

"That did more good for the morale of the soldiers than anything else. That's the kind of man he was. But he didn't let many people see it.

"He gave a lot of young men a chance — and a lot of older men a second chance." ❖

Sparky and the Pope I

September 19, 1987

A few minutes after eight this morning, a slow-moving motorcade will roll down Jos. Campau, and hundreds of thousands of the curious and faithful will crane to see Pope John Paul II on his way to the pavilion built for his speech in Hamtramck.

Shouting the traditional Polish toast to a long life, the crowds scream: "Sto lat! Sto lat! Sto lat!"

As the popemobile comes to a stop in front of the pavilion built for the occasion, a well-tanned, white-haired man in one of the front-row seats leaps to his feet and waves.

"Hey, Holy Father, nice to see you," the man shouts.

"Bardzo mi milo spotkac pana," replies the pontiff, raising his hand and approaching the man. "Jak sie pan nazywa?"

"What did he say, Trixy?" the white-haired man asks, turning to the man next to him.

"He said it was nice to see you, too, and he asked your name."

"Oh. I'm George Anderson, Your Holiness, but most people call me

Sparky."

"Jaki jest pana zawod, Sparky?" the pope asks.

Anderson: "What did he say?"

"He asked what you do for a living," translates Anderson's coach, Dick Tracewski.

Anderson: "Oh. I manage the Detroit Tigers. A baseball team. We've got a game this afternoon, but Trixy here got us these tickets from his church, and we got up at five o'clock this morning to come down here to see you, Your Holiness."

Pope John Paul II: "Czy jestez Katolikiem, Sparky?"

Anderson: "What did he say?"

Tracewski: "He wants to know if you are a Catholic."

Anderson: "Oh, yes, Your Holiness, I sure am. Some of the writers asked about that the other night when they found out I was coming here with Trixy. I told them I was a good Catholic, too, that I sinned all the time. That was kind of a joke, ha, ha."

Pope John Paul II: "Perhaps I do not understand American humor."

Anderson: "What did he say?"

Tracewski: "Sparky, he's speaking English now."

Anderson: "Oh, I must have still been listening in Polish."

Pope John Paul II: "What did he say?"

Tracewski: "Never mind, Your Holiness, it isn't important."

Pope John Paul II: "This team of yours, Sparky, does it win very often?"

Anderson: "Oh, yes, Your Holiness, we've been kicking the ... I mean, we've been beating almost everybody."

Pope John Paul II: "I see. These Tigers, then, they are the champions of the games they play?"

Anderson: "Well, not yet. As a matter of fact, there's this one team from Toronto that we're sort of worried about, you see. We have to play them seven times in the next two weeks, and I was wondering, well, if you could maybe remember us in your prayers or give us a little blessing or something that might kinda give us an edge.

"I know you don't have no idea about baseball or who I am, but since you're the most powerful man I've ever met, I just kind of thought ... "

Pope John Paul II, raising his hands in benediction: "Of course, Sparky. I have something that is fitting. Zostancie z bogiem!"

Anderson: "What did he say?"

Tracewski: "I can't believe it. He said 'Bless You, Boys.' "

Pope John Paul II: "It is something a man in San Francisco taught me on

Friday. His name, I believe, was Roger Craig."

The crowd, unable to see what is going on in front of the pavilion, begins to grow restless and starts chanting: "Niech zyje Papiez! Niech zyje Papiez! Niech zyje Papiez!"

Long live the pope!

Pope John Paul II: "Sparky, it has been very nice to meet you, but my flock calls. I must go now." Then he lays his hands on the man's forehead and says: "Pan z wami. God bless you."

Anderson: "And the same to you, Your Holiness. This has certainly been an experience I will never forget, if I live long enough to see Howard Johnson and Darnell Coles make it into the Hall of Fame.

"I mean, for crying out loud, this is a once-in-a-lifetime thing, like Willie Hernandez saving 32 games in a season or Kirk Gibson throwing a man out at the plate twice in one game."

Pope John Paul II: "What did he say? Oh, never mind."

Then he turns and walks up the steps, addressing the crowd as he goes: "Dominus vobiscum." ❖

Willie Hernandez

October 9, 1987

MINNEAPOLIS — I called my wife this morning.

"Good morning," I said. "I love you."

"Why," she replied, "did he use Willie Hernandez?"

That is how serious the Willie Hernandez problem is becoming in Detroit. Three years ago, Hernandez was Detroit's darling, a carefree reliever with a screwball that helped win the World Series. He laughed and joked and made us smile and feel good about ourselves and our city.

But that was 36 months, a $1 million-plus-a-year contract and many disastrous appearances ago.

The screwball is gone now, largely discarded because he can no longer get it across the plate. The speed is gone, too, a victim perhaps of age or an arm that has been used up.

Most noticeably absent, though, is the confidence. No longer does Willie Hernandez walk to the mound with the self-assured gait of a matador entering the bullring. Now he has the look of a man going to the gas chamber.

And if he is not sure of himself, how can my wife be sure of him?

When Sparky Anderson called him from the bullpen with the outcome of the American League playoff opener against the Minnesota Twins hanging in the balance, all over Michigan people asked the same thing my wife asked: Why Willie?

In his last five appearances, Hernandez faced nine batters and gave up a three-run homer, two singles, two doubles, a triple, walked two and retired one.

"You can't write and say he's pitched well. He hasn't," Anderson conceded. "But beyond that, you have to have some compassion for the person.

"I laid in bed last night and thought about it, and it's scary.... He was really on my mind.

"If he walks out to the mound in Detroit — he brought them the greatest thing they hadn't had in 16 years, the World Series — they boo him as soon as he walks out there. Imagine what is going through the minds of the players in the other dugout, and what's going through the minds of his own teammates. How embarrassing is that?"

Hernandez has told Free Press reporter Joe Lapointe his mind is "messed up," and Anderson admits to genuine concern for his pitcher's mental well-being.

"Absolutely," he said. "This can just torture you beyond torture. I think: 'What if that's my son?' "

In the final months of the season, Anderson has tried to protect Hernandez by rarely using him at home.

But his handling of Hernandez is based as much on expediency as compassion. If, at age 32, Hernandez is washed up, the Tigers' substantial financial investment in him is worthless.

So Anderson must try to rebuild Hernandez's confidence by using him in carefully selected spots. So far the attempt has been a total failure.

"If Willie is going to be any good to us at all, we've got to get him in the first game (of the playoffs) and see if he's going to be any good," Anderson said, going on to concede: "Evidently, he's not making any pitches.

"Remember — what was was, and what is is."

But Anderson continued to plead for mercy in the treatment of Hernandez. "I still gotta have some compassion for this person," he said. "How can I take a guy who gave us everything in '84 — and, by the way, he still has two more years — and tell him: 'You're a piece of shit?'

"I'm supposed to have nine pitchers but just use eight? ... Wouldn't that look nice?

"He earned pride in '84, and I can't take that away from him. I won't."

Anderson would not commit himself to using Hernandez when this series moves to Tiger Stadium over the weekend. "I don't have to answer that question," he said, "because we haven't got there yet.

"He has told me he can face them," Anderson said of the fans in Detroit. "But can you imagine what that man's going through? There's nothing worse than that. You can talk about all the money he's making and everything, but there can be nothing more lonesome or tougher on a human being than what he's going through.

"Money don't take away no pain. It don't solve nothing."

So Anderson has counseled Hernandez. He has pointed out his health and that of his family are more important than his inability to retire batters. "I told him this will go away," Anderson said. "I try to help his mind because I can't help his pitching."

I called my wife back and told her what Sparky said.

"What do you think?" I asked.

"I think I'd have rather seen him use Mark Thurmond," she said. "Oh, by the way, I love you, too."

The Tigers lost the series in five games. Willie — later Guillermo — Hernandez lasted two more seasons in Detroit. ❖

Sparky and the Pope II

October 10, 1987

His Holiness Pope John Paul II.

The Vatican.

Vatican City.

Most Holy Father:

You probably don't remember me, but I will never forget you. We met briefly in Hamtramck a couple of weeks ago.

I was one of the men Archbishop Szoka introduced you to before you spoke there. I was thrilled. I never thought nothing like that would happen to me in a month of Sundays. The most important man I ever met before was Gov. Blanchard. Or maybe Tom Selleck. I can't decide.

Anyway, I'm the guy that manages the baseball club called the Detroit Tigers. When you met me, I was with one of my Polish friends, Dick Tracewski. He coaches for our club — that means he tells runners "go," "stop," "hurry up" and things like that. He also teaches me a few words of Polish from time to time.

He came into my office just now and told me I should ask you: Jak sie masz?

You probably never expected to get a letter from me. And, frankly, I never really expected to write you. But when I called Vatican City information for your phone number, we had trouble understanding each other.

I know you're busy, going to different countries all the time and learning different languages and trying to see that the hungry are fed and the poor are cared for and the weak are protected, but I've got a real problem here, Your Holiness, and I didn't know where else to turn.

Since we know each other, sort of, I thought I'd ask you if you could help.

Remember, when you were here, how you said: "Zostancie z bogiem"? Bless you boys. That was so nice of you. And it worked, too. Remember, I told you we were worried about that team from Toronto and you said "Zostancie z bogiem" and we beat the — I mean, we prevailed over those guys, Your Holiness.

Thank you very much.

But now we've got a real problem.

It is a team called the Minnesota Twins. But the name ain't important. What is important is they — how can I say this to be charitable? — they aren't a real good baseball club. We are the best team. We proved that during the regular season. But, you see, they are beating us like a drum. That's an old American expression. And I don't know what to do about it — not the expression, I mean I don't know what to do about them beating us.

We've used our two best starting pitchers and lost both nights. Our bullpen — that's the pitchers who come in and try to get the other team out when the your best pitchers can't — is so shaky I'm beginning to think it's got the willies, and that ain't supposed to be no knock on poor Willie Hernandez, who can't get nobody out no more. Then we got some problems hitting, too. Kirk Gibson's swing is so messed up he can't even hardly ever touch the ball, and Alan Trammell ain't hitting his weight, and Tommy Brookens and Bill Madlock ain't had a hit in the playoffs at all.

I have been telling everybody that this ain't no life-and-death deal. I know I will still wake up in the morning and be alive, if we win or if we lose, so it don't really matter so much when you put it in the perspective of famine and hunger and war and all of them things, you see.

But to us, Your Holiness, it is still kinda important.

I really hate to impose on you again. But I just thought, with all your wisdom and knowledge, that maybe you could help. I don't even know, sir, what I'm asking for, really. Maybe a prayer, maybe some advice, maybe just being remembered when you talk to Him about those who are in need because, truly, we are among them.

If you could find some way to help us through this one, we'd really appreciate it. We won't ask for no more favors because, if we beat this team, we might have to play the St. Louis Cardinals next, and I think I know where your loyalties lie, if you know what I mean.

Sincerely,

George (Sparky) Anderson, Mr. George Anderson, Manager, Detroit Baseball Club, Michigan & Trumbull, Detroit, Michigan, USA.

Dear Mr. Anderson:

Unfortunately, John Paul II's pressing schedule precludes his responding personally to your letter. However, he has authorized me to say: Since all men are created equal in the eyes of the Lord, and in the eyes of His church, he can officially do nothing further to provide an advantage for your ball-playing team.

Unofficially, though, he suggests you pray more, use your bullpen less and pitch around Tom Brunansky always.

God bless you,

Office of Public Information

The Vatican.

Alas, the Tigers bowed to the Twins, four games to one. ❖

Darrell Evans

October 13, 1987

A nd so it ended, eight days later than anybody had any right to expect.

For the Tigers, the 1987 American League season ended in the gathering dusk, when Jeff Reardon gathered in Matt Nokes' bouncer to the mound and shoveled it to first baseman Kent Hrbek — just as eight days earlier the Tigers had eliminated Toronto on an almost identical play.

There was, with the final out of the season, nothing for the Tigers to do but trudge back to their locker room.

Already, the tributes had been paid.

Already, the Game 5 crowd — held to 47,448 by cold, television and perhaps anticipation of what was to come — had paid its respects. It began with Darrell Evans — who in many ways personifies this team.

Darrell Evans, the weathered warrior of 19 major league seasons, the captain of this team, the first 40-year-old to hit 30 or more home runs in a season, was the goat of Game 4's loss.

He made a mistake, straying too far off third base, and the Minnesota Twins made him — and the Tigers — pay for it by picking him off.

Now he stepped to the plate in the first inning of Game 5.

And it began.

Applause at first. Then cheers. Then an avalanche of noise. Then they were on their feet. All of them.

It was a tribute to a man who had given his best, who at times had succeeded and at times had failed. It was a tribute to a man who might be playing his last game in a Tigers uniform.

"It was," he said when this season had become history in Detroit, "real special. It was something I didn't expect.... You can't pay enough money to have these things happen to you."

Like the Tigers, Evans had a better season than anyone could have expected. He was forced, in the spring, to take a drastic pay cut, then had what he called "my best season in baseball."

Like the Tigers, Evans ran out of adrenaline this week. Out of strength. Out of energy. Out of miracles. Out of the race.

He is, I believe, the leader of a group of overachievers, a bunch of guys who this summer accomplished things they should not have been capable of accomplishing.

He does not agree.

"In a series, or in a month, you could do that. But not in a season," he said. "In a season, you end up where you're supposed to.... For 162 games, we were the best team.

"We had to work hard for it ... and we're proud of it. Even though we didn't win, I got a lot more satisfaction even than '84. This is the closest bunch we've had.

"Because we've been together for a long time, we cherish it."

What they did accomplish — a major league-high 98 wins and an American League East championship — is more special to them because none of us believed.

Believe?

In what? In a catching corps patched together in desperation in the spring following Lance Parrish's free-agent defection to the Philadelphia Phillies?

In a defense that pitcher Jack Morris publicly questioned as spring training ended?

In a pitching staff that was a disappointment the summer before?

In a bullpen of youngsters and one once-remarkable veteran who no longer could get people out?

Believe?

Only the Tigers believed.

We skeptics kept saying: Show us. Prove it. Show us again.

And they did.

Still, the city never got behind them as it got behind the 1984 Tigers. There were empty seats for the playoffs.

If Evans noticed, he chose not to mention it. Instead, he spoke appreciatively of the support.

"This town is a great sports town," he said. "The fans really get involved with the athletes, not just as players but as people. I can't say enough about them.

"I appreciated it very much. People care about what we do in this town. They know how we battled back this season, and I'm glad a lot of them feel a part of it."

A storybook ending would have been nice.

In the end, Evans was supposed to come to the plate with the bases loaded and the Tigers three runs behind and hit a grand slam into the upper deck.

The fans were supposed to erupt in that chant they have adopted: "Dare-ell! Dare-ell! Dare-ell!"

But that is fairy tale.

"It would have been nice to get in position where one swing would make the difference," Evans acknowledged. "But that doesn't always happen."

So in the end, the fans and the Tigers filed silently out of Tiger Stadium, leaving the Minnesota Twins to celebrate their victory in the deserted stadium.

And in their locker room, the Tigers did something you don't often see in professional sports.

On the field, they show us high fives and mob scenes in which men jump on men until they form a pyramid that topples under its own weight, sending grown men sprawling on the ground like a bunch of playground urchins.

In defeat, the Tigers showed us something else.

They walked around the room, quietly embracing, first this teammate, then that one.

Frank Tanana walked up to Larry Herndon, hugged him and said: "God bless you. We gave everything we had."

Then Evans and Herndon embraced. Not a fleeting, self-conscious embrace, but a lingering one — the sharing of two men who have won together and who have lost together. As they hugged, Evans whispered something in Herndon's ear.

And the men and women who were there to ask probing questions stood back silently and in respect and watched the exchange of admiration.

And it was hard to think of the Tigers as losers.

Evans played another season with the Tigers, hitting 22 homers, and concluded his career in 1989 with the Atlanta Braves, the team with which he debuted 21 seasons earlier. ❖

Sparky and the Pope III

September 14, 1988

His Holiness Pope John Paul II.
The Vatican.
Vatican City.
Most Holy Father:
Well, here I am again, Your Holiness, looking for a moment of your time and some divine help.

Probably you don't remember me. It has been just about a year now since we met in Hamtramck when you were touring the United States. I am the gray-haired guy that Archbishop — I mean, Cardinal — Edmund Szoka introduced you to — George Anderson, the guy with the baseball team.

Remember?

You said "Bless you, boys" in Polish, and I'll be da … darned if we didn't go on to win the American League East championship.

I've been meaning to write and thank you, but I been so busy. It seems the only free time I have is in the middle of the night when I should be sleeping, but I can't because of bad dreams. So I pace the floor and try to remember what Kirk Gibson and Lance Parrish looked like in Detroit uniforms.

We've been having some problems, Your Holiness, and I been thinking maybe I should write and see if you could help. Then, son of a gun, Monday night came along and I think I saw your hand in this thing already — even without me asking.

See, we're kind of in the same fix we were in a year ago. We're running out of season here, and we are trying to catch a team called the Boston Red Sox. We are not doing too good on our own, and I was wondering if you could say something else this year, like "good luck" or "kill, Bubba, kill," in Polish, something like that.

For three weeks now we haven't pitched well, haven't hit at all and I swear — I don't mean swear, literally, Your Holiness — if I didn't recognize those guys, I'd think our defense was on somebody else's side half the time.

But like I said, I think I seen your hand in this already, and I really appreciate that. We've got this relief pitcher — what he's supposed to do is just get out one or two guys a game, but he hasn't been real good at that lately. Three times in the last 11 days he gave up home runs — that's when the other team hits the ball into the stands — that cost us the game.

But Holy Father, he is still the best left-handed relief pitcher we have who is healthy. So Monday night, I had no choice but to use him again. Now I'm not saying I was scared about what might happen, but the fact of the matter was I had no choice.

The guys in the dugout all believed in him — we're in this thing together, even if we are in it up to our necks. But I looked up at the press box when he came in, and all those guys had their eyes covered. I think they're infidels, Your Holiness, or at the very least, Protestants.

I told all those writers after the game, I can't be worried about nobody's feelings. I just have to do what I have to do, and Monday I had no choice. You know what, Holy Father? That relief pitcher — he used to be Willie Hernandez, but now his name is Guillermo (that's Spanish; I don't know how to say it in Polish) — came in with runners at second and third and only one out and us up by two runs, and he got two guys out and let only one run in.

Maybe that sounds complicated, but it ain't, really. What it all amounts to is we won, 6-5, and I don't think he could have done it without some help from you or from your boss, you-know-Who.

Up till then, nothing much had gone our way lately. Alan Trammell came into the dugout the other night and said there were so many gulls circling the field in Toronto that he had to keep moving around to keep from getting hit by something, if you know what I mean.

That's pretty typical of what's been happening to us, you see.

We had one guy who thought he was Fred Astaire one night and danced himself right onto the disabled list. I've heard of guys getting hurt on dance floors before, but usually it is when they were dancing with somebody else's wife. I mean, other teams have guys get hurt in bar brawls and automobile accidents and things like that, and we have a guy who can't get on and off the dance floor without hurting himself.

It's things like that that made me gray before my time, Your Holiness.

I know this may be asking too much of you, but it would really help if all those hurt guys would get well. I don't know if you do these sorts of things or not, but I have heard priests pray for a speedy recovery. I don't expect no Lourdes-type recoveries, but I wouldn't complain if we got one. Oh, Lord, no.

I don't expect no reply from you, Your Holiness. I know you've been on the road in all those countries in southern Africa, which is kind of a hard thing to do, I understand, without going to South Africa. Kinda like going from first to third without setting foot on second.

Anyway, I don't expect no reply, like I said.

I'll just look at the standings in my favorite morning newspaper on Oct. 3, and if we're are on top, I'll know you've done it again, 'cause that indeed would be a miracle.

Humbly and sincerely yours,

George (Sparky) Anderson.

One more Hail Mary and the Tigers might have pulled it off; they finished second, one game behind the Red Sox. ❖

Sparky and the Pope IV

April 22, 1989

His Holiness Pope John Paul II.

The Vatican.

Vatican City.

Most Holy Father:

I hope, Your Holiness, I am not getting to be a pest to you — like those guys from the media who keep coming into my office and saying something is wrong with this baseball team of mine are getting to be to me.

Them telling me something is wrong with my team is like somebody telling Edsel something is wrong with his car, if you know what I mean. I don't need no help from those guys who can't help anyway. All they do is stir things up.

So that's why you find my letter in your mailbox again, Your Holiness. When I am in serious need, I know I can count on you.

I understand that in the scheme of things as you see them from the Vatican, baseball ain't the most important thing in the world. I mean, none of my little grandchildren have ever woke up, even one morning, and been in Beirut. And there ain't been no awful disasters here like at that soccer game in England.

Those people know what real trouble is.

But to us here in the USA, baseball is kind of important this time of year.

And if you would take just a minute to look at the standings, you would know we are in a bad way. My team is the Detroit Tigers, remember? And we ain't listed at the bottom because they are doing it alphabetically.

I know when you're talking about the Ten Commandments there ain't really no difference between being No. 1 and being No. 10. But in baseball, there is a big difference. Somebody once told me there was no substitute for being on top.

You have been so kind to me in the past, I thought I would write and see if there isn't something else you could do for us this time, too. And this time it is kind of personal.

I could ask for better defense.

I could ask, Lord knows, for better hitting.

And I could ask for my best pitcher to start pitching good and keep his mouth shut. But that would not be a favor. It would be a miracle. Might need the patience of a saint.

What I think I really need this summer, Your Holiness, is to be blessed with better patience — because this could seem like the "War and Peace" of summers, if you know what I mean. For my players and myself, this summer could be longer than a weekend in Cleveland.

You see, these guys and gals (Yes! There are women in the press boxes now. I mean, they don't let them in the priesthood, do they? Why should they be in the writinghood?) are beginning to cause me to get irritated.

Now I'm a guy with a pretty thick skin, you know. I've been through it all and seen it all and done most of it myself (unless, of course, it was illegal or immoral).

I usually can handle this kind of thing. I tell 'em a few jokes, make up a good story here and there and send them on their way, happy as a bunch of preschoolers with a new box of colors.

I have survived a lot of ups and downs in this business, hitting slumps and dumb plays and even a second baseman who danced himself onto the disabled list right in the middle of the pennant race last year.

But what is happening to us now is beginning to get to me, I guess.

I won't go into the details of what is wrong with this ballclub. Just let me say there seems to have been some mistakes made about the skills and talents of some of the guys in our locker room. It would be a little — I guess — like you promoting a priest to bishop and then finding out the guy doesn't even speak Latin.

That's the kind of trouble we seem to be in here, and it don't help matters none for the press to keep telling me about it.

I even raised my voice to my boys the other day, Your Holiness. And some of what I said, I'm afraid, might not have been very pleasant to His ears.

I've already asked forgiveness for that, Holy Father.

And there is one other thing, too, that I want to make sure He understands — and I hope you can help me with this one. One of the writers asked me what I would do if this team was able to win only five of our first 40 games, and I told him I would commit suicide before that happened. It was supposed to be a joke, Your Holiness. I know it's wrong to do that, and I got absolutely no intention at all of doing it, so I just wanted to make sure He knew I was only kidding.

Well, I won't keep you any longer. I know you are busy, and if there are any miracles to be handed out, they won't go to no gray-haired man whose job is to teach people how to hit a ball with a piece of wood.

I just appreciate your time and your prayers, and I want to say to you what you said to me when we met in Hamtramck a couple of years ago: *Pan z wami.*

God bless you.

George (Sparky) Anderson.

P.S. — Could you say a little prayer for my old buddy, Pete Rose? He might need your help even more than I do.

The Tigers were beyond help in 1989, losing 103 games and finishing last in the AL East, 30 games behind the Blue Jays. ❖

Cooperstown

July 23, 1989

COOPERSTOWN, N.Y. — At eight o'clock Saturday morning, a gauze-like fog spread from the banks of Otsego Lake and hung over quaint Doubleday Field, blurring the images of the groundskeepers preparing for Monday's exhibition game between the Boston Red Sox and Cincinnati Reds.

It was a scene made hazy as much by the passage of time as by the fog. And if you sat in the stands and allowed your imagination to sweep you away to yesteryear, you could believe the young man standing near home plate is was not a groundskeeper at all, but a young man about to become a legend.

Instead of a stadium, there is only a farmer's field in that fog, and the young man, with a stick in his hand, begins to scratch in the dirt the dimensions of a baseball diamond.

That is the way baseball was born. That is what the legend says.

They built Doubleday Field, small and intimate and nostalgic, a monument to the man and to the game and to the legend.

Almost always legends are more palatable, more joyful, more acceptable than truth.

In legends, people live happily ever after. In legends, there is no Lou Gehrig's disease, there is no Black Sox scandal, there is no cloud of suspicion over Pete Rose.

In legend, Abner Doubleday picked up a stick in Elihu Phinney's field one summer day in 1839 and traced the outline for the game that would become America's pastime. And if fact has come to cast doubt upon the legend, then facts don't count for much here any day of the year — and they count for nothing this weekend.

Today four more mortals become legends — Johnny Bench, Carl Yastrzemski, Red Schoendienst and umpire Al Barlick — when they are inducted into baseball's Hall of Fame in this little village, lost somewhere in central New York and sometime in the 19th century.

But even here it is impossible to escape today, or to escape the fact baseball now is as much business as sport because we choose to make it that way.

In Walker Gallery, just down the tree-lined Main Street from the Hall of Fame and Museum, mortals can pay tribute to their heroes by the purchase of expensive icons.

A baseball autographed by Bench, on a stand, along with a baseball card from his rookie season, sold for $250. A Yastrzemski-autographed ball was on sale for $57, and balls with Schoendienst's or Barlick's signature sold for $30.

Those, though, are among the cheaper items available. A Mickey Mantle baseball card is $450. A bat autographed by 17 members of the Hall of Fame is $485. A Ty Cobb autograph mounted with two photos of Cobb in Tigers uniforms is $995.

An autographed photo of Gary Carter and Rose, framed (if you'll pardon the expression), sells for $75.

But even Lourdes, I'm told, has souvenir stands, and commercialism only emphasizes the extent of America's love affair with its game.

Cooperstown this week smells of mowed grass, of the springtime of our youth.

They — the ubiquitous they — say the legend of Abner Doubleday is only a myth. That the game was invented some other way in some other place by some other man.

And perhaps they are right.

Perhaps I did not see Abner Doubleday through the fog, scratching out base lines in Elihu Phinney's field.

But I did walk the halls of the Baseball Hall of Fame and Museum, and if the sport was not born in Cooperstown, it is here that it is most honored and here that its roots and history and meaning are best preserved.

Here, just down Main Street from the village's only traffic light, are the artifacts of 150 years: a ball that reputedly belonged to Doubleday, a flimsy piece of leather that passed as a glove when John McGraw played the game, Al Kaline's Tigers jersey.

For the price of admission — $5 — you can see and touch Babe Ruth's locker, the locker that was used by both Joe DiMaggio and Mantle; you can see the uniform Jackie Robinson wore when he broke the color line in the major leagues and the ball that Hank Aaron hit to break Ruth's career home run record; and you can trace Casey Stengel's marvelous career from rookie to manager of the Mets.

And there — high on a wall in the portion of the museum devoted to All-Star Games — hangs something I had been looking for, something I had been told was there for more than a decade.

It was a blowup of a sports page from the July 14, 1971, Free Press — the day after the American Leaguers beat the Nationals at Tiger Stadium, 6-4 — and at the top of the page was a story ...

By CHARLIE VINCENT.

Ego?

I confess. I liked seeing it there.

I don't know why the Hall of Fame didn't select a page from Detroit's other newspaper. I didn't ask. I just stared at it awhile.

I doubt that anyone else even notices it because when I picked up my credentials, Bill Guilfoile, the man in charge of such things, asked if I was a writer or a photographer.

So much for ego.

I like my name being up there, though, because baseball has always been big in my family.

As clearly as I saw Doubleday, I see my grandmother, who never saw a baseball game, never set foot inside a stadium, sitting in her rocking chair, listening to announcer Ed Dittert broadcast games of the Beaumont Exporters in the Texas League, day after day, well into her 80s.

I see my uncle, standing in the coach's box, but I can't make out the uniform. He wore a few, in Philadelphia and Baltimore and Detroit, in Buffalo and Birmingham and Ft. Worth and Tulsa.

And I see fuzzy, faded pictures from a newspaper clipping in 1927 of my dad, a rookie smiling proudly in his new Miami Marlin uniform.

They made baseball what it is, as surely as all the Alan Trammells and Duke Simses and Billy Beans, and as surely as the thousands of fans who filed into Walker Gallery.

Baseball is Americana.

And the very best who have ever played the game are enshrined here.

The heart of the museum is a shrine — a simple room with a vaulted ceiling — with niches on each side filled with 200 simple bronze plaques honoring the greats of the game.

In the center of the carnival atmosphere, this was a touch of dignity, reserved, ironically, for men who earned their way here by getting sweaty and dirty, by playing America's game with their wits as much as their muscle.

Of all the thousands of men who have played this game, they qualified for admission to this small room because they best met the qualifications set forth on the selection ballot:

"Voting shall be based upon the player's record, playing ability, integrity, sportsmanship, character, contributions to the team(s) on which the player played and not on what he may have done otherwise in baseball."

This is a place of men with great handlebar mustaches and lyrical nicknames.

It is Mordecai (Three Finger) Brown and Rabbit Maranville and King Kelly.

Sandy and Lefty and Yogi. Pee Wee and Duke and Hack.

The Splendid Splinter and Stan the Man and The Babe.

Today four more join them. ❖

Johnny Bench's hero

July 24, 1989

COOPERSTOWN, N.Y. — He hit the longest home run ever and was the greatest baseball player ever.

And he sat in the roasting Cooperstown sun in shirt sleeves and looked on as four others were inducted into the Hall of Fame.

He hit a baseball so far it was never found — deep into an Oklahoma cornfield, where it disappeared forever, lost among the corn rows like a movie fantasy.

He is old now. And gray. A little, leathery man from Oklahoma.

But he has a spring to his step, a smile that covers his weathered face and a friendly wave. And over the weekend, he charmed Cooperstown.

There is no plaque to him in the Hall of Fame, though. And there never will be.

He never played in the major leagues.

He played only with his son, Johnny Bench.

He nurtured him and taught him. He taught him how to catch a fly ball without losing teeth. He taught him how to throw.

And he took a broken old bat, nailed it together, wrapped tape over the nails and showed his son how to hit a baseball.

"I swear," said Bench, "Dad hit it in the cornfield, and we never found that ball. I didn't think there was anybody in the world who could hit it farther than that."

In a little boy's eyes, Ted Bench was the greatest ever.

Standing at the podium on the lawn at baseball's Hall of Fame, Johnny Bench said he still believes it.

"I learned this game from the man who hit the longest home run ever, who was the greatest baseball player ever — my father," Bench said.

This is the stuff of which dreams are made. Days like this prove that American dreams — unlike fairy tales — can come true.

Johnny Bench fooled a lot of people. He did not cry.

"I brought my mom and dad to cry," he said.

But he has cried. Recently.

He cried at the end of "Field of Dreams" because it struck so close to reality for him. At the end of the movie fantasy, the main character stands on the edge of a cornfield and plays catch with his father, who had died many years before.

"At the end of that movie, I saw my dad and I playing catch," Bench said.

And he cried.

Induction day, though, was not for crying.

Induction day was for joy — for the admission of Bench, Carl Yastrzemski, Red Schoendienst and umpire Al Barlick into the shrine at Cooperstown.

And Bench rebuked those who wanted to treat the day any way but joyously.

In honoring those who molded his career once he had left the protective tutelage of the greatest baseball player ever, he reeled off a litany of his managers, "Lou Fitzgerald ... the great Sparky Anderson ... John McNamara ... Russ Nixon."

Some in the crowd stirred. Some booed some of the names.

"Boo some other time, folks," Bench said. "This is a time for celebration."

It was a time for enjoying the completion of a journey from a place few have ever been to a place fewer will ever go.

The cornfield in "Field of Dreams" was in Iowa. The cornfield in Bench's childhood was in Binger, Okla., a settlement of 660 people.

And in that cornfield he began his dream — but it was not to be in the Hall of Fame. It was only to be a major leaguer.

"I never dreamed of being in the Hall of Fame," he said, looking out into the crowd and seeing his father's face. "The Hall of Fame is a place for fantasies. It is where Cy Young is, and Babe Ruth and Ty Cobb.

"This is really the biggest thing in my life.

"It is a great privilege and honor to be up here with my idols ... these men were my dad's idols, and now they are mine.

"When I was in the second grade, our teacher asked us what we wanted to do when we grew up, and I said I wanted to be a major league baseball player, and everybody laughed.

"When I was in the eighth grade, the teacher asked the same question, and I said I wanted to be a major league baseball player, and they all laughed again. But I guess they had every right to because I was about 5-foot-2.

"But in the 11th grade the teacher asked the same question, and I gave the same answer. And I had grown quite a bit by that time, and not so many people laughed."

It has been a long time since anybody laughed at Johnny Bench's ability as a baseball player.

He quit the game at age 35, after he had been moved from catcher to first base and third base.

"Last year," he said when he announced his retirement, "wasn't a good one for me. I thought I'd tarnished some of what I accomplished. I want my name to stay on an upper level. I want to be respected."

His plaque at Cooperstown says Johnny Bench "redefined standards by which catchers are measured."

That might make him the best catcher of all time.

It does not make him the best player ever, though.

The best player ever was sitting in shirt sleeves in the sunshine, a tear in his eye, pride in his heart and memories of a cornfield in his head. ❖

The Griffeys

September 26, 1990

Ken Griffey Sr. didn't see "Field of Dreams," so he didn't know that some fathers have to die to play catch with their children.

He is, at 40 — and after serving four major league teams — now living the dream of every father, playing a child's game for a king's ransom and playing it with his son at his side.

Ken Griffey Sr. in leftfield; Ken Griffey Jr. in center for the Seattle Mariners.

A month ago, they became the first father and son to play on the same major league team, and what has happened since has been, said the older Griffey, "the most enjoyable thing that has ever happened to me."

He worried about it, though.

He worried about going to Seattle and dressing in a locker room beside his 20-year-old son.

They have not always been close.

As a teenager, the younger Griffey struggled living up to the reputation of his father. When the father would show up at one of his son's games, a knot would develop in the younger Griffey's throat and line drives would turn into pop flies, home runs into long outs.

"He always pressed when I came to watch him," the father said. "I didn't want to put pressure on him out here, so when I began talking with Seattle, I called him. I wanted to know what frame of mind he was in. I thought I knew what his answer would be, but I wanted him to reassure himself that he wanted me to come out." The son finished the story.

"He called and asked me: 'Do you want me to … ?' And before he could finish, I told him: 'Yeah!' "

Their relationship is not common. On one hand, it was made necessarily distant by the life of a father who spent his son's growing-up years in distant towns and on foreign fields. On the other, it was made close by a mutual love of the game they play.

And in the month they have worn the uniform of the Seattle Mariners, there has developed a warmth and camaraderie that has melded the best feelings of teammates, friends and father and son.

"It's been better than I ever imagined," the father said before a game against the Tigers. "We're finding more and more about each other. I'm finding how much he has matured, in terms of baseball and off-the-field things.

"It is to me the pinnacle of my career, doing things with him, watching him play. You just have to be in my shoes."

The father has had a career of accomplishments. When his son was 5, Ken Griffey Sr. won his first World Series championship with the Cincinnati Reds. When his son was 6, Griffey hit .336 and won his second World Series championship. When his son was 10, Griffey was named the most valuable player in the All-Star Game.

But nothing compares to this.

It is the ultimate dream of a father, to have a son who wants to be like him, do his work, share his experiences, walk the places he has walked, face the same challenges. And overcome them.

To experience that — and to share it from the same floodlit field, on a perfect early fall night — is almost too grand for words.

"A lot of fathers would like to be in my spot right now," Griffey said.

Everything that has happened — the closeness of dressing together in a major league locker room, the thrill of hitting back-to-back home runs earlier this month, that they are the first to do what they are doing — has emphasized that more than teammates, more than friends, they are father and son.

The father sees the son in garish blue Nike Air Pumps and tells him he will not wear them on the playing field.

There is nearly 20 years' difference in their ages. They are of different generations. In Seattle, the father lives in the son's house ("that's weird," said the older Griffey), but on the road they don't hang out together much.

"I've got to cash his checks because he doesn't have a checking account in Seattle," Griffey the son said. And in his eyes dances the mischief of a son who can now — finally — do something for his father, and he is enjoying it.

Most of us, when our sons are grown, settle for an occasional afternoon with them on the golf course. A Thanksgiving dinner. Maybe a family vacation once in a lifetime.

The Ken Griffeys are sharing careers and life.

"I never thought it would happen," said the father, released by Atlanta midway through the 1988 season. Cincinnati, then managed by Pete Rose, picked him up, but he was released by Cincinnati in August 1990, and those two occurrences allowed a dream to come true.

"I wrote Pete a letter in Illinois (where he is in prison) to thank him for that chance," the father said. "It gave me a chance to play with Junior."

That's when the question of "Field of Dreams" came up.

"Did you see the movie?" I asked.

"No," he said, still patiently sitting in the Mariners' dugout, clutching a bat in both hands.

"At the end, the father and son were playing catch," I told him. "But the father was dead."

"Dead! Wait a minute, man. I'm not dead!" and he bolted out of the dugout, with a laugh, to join his son on the field.

At 40, Ken Griffey Sr. has never been more alive.

Griffey Sr. batted .377 in 21 games for the Mariners in 1990; he played another 30 games in '91 with his teammate and son, Ken Jr. ❖

Diamonds in the rough

June 18, 1991

Baynard Dinkins has seen a lot these past 32 years.

He has seen his city change. He has seen most of his white neighbors move out and more black people, like himself, replace them. He has seen some good people leave and other good people stay and fight long odds for their kids' futures. He has seen opportunities dry up. And he has tried to do something about it.

Around the baseball diamonds on Detroit's east side, they call him Dink. And for 32 years — or maybe it's 31, he's not quite sure — he has been teaching kids to play baseball.

He is president of the Detroit Southeast Little League, and if you're a kid and live between Woodward and Alter and between I-94 and the Detroit River, he's the man who probably hit you your first fungo at Pingree Park or yelled at you when you didn't listen to your coach.

Tony White came to him after a Police Athletic League team folded around him years ago.

"One day, it just wasn't there," White said. He has a family of his own, and when he opened the car door, 5-year-old Renard tumbled out in his baseball uniform.

There isn't enough money for all the teams to have uniforms. Most players show up in tank tops and shorts. But if your team raises enough money, you get uniforms.

White didn't wait.

"He's my son," White said. "I bought the uniform."

Because of baseball, White got a college education, playing at Pratt Community College in Kansas. Eventually he got a tryout, too, with the Minnesota Twins and the Toronto Blue Jays.

He is a product of the inner city.

His mother wanted to save him from the streets, so she sent him to Detroit East Catholic High.

"You know how she did it?" White asked. "She put me through school by gambling. Dice and cards. I love her."

Neither baseball nor his mother could keep Tony White entirely off the streets, though. He said he sold marijuana for a few years. "But that's all past me now. The streets are just hard to avoid. You used to be able to be a kid when I was growing up, but now they're men at 12, selling drugs or knocking people on the head. That's why I bring my kids here, to keep them away from that."

Dinkins said: "When the neighborhood changed, a lot of the activities went out, and baseball was one of them. We're scuffling. A lot of kids don't have the equipment they should have. A lot of them are poor and haven't been introduced to baseball."

High schools in the city have a difficult time fielding teams because the streets have gripped kids by the time they are teenagers.

William Cooper grew up in South Carolina, working in tobacco and cotton fields. He never played baseball. "There were always too many chores to be done in the fields," he said.

He brought his 9-year-old, Chris, a member of the Blue Jays, to Pingree Park. Last year, the boy played with a church team in Warren. It was a good experience, but his father didn't think it was quite right.

"I wanted him to play here, in his neighborhood," he said. "If we don't support this in our own neighborhood and it doesn't succeed, we won't have anybody to blame but ourselves. And I wanted to be here with him. A lot of these kids don't have fathers to bring them."

Some of their dads have died because of the streets, from gunshots or overdoses. Some have just disappeared.

To a kid without a father, with little money and a lot of free time, the streets must look appealing. Fewer and fewer blacks, it seems, are interested in baseball.

The Tigers have never drawn many black fans.

And the Tigers say they are concerned because the number of white fans is dwindling, too, because the stadium is old or the seats are bad. Maybe it's time for the Tigers to take a look at themselves and their city.

Maybe they should ask men such as Willie Horton and Gates Brown and Hank Aguirre to go out into the community and talk to minority youth about the game and about the Tigers.

And maybe they should buy a few dozen gloves and a few hundred bats and a few hundred balls and see that the young men of Detroit have the equipment to play the game.

It's OK to court the rich. It's OK to spend a lot of time in meetings with a bunch of politicians who will see that the Tigers get the land and money they need for a new stadium. It's even OK to devise a plan whereby they can build expensive suites in the new stadium and charge big bucks from the corporations who plan to entertain there.

But how about Chris Cooper? How about Renard White?

How about the hundreds — maybe thousands — like them?

Wouldn't it be a sin if one kid chose to sell drugs instead of playing baseball because he didn't have a glove? Or because nobody took the time to show him how to throw a baseball or how to hold a bat?

Maybe this city will learn to love the Tigers again if they show they really love the city and its people. ❖

Bill Veeck

July 20, 1991

You probably know by now I have some sports heroes.

One of them is going into the Hall of Fame tomorrow.

He was a ragged-looking guy with flyaway red hair, and his shirt was always open at the collar. But often he was more comfortable without any shirt at all, sitting in the bleachers of a ballpark, drinking beer and visiting with fans, his wooden leg — with the ashtray carved into it — propped on the seat in front of him.

Bill Veeck loved baseball, but often it did not love him back.

He was a promoter, a hustler, a gadfly, an irreverent renegade who was never part of baseball's establishment. He was a fan whose gift of gab helped him buy the St. Louis Browns, the Cleveland Indians and the Chicago White Sox twice, mostly with someone else's money.

He was sometimes outrageous, and his promotions sometimes got out of hand, like the night in 1979 when he allowed a disc jockey to blow up a mountain of disco records on the field between games of a Tigers-White Sox doubleheader. The fans rioted, and the White Sox had to forfeit the second game. Al Kaline said: "I never thought I'd see something like this happen in America."

But if Bill Veeck was anything, he was American. All-American.

Forget that it was a World War II injury that eventually cost him his leg. A lot of Americans of his generation paid heavier prices for their country in wartime.

You should know other things about him, though, such as the fact he stood in line for seven hours to walk past President John F. Kennedy's casket. When a guard recognized him and offered to move him to the front of the line, Veeck refused: "I'm not here for any special treatment. I'm here because our president died."

You should know he insisted on riding in the front seat of taxi cabs because he felt uncomfortable being chauffeured.

You should know what Larry Doby said of their first meeting.

"When I first met him," Doby recalled, "I said: 'Mr. Veeck ... ' and he said: 'Call me Bill.' "

Doby was the first black player in the American League, signed by Veeck in Cleveland in 1947. The next year, he signed Satchel Paige.

Several years earlier, Veeck had proposed buying the Philadelphia Phillies and stocking the team entirely with American-born blacks. The Phillies were quickly sold to someone else.

Veeck always had that effect on baseball's establishment. He was never one of them. He was always one of us.

When Veeck was around, baseball was fun.

"To be successful in baseball, you must have more than a winner," he once said. "You have to sell baseball to the customer other than from the field of play. This is the entertainment business, not religion."

It was Veeck who sent 3-foot-7 Eddie Gaedel to pinch-hit for the Browns against the Tigers in 1951.

Veeck hung the ivy at Wrigley Field as a youngster working for the Cubs. He was the first man to put players' names on the backs of uniforms because he thought fans shouldn't have to buy scorecards. In the early '40s, when he owned a minor league team in Milwaukee, his team played morning games so swing-shift workers would not be excluded from the sport.

He scheduled a night for veteran player Kenny Keltner in Cleveland once, but then a fan wrote: "Here I am a GI like thousands of other GIs, and you have a day, and you're giving this guy a car and gifts to ballplayers who make 10 times as much as I do. Your fan, Joe Earley."

Veeck canceled Keltner Night and held Joe Earley Night instead and gave him a car and burned his mortgage.

That was Bill Veeck. And that's why no one was ever more deserving of his place in baseball's Hall of Fame.

It was Veeck who saved the White Sox from being taken over by the league when their owners were wallowing near bankruptcy in the mid-70s. He put together a syndicate and bought the club. Then, to the horror of the establishment, he placed an "Open for Business" sign and an American flag on a desk and began conducting trades in the lobby of Miami's Diplomat Hotel.

Three years later, a 34-year-old minor league manager caught his eye. He had managed only 183 games when Veeck made him manager of the White Sox, but among active managers today only Sparky Anderson has a better winning percentage than Tony La Russa.

When Veeck finally left the game for good, he was presented with a lifetime pass to every baseball park in America. He never used it.

"I pay for my tickets," he explained, "so I can complain."

When he died on Jan. 2, 1986, kids showed up at his funeral in baseball caps, adults in warm-up jackets, and Minnie Minoso attended wearing one of those turn-of-the-century-style White Sox uniforms Veeck brought back for a while.

In his autobiography, "Veeck — as in Wreck," he wrote: "Sometime, somewhere, there will be a club nobody really wants. And then Old Will will come wandering along to laugh some more. Look for me under the arc lights, boys, I'll be back."

Of course, he won't.

And there won't be any other like him, either.

That's too bad for us. And I think it's too bad for baseball, too. ❖

Sparky and the Pope V

March 3, 1992

His Holiness Pope John Paul II.
The Vatican.
Vatican City.
Most Holy Father:
I hope you remember me and that it is not an intrusion for me to write every now and then. We met a few years ago when you were in Detroit. You might remember because that's where somebody in the crowd shouted: "Who's that guy with Sparky?"

I thought that was pretty rude, but I am well-known in Detroit. Sometimes I wish I weren't, you know. Sometimes people expect more than can be delivered, but in your line of work, you probably run into that, too.

I mean, when people expect miracles from you, at least you are close to someone who might help. In my line of work — I manage a baseball team called the Detroit Tigers — people expect miracles, too. But when I try to perform one, I have only other mortals to ask for help. Some of my mortals have weights that are higher than their batting averages, so you can imagine how I'm doing in the miracle category.

Well, holy smoke — if you don't mind me saying that — there are a lot of things going on around this ballclub that people on the outside don't take into consideration.

You're lucky, Your Holiness, that from the day you were ordained you knew who you were working for. Well, here we don't have that luxury. Some people say Tom Monaghan is going to own this ballclub for a while yet, and some others say one of the Fords is going to buy it, and there's even some guy in Lansing who says he wants it, but I understand he wanted to buy the team with his Discover card.

Oh, my gosh, I told the writers when they started showing up here that I'd talk about almost anything, like I always have, but I wasn't about to talk about the sale of the club. There's nothing to be gained there, and I don't know anything about what's going on, anyway. Somebody told me that Mr. Monaghan is about as broke as Humpty-Dumpty, but I don't know that I believe that.

I've got my hands full with what goes on right here in my locker room and on the field here at spring training.

Maybe you remember, I wrote you once about my second baseman. He's the guy who got hurt on the dance floor, which I thought was unusual at the time because he was dancing with his own wife. Anyway, he's talking about wanting a lot more money when he signs his next contract, and the writers who hang around here and sun themselves this time of year are listening to him and writing down what he says.

The writers, in general, aren't too bad. I like to joke with them, but sometimes you have to put them in their place. There's this columnist from the Detroit Free Press, Charlie Vincent, who thinks he knows something about baseball, but I swear I think if he heard somebody scream "Suicide bunt!" he'd call Jack Kevorkian.

I call him Standing Eagle because a standing eagle is one that's too full of something to fly.

We're in spring training now, in a place called Lakeland, Fla., and it seems all the writers here want to ask me questions about things that don't have nothing to do with hitting or catching a baseball.

For instance, there's a big fuss over building us a new stadium, which you might find kinda odd, since the Vatican was several hundred years old when we built the stadium we're playing in now. But in the United States, we don't keep things around as long as you Europeans do. If we had the Sistine chapel here, we'd probably tear it down and sell pieces of the ceiling for souvenirs, like they did with the artificial turf out at Michigan Stadium.

I guess you don't really have any use for luxury suites at St. Peter's Basilica. We didn't seem to need 'em in baseball either for a long time, but now people tell me we've got to have 'em, so I guess someday we'll have them in a new stadium, but nobody seems to know when or where or how, or who'll own the team by then.

Somebody suggested to me a minute ago that I might ask if you were interested in buying the team. I hope you're not, Your Holiness, because the commissioner wouldn't let you do that. He only trusts American money. No Japanese, no Italians and no Polish people. I hope you don't take that personally.

You know, when I write you, I usually have a favor to ask, usually something for myself or my baseball team. Sometimes I've asked for a prayer to help us through, or something like that. But this time, I'm not asking for nothing for myself or my team.

I'd appreciate it if you'd say a prayer or two for Millie Schembechler. She's Bo's wife — probably the name doesn't mean much in Rome, but people here

My father was the athlete in the family. Charles Eager Vincent — better known as Slick, a tribute to the things he could do with a basketball — was a prep and college star. He went on to play pro baseball in the Florida State League and semipro basketball in the late 1920s and early '30s.

EARLE CARDINALS
EARLE, ARKANSAS
South's Greatest Basketball Team

SLICK VINCENT

– Presenting –

1933-34 LINE-UP

– of –

EARLE CARDINALS

Greatest

BASKETBALL TEAM

To Ever

Represent

EARLE, ARKANSAS

"The Cardinals Play Them All"

Two of my daughters — Dixie, center, and Lisa, right — meet their idol, tennis great Billie Jean King, who later admitted to having an affair with her female secretary. King asked for understanding from fans; I didn't think that was necessary.

For 13-plus seasons, Bill Laimbeer displayed great heart and made the most of his abilities, but the Pistons center never knew when to drop his game face. He retired after 13 games of the 1993-94 season as the most-disliked, most-fined player in the NBA.

MARY SCHROEDER

WILLIAM ARCHIE

Dennis Rodman fights back tears after being named defensive player of the year in 1990. GM Jack McCloskey looks on. Rodman's helter-skelter behavior forced the Pistons to trade him, to San Antonio.

When I first met Isiah Thomas in 1981, a few weeks before the NBA draft, he told me that he hoped to play for the Bulls instead of the Pistons. But when he retired in 1994, after leading Detroit to two NBA titles, he said: "This has been a great life for me." Along the way, I met his mother; saw where he grew up; and watched the kid from Chicago evolve into an NBA legend.

MANNY CRISOSTOMO

The brothers Fontes — head coach Wayne, left, and assistant coach Len —
pal around on the Lions' sidelines.

Martha Louis and heavyweight husband
Joe, in 1970 photos. She was a fighter, too
— the first black woman to practice law
in California. I met them in 1979, two
years after an aneurysm, followed by a
stroke, left Joe virtually helpless.

Outspoken heavyweight champ
Muhammad Ali was still drawing
crowds when we met in 1989.

*Tigers manager Sparky Anderson spends a quiet moment at Lakeland, Fla.,
no doubt contemplating another letter to the Pope.*

*Former and future
teammates Kirk
Gibson and Alan
Trammell were
friendly rivals in
1991, when Gibson
played for the
Royals. Gibby
proved you can go
home again,
returning to the
Tigers for two
productive
seasons,
beginning in 1993.*

Fun-loving Lions quarterback Bobby Layne drinking milk? He didn't always.

I caught up with Arnold Palmer, left, and Calvin Peete, above, at the '87 Masters. Arnie's Army hadn't deserted him, but his game sure had. Peete, a Detroiter and one of 19 children, took up golf relatively late in life. Only one other black, Lee Elder, played the Masters before him.

Bill Frieder was a Michigan man in early '89, but his days were numbered.

Bo Schembechler, far left, chats with Notre Dame coach Lou Holtz. Schembechler, also serving as U-M's athletic director at the time, fired Frieder on the eve of the 1989 NCAA tournament after Frieder announced he had agreed to coach Arizona State the following season.

Mario Andretti enjoyed one magic moment at the Indy 500 — and countless other disappointments.

The saga of Tonya and Nancy began in Detroit and ended in Lillehammer, Norway, where Kerrigan, left, won a silver medal at the Winter Olympics while Harding, above, faltered and came home empty-handed. Harding was implicated in the attack on Kerrigan and forced to resign from the U.S. Figure Skating Association.

JULIAN H. GONZALEZ (3)

Alexi Lalas and the U.S. soccer team shocked Colombia and reached the second round of the World Cup.

know who they are. She's been sick, and we've been praying for her here, and I thought, with your connections, it would be nice if you would, too.

I gotta go now.

Thanks for your time and your prayers. I'll leave you with a word of Polish I remember from your visit here: Wappakaneta.

Sincerely,

George (Sparky) Anderson. ❖

Prince Hal

March 18, 1992

For 30 years he waited, usually impatiently.

For 30 years he wondered why his phone didn't ring, why the names — when they were announced at this time of year — were always someone else's.

For 30 years, Hal Newhouser wondered whether he would go to his grave without receiving the ultimate award baseball can bestow.

Today, he has his answer.

Today 70-year-old Hal Newhouser and umpire Bill McGowan — who died in 1954 — are the newest members in baseball's Hall of Fame, named by the Veterans Committee for induction Aug. 2 along with Tom Seaver and Rollie Fingers, who were voted in earlier by the Baseball Writers Association of America.

After learning that his wait had ended, Newhouser's first call was to his 95-year-old mother. "I called my mother and said, 'Are you sitting down?' She said, 'Yes, why?' And I said, 'Are you going to come to Cooperstown to see your son inducted into the Hall of Fame?' "

And they both wept.

Hal Newhouser was the best news Detroit had during World War II. He was born here in the years before the Depression, and by 1940, at 19, he was attending Wilbur Wright Technical School in the morning and pitching for the Tigers in the afternoon.

Within a few years the war was taking an awful toll, but baseball struggled on, giving Americans something to cheer about, to feel good about, to talk about during dinner, after the war news had been digested. And young Hal Newhouser, nicknamed Prince Hal, dominated the American League the way no other pitcher did.

He was the league's most valuable player in 1944, when he was 29-9 and the Tigers finished a game behind the first-place St. Louis Browns.

And in 1945, he led the league in wins (25), winning percentage (.735), ERA (1.81), starts (36), complete games (29), innings (313⅓), strikeouts (212), shutouts (eight) and hits allowed per nine innings (6.86).

He won two games in the World Series that fall, including the Tigers' decisive Game 7 over the Chicago Cubs. And he was named MVP for the second consecutive season — something no other pitcher has done.

But when Hall of Fame balloting time came, a sad, old refrain always filled Newhouser's ears.

Wartime pitcher … wartime pitcher … he was a wartime pitcher, that's all.

His records and accomplishments were discounted like a cheap suit because some of his biggest successes came in the years when some of the game's biggest names were in military service.

In 1962, the first year he was eligible for the Hall of Fame, Newhouser received four votes. In 1975, the final year he was on the writers' ballot, he received 155 votes; 272 were needed for induction that year.

George Kell, a Tigers teammate of Newhouser's in 1946-52, was inducted into the Hall of Fame nine years ago. And he has thought for a long time that Newhouser should be in Cooperstown, too.

"He was one tough pitcher," Kell said. "He was a real live wire around the clubhouse most of the time, but on days he pitched, he didn't even want anybody to smile. I liked that. I liked to play behind him.

"I've always heard that wartime pitcher stuff, but he won 29 games in 1944, 25 games in 1945, 26 in 1946. Nobody else did that, and I think this is well-deserved, wartime years or not."

For a lot of years Newhouser, who lives in Bloomfield Hills, would read the newspapers to find the date of the Veterans Committee balloting. Then he would pull a chair up to the radio at midday to listen to the news. Every year, someone else's name was broadcast, or no one's at all.

One year, the committee named Earl Averill to the Hall of Fame. Another year it was Bobby Doerr. Another it was Pee Wee Reese.

Exasperated, disappointed and a bit bitter, he wrote all the members of the Veterans Committee one year.

"I just wanted to find out if there was a reason for me not making it," he said in 1988. "I received nothing back. Not a single reply."

He won 207 games in his major league career, had a 3.06 ERA, struck out 1,796 and was named to six All-Star Games before retiring after the 1955 season. He pitched against Ted Williams and Joe DiMaggio, Bob Feller and Whitey Ford. He thought he had done well enough to join them all in the Hall of Fame.

But each year he was denied. And he admitted: "Not a day goes by that I don't think about it. It bothers me, and I think it will bother me until the day I get into the Hall of Fame."

As time passed, though, he all but gave up hope.

One year he read a story in the Free Press that quoted a member of the Veterans Committee as saying Newhouser's name was hardly mentioned in their deliberations. He wadded up the paper, pressed his lips together and accepted the fact that his time might never come.

"I was discouraged because I kept thinking instead of them looking at the record, all they looked at was that I played during the war," he said. "I always felt my record was there. I felt I was of good character and had integrity and I helped my team, so I could never understand it.

"Now, after all of these years, what's going to be so nice is to be able to write back a different message to all the people who have written me over the years, asking for my autograph and asking why I'm not in the Hall of Fame.

"Now they're going to ask how I feel about being in."

The years of bitterness fell away like dead leaves in the winter. Hal Newhouser will never be a kid again, but for now he feels like one. For now there are no thoughts of rejection, of denial, of bitterness.

For now there is the glow in his heart that tells him his work in baseball has been recognized as being among the best the game has ever seen.

"I was born at the right time," he said, discounting the multi-zeroed salaries of today. "My salary was tops for that era.... I played against DiMaggio and Williams, and I pitched against Feller. I played with Hank Greenberg and Charlie Gehringer. I'd take the '40s anytime."

Hal Newhouser has never been to Cooperstown.

He has never walked into the gallery that contains nothing but the chiseled plaques of baseball's most honored players. He has never seen the people who file by in awe, whispering — as if in a church — as they reach out to touch the images of the members of baseball's Hall of Fame.

Babe Ruth.

Ty Cobb.

Walter Johnson.

Stan Musial.

And in August: Hal Newhouser.

"I don't know what could be better," he said. "My mother just turned 95 and is in good health and will see her son inducted into the Hall of Fame. I'm the first Detroit-born Detroit Tiger to be inducted into the Hall of Fame. I will turn 71 in May, and I just passed my physical with flying colors.

"What more can you ask?" ❖

Jack Morris

October 7, 1992

M y friend was upset.

He is a baseball fan and a family man, and he works hard for a living and thinks of himself as fair.

He will not want to watch the American League playoffs tonight. He does not trust Jack Morris. Morris just might pitch a shutout. Or a no-hitter. And my friend's evening will be ruined.

We have talked about this. I have tried to rationalize with him, but he didn't want to listen to baseball statistics. He wanted to quote history.

I told him I have made peace with my remembrances of Jack Morris as a Tiger. I told him the man has earned a place in the Hall of Fame. He has made winners of three teams that might not have been winners without him.

I told him the Tigers have not been the same since Morris left. I asked him where the Minnesota Twins, without Morris, finished this season. I told him these are the facts, and the facts do not lie.

My friend said something that cannot be printed in a family newspaper.

"He's a jerk," he said.

I know people who would argue, though they might admit there were certainly times when Jack Morris acted like a jerk. He was misunderstood, his old teammates think, skewered by a vengeful press. I ate lunch with a few of them the other day, and they talked of how they miss Morris' company.

My friend was profane again at the mention that there are people who like Jack Morris.

"Look at all the kids he ignored," he said. "All the autographs he could have declined politely but sneered at instead as he walked away. Look at all the ill will he spread where he could have been an ambassador for the sport."

"He's won 237 games," I countered.

"He's a jerk."

"That's not the issue," I tried to tell him. "He has won more games than

Dizzy Dean. More than Whitey Ford. More than Sandy Koufax."

My friend was not listening.

"Don't you have any memory at all?" he asked me. "Don't you remember when Morris turned down $3 million from the Tigers? Don't you know a regular Joe would have to make $60,000 for 50 years to equal that? What kind of loyalty is that?"

I tried to remind him that as much as we would like baseball to be about loyalty, it is — in the real world — about business, instead.

"Loyalty," I told him, "won't come into play this winter if the Tigers decide not to re-sign Dave Bergman or Frank Tanana or Alan Trammell or Lou Whitaker."

My friend was not listening; he was turning red.

"He's a jerk," he said again. "Don't you remember the crude and insulting things he said to Jennifer Frey when she was an intern at the Free Press a few years ago? I hate it when he does well."

"Look," I tried to tell him, "we're not talking about sainthood here. We're not talking about nominating the guy for model citizen of the half-century. We're talking pitching. Besides, Jennifer Frey has recovered nicely, thank you, is working for the New York Times and is on the way to a better career than Morris."

"How about all that crap when he cried because he was so happy to be going home to Minnesota?" my friend wanted to know. "How about the way he'd glare at an infielder after an error? How about … "

We will not agree. My friend let Morris get under his skin.

He remembers Morris walking away from Minnesota's $8 million offer to accept Toronto's for $10 million-plus by saying: "Who knows when the kids are going to get sick?"

He remembers Morris saying: "I guess I don't think too much about yesterday. The game of baseball isn't much different from one uniform to another," and he wishes there was more loyalty in Morris' soul.

What he has instead is heart, a tireless right arm and a 7-1 record with a 2.59 ERA in postseason games.

The Toronto Blue Jays have never quite fulfilled the expectations for them. When they were expected to win the American League East, they would fail by a game or two. When they were expected to win the American League championship, they would come up short in October.

And that is why they gave Jack Morris all that money. He has a history of winning in the clutch. In October.

He cannot rewrite the Blue Jays' history and make their failures disappear, but by starting him tonight, in the first game of their American League playoff series against Oakland, the Blue Jays are asking him to do for them what he did for Minnesota a year ago, for Detroit in 1984.

They are putting their hopes in his 37-year-old hands, counting on him to give them a one-game advantage toward a place they've never gone: the World Series.

My friend cannot bear to watch because he knows — despite all the baggage he carries with him — Morris, more than anyone else, is likely to take the Blue Jays where they want to go.

"He's a jerk," my friend said.

"He's a winner," I countered.

And probably we both are right.

Morris went on to pitch for Cleveland and surpassed the 250-win mark during the 1994 season. He was released by the Indians on Aug. 9, 1994. ❖

The man in blue

November 25, 1992

We've seen managers kick dirt on an umpire's shoes or shoot a stream of tobacco juice in his direction.

We've seen players say things to umpires that they would not say in front of their mothers. Or their children.

And we've seen umpires say worse things in retaliation.

We've seen the greedy side of baseball — players who won't play for less than $5 million, teams that say good-bye to loyal, longtime employees because $300,000 is too much to pay an aging player.

Take a couple of minutes to hear about a more noble side — a sad, but noble, story.

John Hirschbeck has been umpiring in the American League for nine seasons. Usually, umpires have only themselves, other umpires and their families. Every game is a road game, no one cheers for them and most relations with players or managers are adversarial.

"Kill the umpire!" is one of the first things we learn to shout at the ballpark.

But early next month, baseball will do all it can to save the umpire's son. And while it is probably too late to save one, there is great hope for the other.

John Hirschbeck was in Seattle last April, preparing to walk onto the field for the season opener, when he got a call from his wife, Denise, in Poland, Ohio.

The news was bad. About as bad as it could be.

Their 8-year-old son, John, had been acting strangely.

Though he had been a bright child, his report cards in the first grade were not good. He became a discipline problem. And, even with the help of his parents, he had trouble counting and reading.

In February, a pediatric neurologist diagnosed John's problem as attention deficit hyperactivity disorder. But his behavior became increasingly bizarre, and on a flight from spring training to Ohio, something happened that frightened his parents.

"A man, just being nice, asked where he was going," his father recalled, "and he didn't know. We'd been worried because, at a spring game, a girl asked him how old he was and he told her the wrong age."

And now, with a new baseball season beginning, 2,400 miles from home, John Hirschbeck picked up the phone and heard his wife say: "They think they see something in his brain ... some gray in what is supposed to be the white area."

Adrenoleukodystrophy didn't mean anything to them then.

Fewer than 80 cases a year are diagnosed in the United States and Canada. Nobody gets it.

And then your son does.

"I flew home the next day, and that's when the doctor told us about the disease," Hirschbeck said. "It affects the central nervous system, and it's so rare we didn't even worry about the other three kids right away. But when we got their blood samples analyzed, it turned out all of them have it. We were just devastated."

Doctors told Hirschbeck that nothing could be done for his oldest son. He had a year, maybe. They went to the University of Minnesota Medical Center, where the disease was understood, and learned that Erin, 4, and Meghan, 1, probably would never show active signs of the disease but would be carriers.

But a brain scan showed that Michael, 6, had two small gray spots. Last July, during baseball's All-Star break, he underwent a bone marrow transplant, hoping the new marrow would correct the enzyme imbalance in the brain that causes the disease. The donor was his 1-year-old sister.

It was more difficult finding a match for John, and as the disease progressed, the chances of a successful transplant have decreased.

"We have been commuting between Ohio and Minnesota every other weekend with one boy or the other," Hirschbeck said. "The damage that is there is not reversible, but Michael shows no symptoms." Even over the telephone you could hear the catch in his voice and imagine the pain in his heart as he said, "Because of John, we knew what to look for."

A 6-year-old hardly knows what to make of it. He watched his big brother change, and one Sunday, just before the transplant, his parents sat him down.

"We said, 'You know John is sick. Well, you have the same thing. But because of John, we can help you. Everything is going to be all right.'

"But we could tell he was nervous, and his mom said, 'It's all right to cry.' And he started crying."

John succumbed to the disease. Michael continues the battle. ❖

Pete Rose

March 3, 1993

BOCA RATON, Fla. — Fifteen or so miles down the road, Steve Howe is in a baseball uniform and George Steinbrenner is back in charge of the New York Yankees, and neither fact is lost on the man who has just emerged from a broadcast booth in his restaurant.

What he did on baseball fields for 24 years should have put him into the Hall of Fame, but what he did off the fields made baseball say, nope, you're not going to Cooperstown.

And seven seasons after he played his final game, Pete Rose is still trying to cope with the rejection.

He sees Steinbrenner given a second chance after a "lifetime suspension." He sees Howe back after seven suspensions for drug and alcohol abuse. And he believes there will be a day when baseball welcomes him back, too.

"It gives you optimism," Rose said of the game's leniency with Steinbrenner and Howe. "All you want is somebody that's going to be fair, and it was very obvious (former commissioner) Fay Vincent wasn't going to be fair."

Not everyone will agree. There are still those who say, "Where there's smoke, there's fire," and maintain Rose must have bet on baseball games, though there has never been any evidence released that he did. He was suspended for betting unrelated to baseball and went to prison for five months for income tax violations.

Now he is reconstructing his life and image.

Rose does a syndicated, daily two-hour sports talk show from the Pete Rose Ballpark Cafe in Boca Raton that is heard on 30 stations. He is involved in other projects, including an about-to-be-introduced "power drink" that he said "could get me in the category of a .388 hitter, and you know what a guy who hits that would make today."

That earns him a living and keeps him busy. And perhaps the latter is more important because being busy keeps him from dwelling on being denied his spot at Cooperstown.

He makes a point of saying that when his world fell apart, "I didn't whine. I kept my mouth shut, paid my debt to society and went on my way."

Someone gave him good advice. That is the only way baseball will accept him back. Rose was a fireball, a bare-knuckle throwback to when spitballs were winked at and baserunners were supposed to take out an infielder with every slide.

The game loved him that way then. But now it wants him humble. You get the feeling it wants an apology. You get the feeling it wants Rose on his knees and then, maybe, somebody will invite him back into the family.

Getting on his knees, though, just isn't Rose's style. Someday, he will ask for his ban to be lifted. Not today, though. Or tomorrow.

"Who would I send it to?" he asked, noting that baseball does not have a commissioner. "I want somebody who will really consider it, not just file it away. Timing is everything, and right now is not the right time."

On this night, Rose, 51, his hair as brown as ever, thanks to the wonderful world of chemicals, finished his radio show and slid into a chair to talk to a couple of reporters, plopping on the table a four-inch stack of pre-autographed cards for the dozens of diners he knew would stop by to ask for one.

He sees himself as baseball's best ambassador. And if baseball doesn't like that, too bad.

The people who come to him for autographs seem to remember only his good days. They are kids too young to have seen him play; young women still enamored by his dashing image; older couples who winter here and guard memories of the old days at Crosley Field and Riverfront Stadium.

"I don't go home every night and pray I go into the Hall of Fame, but if I do go in, I'll be the most appreciative guy there," he said, and it had the sound of a practiced response. "I appreciate the things that Babe Ruth did and Ty Cobb and Lloyd Waner. I understand the history of the game. Every ballplayer should thank God for Babe Ruth and, if he's a black ballplayer, for Jackie Robinson."

Only on the subject of Howe does there seem to be a twinge of raw emotion in Rose's voice. Howe has had so many second chances, and so far baseball has given Rose none.

"I met Howe and his wife and little children a few years back," he said. "I keep hoping the SOB takes advantage of the opportunities because he has that young family growing up... . When you hurt yourself, you usually hurt people around you, too."

Rose, who should know about that, doesn't allow himself to believe he will be forever banned from the Hall.

"You'll never get me to say I don't think I'm going to go into the Hall of Fame because I bet on "Monday Night Football," and that's where it stands now," he said. "I never was a bad citizen. I never was a bad guy... . A lot of people are willing to give me a second chance. I won't need a third.

"I think everything will be OK."

Rose has made mistakes. He probably will make more. But no one was ever more committed to playing the game of baseball, and not many played it better.

In America, we are taught to forgive even if we cannot forget.

It is time for baseball to forgive Pete Rose and to allow his name on the Hall of Fame ballot.

Rose has yet to be reinstated or listed on the Hall of Fame ballot. ❖

Mike Ilitch

March 6, 1993

L AKELAND, Fla . — Mike Ilitch has all the money and half the pizza in the world.

And yesterday, for the first time, he saw his major league team play an exhibition game. It was the first time in 40 years he was able to bring himself to come to Lakeland to watch an exhibition. He has been to Florida a hundred times. Been to games more often.

But when he hung up his glove for the final time, conceding a professional career to an injured knee, something happened inside him. Lakeland — where he was a member of the Tigers' minor league organization — became a town of bad memories. Maybe the worst memory.

The town where he dared dream the dream of all boys.

And when he realized he could never again come here with his glove and his shoes and bats to play the game, he could not cope with being here at all. His dream had died. He had failed.

"This isn't going to sound right," he said after the Tigers had lost their exhibition opener to the Chicago White Sox, 7-6, "but I never came back here to watch an exhibition because it kind of hurts you that you didn't make the major leagues.

"It's one challenge in life that you faced that you didn't achieve. You never get over it. It's like your first love, your first date."

The experience left Ilitch with a feel for the game that most owners don't have. Probably he will never be the overbearing owner that George Steinbrenner is, but neither will he be Tom Monaghan, who once said he would sell the Tigers if they became "a distraction."

Probably Ilitch will not meddle, but certainly he will be aware.

When he was vacationing in Arizona last fall, he spent a couple of nights scouting Tigers players in the Arizona Fall League. He kept notes and observations, and when he was done, he called Detroit to let the front office know he liked the looks of a right-hander named Tom Schwarber, who eventually went 4-0 in the fall league.

He laughed at the memory.

"As soon as I hung up, they probably said: 'Did you hear that?' " Ilitch said.

He kept notes of a sort this day, too.

He spent the first 4½ innings in a seat beside the dugout along the first base line, then moved to a booth in the press box, where he and general manger Jerry Walker and assistant general manager Gary Vitto could talk in private.

"I like to sit with Jerry and get briefed on the minor leaguers, what kind of kids they are, what their attitudes are," he said.

He likes, too, to be left alone to evaluate what he sees.

He paid $10 million for Mike Moore, who will be the Opening Day pitcher. And in this exhibition, Moore gave up seven hits, five earned runs, two walks and three wild pitches in three innings. An ERA of 15.00.

And Ilitch understood. Or said he did.

"I kind of feel like the players feel," Ilitch said. "This is the time to get into shape. There are some things that don't show up. Like Moore throwing those balls into the dirt, pitchers trying to keep the ball down, working on keeping it low. I ask myself: 'What's he working on?' "

He watched Alan Trammell play his first game in centerfield, a typical workmanlike effort by the veteran shortstop who is in his 17th season as a Tiger and trying to adjust to what is best for the team.

"There's not a better place to break in for a centerfielder than here with this vicious wind," Ilitch said.

The first time Ilitch came to Lakeland, he was a rookie whose baseball playing had been done at Cooley High and in the Marines. They had given him $3,000 to sign, and even in 1952 that did not seem like all the money in the world.

"We had a guy in my group that got a $25,000 bonus, and he had a silk shirt and nice pants.... I had a little different wardrobe on," he said.

When Ilitch returned to Lakeland, he could afford to dress any way he wanted. But he still identifies with the guys who came here this spring with a dream because he left one of his own here 40 years ago and arrived yesterday with a new one.

Detroit Tigers: World Champions.

Hey, you might as well dream big.

Trammell's move to centerfield didn't last; Ilitch is still looking for that elusive world championship. ❖

Tram

April 2, 1993

L AKELAND, Fla. — There are traits that reveal a champion.

They do not show up in a batting average.

They are not in the box scores. And, too often, they are not in the stories you read, either.

But if a guy hangs around long enough, you can tell if he's a champion or a chump or something in between. And sometimes you get the best glimpses of a champion — corny as that sounds — when the batting average is at its lowest, his name is absent from the box score and his career is in jeopardy.

In Oakland, for the first time since 1980, the Tigers will field an Opening Day lineup without Alan Trammell.

Long before he suffered a pulled groin muscle in an exhibition win over St. Louis, it was decided there was no place for Trammell in the Tigers' starting nine.

He has missed 194 games the past two seasons because of injuries but came here healthy and happy and hopeful. When Sparky Anderson said he wanted to experiment with the 35-year-old, who had never played anywhere but shortstop in his 16-year major league career, Trammell said sure.

It was great for the photographers. They snapped dozens of pictures of him walking onto the field with gloves in his arms — infielder gloves, first baseman mitts, outfielder gloves.

Trammell smiled and said he'd do whatever he was asked.

So he started a couple of games in centerfield before Anderson decided that wasn't where he wanted Trammell.

Then he played awhile at third, replacing Scott Livingstone. And it looked like Trammell might be there Opening Day. But Anderson changed his mind again, and Trammell played a little more centerfield, a little shortstop.

And now he is a little left out, but not put out.

Milt Cuyler will be in centerfield for the opener, Livingstone will be at third, Travis Fryman at short and Cecil Fielder at first.

Alan Trammell will be in the dugout. And Anderson's most recent judgment is that he doesn't know when or where Trammell will play once the season gets started.

If you are 35, if you have played your entire career with one organization, if you have a history as someone who has done whatever that organization asked, you'd have a right, I'd say, to be upset.

Maybe that means I might not be a champion.

Trammell is.

In the exhibition against the Cardinals, Trammell played shortstop only because Fryman was sidelined with the flu. Trammell aggravated a groin pull as he pursued a ground ball by Ozzie Smith in the first inning. "I did it on the first step," Trammell said. "But I knew I could get there. I just had to keep dragging the leg and saying: 'C'mon! C'mon, you can get there!' "

He made the play, made the throw, then limped straight into the Tigers' locker room.

That one play meant nothing in the context of his career, and it meant everything. It would not win him a starting spot or detract from his accomplishments. But it would define the way he has always played.

He has always played the game with his glove and his bat and his body, never with his mouth.

Now, though, there is nothing he can do but sit and wait — and that was true even before he hurt himself on a meaningless ground ball. But if Trammell is resentful or unhappy about the situation, he is not telling me so I can tell you.

"If I have a problem," he said, "I can talk to Gibby (Kirk Gibson) about it. We've talked a lot this spring. I talk to my wife, too, but she brings me down to earth. She tells me: 'I've got a family to raise here — I don't have time for that.' "

He said it with a smile that said he understands the world has little reason to care about his professional problems if his wife belittles them.

At the bat, Trammell's spring has not been impressive. He has hit .231 and concedes: "Early on, I was lost. I was rusty, but it's getting better."

Despite all the position changes and that he had never played anywhere but shortstop, he has not made an error. And all the gloves he collected when training camp began are still nestled in the top of his locker, ready to be used at Anderson's next whim.

"I found I really like playing centerfield," Trammell said. "And I think I can do a good job out there. But that's the way I feel about everything."

He has talked to one other person about his spring and his plight. Dave Bergman, a former teammate and an old friend, had some advice.

"I know this may be it for me," Trammell said, "but I want to stay in the game — coaching, scouting, something, whatever — and Bergie made the point that going through this spring might help me in the long run. I'll be able to relate."

So Alan Trammell's batting average might not look like much this spring. And on Opening Day, his name won't be in the starting lineup.

But that's not the test of a man or of a champion.

If there were ever any doubt, Alan Trammell passed those tests this spring. And there's a lesson there for all of us.

Tram made 58 starts at shortstop, 27 at third base, four in centerfield, four in left and four at DH in 1993. Overall, he appeared in 112 games — and batted .329. ❖

Detroit's own

April 14, 1993

Some things are just Detroit.
White Castle.
Vernors.
General Motors.
Kirk Gibson.

Sometimes we curse them. The burgers are too small, the Vernors too warm, the automobiles too expensive, the ballplayer too self-centered.

But in the end, they are ours. And they are ours all the more when we have been without them awhile or when one has gone away, then returned, as Gibson did yesterday afternoon in Tiger Stadium.

When he came to bat for the first time, most of the people in the Opening Day crowd of 49,674 rose and applauded. Applauded and cheered and stomped their feet.

Gibson has not always been so beloved here. We remember, and so does he, when he was booed and jeered — and even he said there were times he deserved it.

"I've got my strengths and my weaknesses and my faults," he said.

There were times in his youth when he was self-centered, too full of himself and his accomplishments, when he seemed to tell us he was more important than you or I, and worse, more important than our children, who too often were ignored as they looked up at him with pleading eyes and offered little fists clutching pens and scraps of paper.

But his faults never included forgetting his love for his hometown or for his sport. Never, in a career filled with controversy, did anyone accuse him of loafing or giving up or saying his hometown was the pit that so much of America seems to believe it is.

Eventually he outgrew most of his youthful arrogance, and in time we gave more weight to his work ethic and his love of this city than to the mistakes he made as a young man.

So when he came home, Detroit was ready. And Detroiters stood and let him know how they felt.

"I felt like I was a rookie," Gibson said after the Tigers' ridiculously easy 20-4 victory over the Oakland Athletics. "I was almost out of control.... I guess it brings out the boy in me."

He struck out his first time, looking for a way to return what the fans had given him. Looking for a way to jack an inside fastball into the rightfield seats.

"I was going to try to hit the ball out of the park, and I was setting up inside," he said of facing Oakland starter Storm Davis. "But he never came in there. He threw the ball right over the plate.

"My first at-bat was as good a stress test as you'll get, and I was kind of fighting my emotions all day. I guess I don't have any excuses from here on."

He had a walk and run-scoring double in four tries.

It was among his least eventful Tiger Stadium Opening Days.

The last time he was in the Opening Day lineup — in 1986 — he drove in five runs with two homers and two singles against Boston. Three years before that, he got hit with a fly ball he lost in the afternoon sunlight.

He and Sparky Anderson laughed about that.

"I remember some of the lowlights," Gibson said. "Even though it was 10 years ago, I remember it."

He also remembered being booed that day.

"When bad things happen, I do worse things to myself than boo. I condition myself to believe I'm going to do things in the clutch, and they believe it, too," he said of Tigers fans. "I take it very hard when I fail. It's not something I throw off and say, 'That's just the way it goes.' "

It's that attitude that makes Detroit love Kirk Gibson.

That, and the way he feels about the city.

Somewhere else, people might think it's corny to say you love a town. Here we long for love, for someone else to feel as we do about this city. It was a feeling Gibson experienced on the drive in from his new home in Grosse Pointe — the home his wife moved into last week while he was on the West Coast with his new teammates.

"Coming in today, I got on the freeway and it's Detroit. The stadium's Detroit. These are things I've related to my whole life.

"It's just not as bad a place to live as everybody thinks it is. We're the only ones who know that. But I'm glad to be back here and proud to be back here."

His sons, Kirk and Kevin, were in the stands for the opener, and the man who once found it so easy to walk past little kids said: "It was great to look up there and see my boys. They were really excited to come to the game, and I was excited to be back here and be able to perform here.

"I think it's very obvious the fans appreciate my work ethic, and that's what they were applauding. I appreciate what they were saying. But what they did for me today was a courtesy. I want to hear it in October... . I said to the guys earlier to listen to the crowd and to picture it in October. This was nothing compared to what I remember it being in October, every day for a week."

We can only hope Kirk Gibson can again be the ballplayer he was, but the thing we should appreciate most is that he has become a man he never was.

And it's good to have him back home.

Gibson hit .261 with 13 homers in his first season back with the Tigers. ❖

Skeeter Barnes

March 29, 1994

LAKELAND, Fla. — No one will ever make a movie of Skeeter Barnes' life.

No one will write a book about what he accomplished in the baseball career that probably ended yesterday.

But he is my favorite Tiger story of the last five years.

The day we met, in March 1991, he was a 34-year-old career minor leaguer, playing for peanuts and pride. He had been a pro for 13 years, playing in such places as Billings, Wichita, Waterbury, Nashville and Portland. In those 13 years, he had 109 major league at-bats in appearances with Montreal, St. Louis and Cincinnati.

He was in the Tigers' minor league camp that spring, headed for Toledo, with no promises he would ever again play in the majors.

"If it ended tomorrow," he said, "I wouldn't feel bad about anything. I've played hard and, if anything, I've been an overachiever."

He was a classy man with pride in himself and an appreciation for how difficult it was to become a major leaguer. He hit .330 in Toledo that spring. And in June, the Tigers called him to Detroit, where he batted .289 against American League pitching.

He hit .273 the next year. And .281 last summer.

They were his summers in the sun, three seasons in the majors at an age when many players are retired. He had 484 at-bats, mostly when somebody better needed a rest. But he did not just fill in. He contributed. Last summer, he hit .294 with runners in scoring position, .313 leading off innings. Those are numbers a manager looks for in a hitter. But only if the hitter is young. Only if the hitter has a future.

At 37, Skeeter Barnes does not.

So Sparky Anderson called him into his office, told him to shut the door, and told him good-bye.

"It was awful," said Anderson, who dreaded the day because he likes Barnes and because he knew Barnes' statistics did not justify his release. "I told him: 'You done 2½ years of outstanding service for this club.' Skeeter got caught in a thing. There was no way to ever play him.

"He did everything. He could not do more to secure his job than he has done, and he couldn't secure it. You look at him and tell him that and tell him he hasn't got a job. If he would say: 'I'm looking at an idiot,' I would take it and not bat an eye."

Barnes, classy to the end, did not say that.

"I got my fishing papers," he said when solemn teammates approached and wished him well. "It just didn't work out. Don't look so sad. I'm not dead. Take care of yourself, and maybe I'll see you down the road."

The Tigers say he can go to Toledo if he likes. But after he finished shaking hands, Barnes flew to Indianapolis, to his wife and family, to contemplate his situation.

"Maybe somebody out there will claim me," he said.

Inside he had to be hurting.

When he was a kid, he wiped off the seats at Cincinnati's Riverfront Stadium when Anderson was manager of the Reds. He dreamed then of "what it would be like to run down there and jump around."

He earned his way onto those major league fields. He proved himself after years in the minors. He proved to all who doubted him for 13 years that they had misjudged his ability and dedication.

"There just wasn't enough room this year," he said without bitterness. "When you have a decent year, you don't think it'll end like this. But when they don't want you and don't have a place for you, there's nothing you can do."

He did not say he had been treated unfairly. He did not say the Tigers had made a mistake. He did not say this was an injustice.

When reality sank in, he turned toward his littered locker and said: "God, I hate packing all this stuff up."

"A lot of memories are there, huh?" one writer said.

"It's not that," Barnes said. "I just hate packing all this stuff up."

That is Skeeter Barnes. He never fooled himself, and he never tried to fool anyone else. He was a kid who wanted to be a major league ballplayer, and he grew into a man who became one.

And though he was never a star, his commitment earned the respect of his teammates. When Kirk Gibson learned Barnes had been released, his shoulders slumped, and he looked as if he had been hit in the stomach.

"Where is he?" Gibson asked, then headed off to see whether Barnes needed help handling his situation.

"He's one of the hardest I've done," Anderson said, "and I've done better players. He did more with the tools he had than any player I've ever had. I'd like to see him play one more year (in the minors) and then get into coaching."

In the Detroit organization?

"I'd hope so," Anderson said. "I can't believe anybody in his right mind wouldn't want somebody like that around young people."

That isn't a major league job, but it's a powerful testimonial to the worth of the man. ❖

Gibson revisited

August 11, 1994

It was barely 4 o'clock, three hours before what might be the season's final night baseball game in Tiger Stadium, and out on the emerald field a man mostly gone bald was twisting his upper torso back and forth, back and forth, working out the kinks, loosening his muscles as if a lifetime of games lay before him.

Others might have gone into a strike mentality. Others might have plane tickets bought to their off-season homes. Others might be content with going though the motions.

Kirk Gibson has never been content with that, and, in his 38th year, he is having one of his most productive seasons just when the owners and the players are telling each other to get lost.

Congratulate him on his 23 home runs, his 70 RBIs, his .276 average and he will fix you in a steely glare and tell you he cannot accept that as praise.

"We're 20 out on Aug. 10," he said. "We haven't played well as a team all year, and I can't accept it when people tell me I'm having a good season. I feel I'm a motivator, and I look at it as a failure on my part. I haven't been able to motivate them."

He has handled the problem the only way he knows: He has confronted some of his teammates. Told them what he thought of the way they played the game. "Light confrontations," he called them.

A few years back, during his Angry Period, Gibson probably would have named the offenders. Maybe he even would have pulled them out by the ear to show them off as the guilty parties.

He has mellowed with time, though. Anger seldom shows itself publicly. And when you scratch the surface of Kirk Gibson, you find the pride and competitive spirit remains from his younger years while the combativeness has disappeared.

"Our opinions and our theories about this season are irrelevant," Gibson said, sitting in the Tigers dugout — perhaps for one of the final times — and staring straight ahead at the vacant field. "What is relevant is we didn't do it, and we all need to share the responsibility."

The game was more than the potential final night game in Tiger Stadium this season. It might have been the final night game of Kirk Gibson's career.

No one knows what next season will bring.

No one knows whether Sparky Anderson will be back, so certainly no one knows whether Kirk Gibson will.

Seldom has an athlete in our town gone through the metamorphosis he has. As a youth, he was smug and arrogant and swaggered his way past people who wanted only to touch him or hear him say hello. He said he feels bad about it.

"I've changed as a person," he said, and there is no reason to doubt him. "I've got some bad things about me, but I've grown up."

Becoming a father gave him greater respect for other people's children, and signing autographs became less of a chore.

The one thing that never changed is his approach to the game. His single-mindedness to it comes with competition.

"I know this strike might end my career," he said. And he pauses for a minute, allowing the thought to sink into his brain. "Every game is fun, and the fun of it is the challenge.

"In Toronto the other night, I was retired three times in a row, and the next time I won the ballgame. I got up there and it was 1-0, 2-0, 3-0, and I sat on the next pitch for a home run and we win, 8-7. That's fun."

When he comes to the plate, the same people who booed him during his Angry Period cheer. Sometimes they even stand and cheer in honor of the work ethic they have come to appreciate.

"The fans have been great, and it is very gratifying, almost embarrassing to me," he said. "But it's disappointing that that's the predicament we're in.... It bothers me to sit there and watch it.

"Honestly, if I'm hitting .220 with six homers and we're in first place, I'd have to say I must have done some damage. That's just the way I think. Some people tell me they don't believe me when I say that. Those people don't know what it takes to win."

Neither, obviously, did enough of Gibson's teammates in this abbreviated summer.

From the first day, the Tigers were a dull, uninteresting team — lethargic and unable to command the attention of a city that has always maintained a love affair with baseball.

It seems the business is about to shut down, and Gibson assessed the importance of the strike perhaps more eloquently than anyone: "I would rather be here. But I refuse to waste nervous energy on something I have no control over.

"I've got a wife and four kids that mean more than any game to me... . This weekend I hope to be here, but if we're on strike, I'll spend every single day with my family. It doesn't matter what kind of day I have at the stadium, when I get home, if one of my kids jumps in my arms and says, 'Hi, Daddy, I love you,' that makes me feel great.

"So if there's a work stoppage, don't get upset. There's more constructive things you can do with your time."

Kirk Gibson, it turns out, is not only an honest laborer, but a wise man, too. ❖

Auto racing

CHAPTER

5

PETTY

ANDRETTI

A.J. FOYT

Every man for himself

May 28, 1982

INDIANAPOLIS — They held a meeting between the pit road terrace seats Thursday.

Thirty-three men who know their lives will depend upon one another Sunday afternoon talked about courtesy, the rules of the road — and how they could all come out of the 66th Indianapolis 500 with all the body parts they have today.

It may be the only time they are all in the same room. They are not friends, comrades, drinking buddies. They aren't a bunch of good 'ol boys just out for a helluva time.

The ones who have done this before — men such as A.J. Foyt, who has won this race four times; Mario Andretti, who has been in this field 17 times; Gordon Johncock, who has run here every year since 1964 — know what to expect.

They are survivors, plain and simple. There's no other way to put it.

And Thursday, they invested a few minutes to ensure they would be survivors once again when the checkered flag dropped.

They shared their experiences with the nine rookies in this year's field: Chip Ganassi, Danny Sullivan, Herm Johnson, Hector Rebaque, Bobby Rahal, Roger Mears, Dale Whittington, Jim Hickman and Chet Fillip.

They talked about how to blend in when coming out of the pits. They talked about not trying to win the race in the first lap. They talked about how to avoid trouble and how to get out of it when it is unavoidable.

They didn't do it out of a sense of duty but out of self-preservation.

It may be the only words they speak to these rookies all month.

"There's no Welcome Wagon around here," Hickman admitted. "Nobody's going to go around and shake every rookie's hand.

"Speak when spoken to is my policy. I generally don't go around asking a lot of questions."

In auto racing, it is an unwritten law: Every man for himself. If you've got a problem, that's your tough luck, bub.

Foyt and Andretti and Johncock didn't get where they are by whispering hard-earned bits of information into the ears of perfect strangers.

They may tell Jim Hickman how to counteract a spin in Turn 3 but never how to adjust the wing on his car; how to move over for a faster car, but never how to catch a faster car.

Rookies generally are considered by the old-timers to be dangerous people, men with more guts than brains, more spunk than skill.

They are to be avoided — especially on the track, but off it, too. A lot of them won't be around long, anyway. Lack of talent or lack of luck will eliminate them one way or another. Next May, some will be selling shoes in Tacoma, some will be back in the minor leagues of auto racing, and some may have their last earthly resting place marked by a simple stone.

A lot of them, the veterans believe, just don't have enough experience to drive this race, in these cars, at these speeds.

Take Hickman.

A fifth-generation rancher from Oklahoma, he began racing five years ago at 34. He has driven just one IndyCar race, finishing seventh in Atlanta earlier this month.

Sunday, he will start in the eighth row after qualifying at more than 196 miles an hour.

His driving has been the target of criticism at least once this month. Kevin Cogan looked in his rearview mirror one day and saw Hickman's car spinning out of control, about to tag the back of his Penske-Cosworth.

Cogan, 13 years younger than Hickman, had some stern things to say afterward about "these rookies trying to get a few extra miles out of their cars."

Hickman said: "After you've been here awhile, you are an accepted person. Anybody else is an outsider. There's a reluctance to accept anybody regardless of his credentials in other forms of racing.

"But it's an attitude you have to expect. And it's somewhat justified."

It's justified because here they play for keeps. Too many men have invested their lives, literally, in this sport.

That's why they held Thursday's meeting.

That's why the veterans, for one day at least, had time to accommodate the rookies.

Sunday, they only will motion for them to move over.

Veterans Gordon Johncock and Rick Mears dueled to the finish of the '82 Indy 500, with Johncock winning by a fraction of a second. Hickman died three months later in a crash at Milwaukee. ❖

Al Jr.

July 20, 1985

BROOKLYN, Mich. — The cockpit of a speeding race car is a lonely place. There is no one to ask for advice or to pay the price for a mistake. There is no one to look to for help.

No one to dry sweaty palms or soothe nerves as the world goes by at 200 m.p.h.

Once he wedges himself into the hull of the red, white and blue Domino's Pizza Hot One at Michigan International Speedway for the Michigan 500, Al Unser Jr. — like the men in the cars surrounding him — will be on his own.

Just three months past his 23rd birthday, the redhead with the familiar name, the winner of the last two races, already ranks 17th on the sport's all-time money winnings list, just $22,002 short of a million bucks.

He got there with an uncommon amount of skill and poise for a man so young. But he doesn't mind admitting he didn't get there without a lot of help.

There's his dad, Al, of course.

And his uncle, Bobby.

There is Doug Shierson, owner of the car he's driving.

Then there's John Paul Jr., whose contract as Shierson's driver was ripped to shreds when he was indicted for drug smuggling.

And there's a guy named Walter Judge, to whom the older Unser entrusted his teenage son when his racing career was in its infancy.

Judge had a Maxwell sprint car. "A tank," said Unser. "But well mechanized.

"He was an old guy — about 60. And I was 16," Unser recalled after qualifying at 208.932 m.p.h. "We went around traveling the Midwest together. He taught me a lot about racing attitudes that a father couldn't teach — attitudes toward the fans and things like that."

Unlike many of his peers, Al Unser Jr. never had to risk his life in the cockpit of a jalopy strung together with baling wire and bonded with Krazy Glue. His cars were always safe and usually competitive.

"My dad got me in the door," he said. "I always had a good car, and that has helped tremendously on how my career has gone."

Seldom in these United States does a son follow the career footsteps of his father. No longer do cobblers pass their skills from generation to generation.

Farmers' sons leave the land for the bright lights and economic promise of the big city.

Those who stay behind and learn at the knee of the father sometimes are the beneficiaries of uncommon lessons, though.

Al Unser Jr. believes he is one of those.

"It is very gratifying to be able to win at doing what my dad's been doing all these years. He's taught me an awful lot. I didn't pick up just a couple of things, there's been so much."

Before the 1985 season began, the younger Unser had won once in 30 IndyCar races. His career was progressing, but he was hardly front-page news. Then his dad's name helped open another door.

This season Al Jr. had a contract with Team Lotus, one of the Formula One teams that have been talking of coming to the CART circuit. But the team came up short of sponsorship money and postponed coming to the United States.

If he thought that was bad news, though, Unser should have been in Paul's shoes.

Just as Lotus was calling Unser to tell him of their plight, a grand jury was returning an indictment against Paul. And Shierson decided that was more than enough reason to cancel his contract with Paul.

"The next day, my dad and I talked to Doug. Dad set it up. He knew John was in trouble; I didn't. It was really something else, the way me and Doug got together."

Unser became Shierson's fourth driver in just more than a year. First Johnny Rutherford quit his team at Indy a year ago because his cars were sub-par. Then Danny Sullivan accepted a better offer from Roger Penske at the end of the 1984 season. Paul left quietly after the indictment.

But Unser took over the car as if it had been made for him.

Inherited or learned, he demonstrated a coolness that has marked him as a driver with a future — something few in this sport can count on having.

Lack of success or lack of caution ends careers and lives quicker than in most sports. The Unsers have been exceptions. His dad is in his 22nd year as a driver. His uncle, Bobby, walked away in one piece after 21 years.

Throughout their careers, they lived with the knowledge that the career or the life of an acquaintance could come to an end in the blink of an eye — because of his error, or because of someone else's.

Friendships that can be terminated so quickly or so violently are to be avoided.

"I've been warned," said the youngest Unser. "My uncle Bobby told me.

"The only one I'm really close to is my father, and that was done long before racing."

The cockpit of a speeding race car is a lonely place.

Unser Jr. had a future, all right. He won his second Indianapolis 500 in 1994. ❖

Darrell Waltrip

February 15, 1986

DAYTONA BEACH, Fla. — Darrell Waltrip couldn't get the picture out of his mind. It was there if he looked at the television screen. It was there if he stared at the wall. It was especially vivid if he shut his eyes and tried to blank it out.

Christa McAuliffe's parents were clutching each other and staring in shock at the empty Cape Canaveral sky where moments before had been the space shuttle Challenger, carrying their daughter and six other astronauts.

"For the first time in my racing career I knew how my family felt when I'm racing because I saw it firsthand," Waltrip said.

"It was grim reality standing there, watching that girl's parents and that confused look on their faces, and they knew something terrible had happened, and they didn't know what to do, and they didn't know whether to smile, they didn't know whether to cry. It was incredible."

For Americans, space shuttles had become routine, almost as routine as it has become for Waltrip to drive 200 miles an hour. The comparisons were inescapable and too much for Waltrip, 39, to handle alone.

"It really bothered me," he said. "I really felt like I needed to call home. It just made me really sad. I'm sure the whole world felt that way. I know I'm no different than anybody else. I know everybody was grieving, but to see it and to be in the profession I'm in and to be able to relate to it was a real good lesson for me.

"My family has watched me race for 20 years, and I've never thought about — I hope it doesn't sound selfish — but I never thought about how they felt."

Waltrip called his wife, Stevie, as soon as he saw the Challenger tragedy. He called her again that night. And again the next morning.

He could not get it out of his mind.

Speed kills.

They talked about that. They prayed over it, something they do almost daily. And they think they learned something from it.

"I used to assure my family all the time that, hey, nothing's going to happen to me," he said. "Now rather than hiding the fact from them that that could happen to me, I feel more comfortable about talking about it, which I think helps.

"They knew I was just saying it. Now rather than making a fool out of myself and making them feel bad, I feel more comfortable about telling them: 'Hey, I know I can get hurt, and I want you all to be prepared for that. Let's don't fool ourselves.' "

Most racers and their wives usually give you that, "Aw, shucks, 'tain't nothin' " answer when you ask about the dangers of what the drivers do. Some may believe it. Waltrip doesn't. And neither does his wife.

"Usually when somebody asks me about it," Stevie said, "I say: 'That's part of racing.' Something like that. Something real shallow."

She says it, but she doesn't mean it. Or feel it.

Especially here.

Stevie doesn't watch her husband race. She's here, but she won't watch. She'll be in his pits, keeping lap charts, timing pit stops, anything to keep her busy and her mind off the dangers of what her husband is doing.

The work, she said, "is therapeutic."

She's been preparing for the Daytona 500 since they arrived a couple of weeks ago. A couple of times, she has made the hour drive to Orlando to attend a Bible study group.

"I have to fortify myself spiritually, especially for this race," she said. "I guess it's because of the speed. And for a lot of rookies, this is their first race. It causes some anxiety.

"You face the fact that the same thing can happen to your husband as happened to Butch Lindley or Bruce Jacoby," drivers who have been hospitalized more than a year because of racing accidents.

There's no way to remove risk from auto racing. But there are ways to reduce it.

NASCAR has fortified its cars so they can take a 200 m.p.h. smack into a concrete wall, or an airborne flip.

They are more tanks than cars.

"It is," Waltrip said, "an evolution. Every year something breaks or falls off of one of them, we make it bigger and better. Stock cars are the safest form of racing there is in the world."

Years ago, Jim Murray began his Los Angeles Times column from the Indianapolis 500 with the sentence: "Gentlemen, start your coffins."

The cars here are not coffins. Here they are tanks.

And tanks are every bit as safe as space shuttles.

Darrell Waltrip won the Daytona 500 in 1989. ❖

A day in the life

June 15, 1986

BROOKLYN, Mich. — At 7 o'clock Saturday morning, I climbed back into my bed in a motel room in Jackson, pulled the covers up under my chin, set a cup of coffee on the nightstand and began to read the Free Press.

A few miles away, Rick Baldwin, a 31-year-old race car driver who was sharing a hotel room with his crew chief, Joey Arrington, was trying to overcome the handicaps of two men and only one bathroom so they could get to Michigan International Speedway in time to run some practice laps before qualifying.

Baldwin is one of the men who fills out the field of big-time stock car races. He never has been in the right place at the right time. He never had the right equipment and, maybe, never had the right talent. He had run at MIS only twice before — finishing 28th last August and 36th in 1983.

In four years, he has driven for five teams, always looking for a way to overcome anonymity.

At 11 o'clock Saturday, I was walking around the garages at MIS, looking for familiar faces. I made small talk with Benny Parsons and chatted with his brother Phil about the state of the Detroit Tigers.

A few feet away, Rick Baldwin was chatting with Arrington and his father, Buddy, who owns the automobile Baldwin was to qualify within the hour. A Texan by birth, Baldwin has practically become a member of the Arrington family, living with them outside Martinsville, Va.

Baldwin — qualifying the car for the older Arrington, who suffered a concussion in a wreck at Pocono, Pa., last weekend — tinkered with the car some and made some suggestions. Then he settled back to wait for his number to be called.

A few minutes before noon, I was sitting in the infield press room, recording speeds of drivers as they attempted to qualify for the Miller American 400. Jonathan Edwards, 162.177 m.p.h.; Bobby Hillin Jr., 169.264; Chet Fillip, 165.010; Ricky Rudd, 168.500.

Half a mile away, Rick Baldwin was just getting Arrington's race car up to speed on the first lap of his qualifying run when, heading into the first turn of the two-mile race track, the car took control of the man and his fate. The car spun, slamming back-end first into the wall, then the front end whipped around, smashing the driver's side of the car into the concrete with such force that Rick Baldwin's head snapped forward. And in an instant, he lost consciousness.

It took 28 minutes to cut him from the car, and once he was placed on the slab of wood designed to prevent further injury, he was gingerly carried to an ambulance, where an intravenous needle was shoved into his arm.

At 1:15, I was standing beside the crumpled remains of Baldwin's car, with the number 67 scratched and ripped from the impact with the wall, when the voice of MIS's public address announcer informed the crowd of 40,000: "Rick Baldwin of Martinsville, Va., sustained head and neck injuries when his car made contact with the outside wall between Turns 1 and 2 during his qualification attempt today. He has been transported to W.A. Foote Hospital in Jackson for further observation and testing. Dr. Greg Baumann, MIS medical director, has termed his condition critical."

Eighteen miles away, doctors were checking Rick Baldwin's vital signs, looking for a way to help him.

At 2:30 I was talking to Terry Labonte, who had just qualified at 170.193 m.p.h. "When we were both 17 or 18, I ran against Rick a lot back on the dirt tracks around Corpus Christi (Texas)," Labonte said. "Usually he won or I did. He just never had as much success on asphalt. How is he?"

Eighteen miles away, Rick Baldwin, clinging to a thread of life, was in an operating room, doctors feverishly trying to repair the damage done in an instant.

At 6 o'clock Saturday, I packed my briefcase and walked to my car in the parking lot behind MIS's infield press room. My wife was with me. We were going to a reception in Jackson honoring Richard Petty on his 1,000th NASCAR Grand National start. There would be food and drink and conversation, people would be laughing and talking about the big race.

A few miles away, Rick Baldwin, father of two little girls — who began the day an aspiring race car driver — lay in a coma.

Baldwin remains in a coma, eight years later. ❖

J.D. McDuffie

August 17, 1986

BROOKLYN, Mich. — I've never really understood this thing about role models. Kids grow up wanting to be just like Nolan Ryan or Chris Evert Lloyd or Magic Johnson. Or like Prince or Madonna or Arnold Schwarzenegger.

The American dream is to grow up rich and successful, good looking and famous.

When you're a kid, you never want to grow up to be just like Bishop Tutu or Jonas Salk. Or like your mom or dad.

Our idols change as we get older.

Young auto executives want to be like Lee Iacocca. Young attorneys want to be like Melvin Belli. Young sports writers want to be like Red Smith or Jim Murray. Or Mike Downey.

I guess I've never really had an idol. But I met a guy the other day who should be somebody's idol.

His name is J.D. McDuffie.

And I like his attitude.

J.D. McDuffie will be in today's Champion Spark Plug 400 at Michigan International Speedway. Look for him at the back — he qualified second-to-last — in car No. 70. Look quick before he's lost in the shuffle.

J.D. McDuffie is 47, you see, and today's race will be his 606th Grand National start. And never — not once since he started doing this for a living in 1963 — has he won.

He hasn't even finished second.

In his youth, his heart harbored hopes that some Sunday the car and the breaks would be just right, and he'd look in his rearview mirror at the finish line and see the Richard Pettys, David Pearsons and Darrell Waltrips struggling to catch him.

But long ago he stopped believing that would ever happen.

He came to grips with reality and compromised. Not everybody can take the checkered flag, but maybe winning doesn't always mean finishing first.

"Really, you know, if you finish in the top 15, you done a bunch — having no more than I've got," he said.

Things have not come easy for J.D. McDuffie. Long ago, when he was racing against other guys from the hills and the farms of North Carolina, he sometimes had a chance. Today, racing against the money of Budweiser and Crisco and Kodak and the technology of Ford and Chevrolet and Oldsmobile, he has no chance.

When he climbs into his race car, he thinks only of doing the best he can, of arriving back at the garage with his car and body intact. Only on the rarest of occasions, he said, is there a thought "way in the back of your mind about winning."

"Used to there was a time when we run in the top 10 regularly," he said, "but there's so many beefed-up teams now it's rough. And don't none start like I did: With nothing."

J.D. McDuffie has taken what God, and token sponsors, have given and has done the best he can with it.

There is grease under his fingernails and sweat soaking through his driver's suit because he has never been able to afford the luxury of supervising from a high-backed chair.

"The only way I've survived all these years," he said, "is to do my own work.

"It gets tough sometimes when you don't have enough equipment to run with. We just try to run as high as possible without ruining the equipment 'cause we got to run the same car next week."

In a time when family garages routinely contain two cars, McDuffie's racing garage routinely has just one.

But because of his persistence, he is one of only 21 men who have earned more than $1 million in this sport. Divided over 23 years, though, that amount is not so impressive. And reinvested in parts, cars and overhead, there has been little left over.

"I make a living out of it," he said, waving a long, unlighted cigar in the afternoon sunlight. "But that's about all. But can't many people say they've done what they want to, and I can."

On the darkest days, he has felt sorry for himself and thought of giving up the chase — despairing, but only momentarily, at the futility of it all.

"You think about it once in awhile," he said, "but an hour later, you're ready to go again.... We're gonna run better, you know.

"You couldn't call me a quitter."

I like J.D. McDuffie's attitude.

He should be somebody's idol.

McDuffie was the subject of another Vincent column, in August 1991. It read, in part:

Sometimes news is dated. Sometimes it makes no sense to write about something that happened 10 days before. But I don't believe it is ever too late to write about the death of a man who was out of the ordinary.

J.D. McDuffie was one of my heroes. He died in a crash during a NASCAR event on Aug. 11, while I was in Cuba for the Pan American Games. He was 52 years old and had raced in 653 races over 28 years, without ever winning.

"You couldn't call me a quitter," he told me once.

He never did quit, and he died 10 days ago when the front-left tire came off his Pontiac while it was doing 160 miles an hour during a race at Watkins Glen, N.Y.

He left a wife and two children.

And he left an example of perseverance I will always admire. ❖

Mario

May 25, 1987

INDIANAPOLIS — Mario Andretti makes me want to believe in reincarnation.

I think he raced at the Indianapolis Motor Speedway in another life. I think he was Ralph DePalma.

How else do you explain what has happened to him here in the past seven years? How else do you explain that, when he cannot be beaten, he is beaten?

It happened again Sunday, when the unbeatable driver in the unbeatable car finished ninth in the 71st running of the Indianapolis 500 after leading 170 of the first 177 laps.

Only one guy in the history of this race has had luck like that.

Ralph DePalma.

In the second running of this race, in 1912, DePalma led 196 laps — the third through the 198th — before a piston broke, and DePalma and a mechanic pushed his car across the finish line in 12th place.

In 1920, DePalma led by two laps when he ran out of gas on the 187th lap, and that poor mechanic had to run back to the pits for more fuel.

In 1921, DePalma led by three laps at the halfway mark when his car threw a rod.

They don't run fuel to troubled cars anymore, and they don't push cars across the finish line anymore.

But the spirit of DePalma, beating inside Andretti, must have wanted to do something like that.

Seldom has a driver had a car more dominating than the one that encased Andretti. "After 10 laps, I could sort of feel the measure of the competition, and I knew unless something drastic happened, we were going to be all right," he said. "It was picture perfect."

By the time he reached the 130th lap of the scheduled 200, he was on the lead lap alone — more than 2½ miles ahead of second-place Roberto Guerrero.

It was a Sunday drive.

It was what he had been waiting for since 1969, when he won his only Indy 500 championship.

Some people think Mario Andretti — like DePalma — is jinxed here.

"I don't want to talk about jinxes," Andretti said in the steamy concrete garage, where his 22nd Indy ended. "It just wasn't my day. That's all. We had a great month, nobody got hurt, and we've got another race next week."

But with his next breath, Andretti — whose qualifying speed was two miles an hour faster than second-fastest qualifier Bobby Rahal's — admitted losing did not seem like the natural thing to happen.

Asked whether his car was running so well that he reached a point when he believed he could not lose, he replied: "I had every reason to feel that way.

"It was not one of the best rides I've ever had here, it is the best. I really thought I had it handled."

But then that something drastic happened, and somewhere the spirit of Ralph DePalma must have nodded in sad understanding.

On the 176th lap, with nothing but clear track ahead of him and nothing but also-rans in his rearview mirror, Andretti heard the sound that warned him his Sunday drive was over.

"All of a sudden," he said, "the thing backfired. The fundamental part of the engine was working picture perfect, but something got screwed up in the fuel system, it wasn't regulated any longer, and it was pouring raw fuel into the car.

"I couldn't keep it running. Every time I tried, it would flood out.

"I had no warning whatsoever. There was not a sign."

Andretti tried to diagnose the problem himself, bypassing an opportunity to pit after the backfire warned him of trouble in the fourth turn. Instead, he struggled through another lap, his car sputtering and wheezing before he could get it back to his pit.

"Everything humanly possible was done to prepare this car," Andretti said. "We got it blessed and everything."

You know, of course, this is not the first time this has happened to Mario Andretti at Indy.

You know he led 19 laps a year ago before a handling problem forced him out.

You know he qualified third in 1982 before the infamous Kevin Cogan accident knocked him out at the start.

And, of course, you remember he was named the winner in 1981 when the apparent winner, Bobby Unser, was penalized one lap the day after the race. And you remember five months later, that penalty was overturned, and he was dropped to second place.

Mario Andretti.

Ralph DePalma.

Reincarnation?

Like DePalma, Andretti would win only one Indy 500. ❖

The driver's wife

August 1, 1987

BROOKLYN, Mich. — You know how it is when you come home from a hard day at the office, kick off your shoes, flop into an easy chair and your wife asks how your day has been?

"Aw, honey, I work so hard and my boss doesn't appreciate me," you complain. "They work me too hard and don't pay me enough."

"Ohhh," she sighs sympathetically. "That's not fair. You've done so much for them. I'm going to call him and give him a piece of my mind."

"No!" you shout. "I mean, I appreciate your support, dear, but that probably wouldn't be productive. Not a good idea, but thanks anyway."

Tom Sneva knows about that.

Sneva has won an Indianapolis 500, has been on the pole there three times, has earned almost $4 million driving racing machines and has won $309,863 for Mike Curb's racing team in the first eight races of the 1987 CART season.

But at Michigan International Speedway, he sat in a big hospitality tent at 3 in the afternoon when everyone else was qualifying for the Marlboro 500.

He sat there and visited with a sports writer, sipping on a soft drink, wearing shorts and a knit shirt and a pair of canvas shoes over stockingless feet.

He might have been there because his wife, Sharon, made a phone call to his boss.

You see, Tom Sneva got fired a few days ago. At midnight.

The telephone rang in his hotel room, and on the other end of the line Curb's attorney said something like: "Tom, we understand you're unhappy, so for the good of everyone, we've decided to make a change. Ed Pimm will drive the rest of the season. Thanks very much, and good-bye."

That's the way Tom Sneva told it as his turn on the qualifying line came and went.

Rumors at the track said the rift between driver and owner came after: A) Sneva began shopping around his Skoal Tobacco sponsorship to other teams for next season; B) He demanded to immediately negotiate a more lucrative contract for 1988; C) His wife called Curb and said, "Pay up the money you owe us or we're not racing at Michigan."

"Well," Sneva said, sitting in the shade of the tent while Pimm prepared to take out the Curb automobile, "the first two rumors aren't true, but Sharon did call him.

"She's the one who pays the bills, and they are behind in what they owe us, and we had to go to the bank to take out a loan to pay our bills. She called and told him we wouldn't run here if we didn't get the money they owed us.

"She didn't ask me about it. When she told me later, I said: 'Maybe we shouldn't have gone quite so strong on that, honey.'

"I mean, we could have gone to the bank and got the money. It's just a cash-flow problem, really."

But Sharon Sneva wanted to help. She wanted to stand by her man. She does that a lot, Sneva said.

"When she really gets upset, she usually writes letters and she clears them with me before she sends them. Sometimes we decide we shouldn't send them. But this time, she didn't check with me."

Tom Sneva tried to repair the damage.

He called Curb.

"I apologized for Sharon's call," he said. "And we discussed the other rumors that were going around, and I thought we had everything resolved."

He thought he had been rehired.

But when he got to the track here, Curb's team manager, John Anderson, said he didn't know anything about a reinstatement.

He told Sneva to sit tight.

Hang out.

He told Sneva he would get a car set up for him, just in case, but that he couldn't drive it until Curb got to town and cleared up the situation. Late in the day, Curb gave the OK. Sneva will try to qualify.

But Sneva knew it probably would be a futile drive because driver and car need some time to grow accustomed to each other again.

He sat and sipped his soft drink and cooled his heels while Pimm — who hadn't driven an IndyCar since the Indianapolis 500 — qualified at 206.706 m.p.h., 18th fastest.

He sat and waited for Mike Curb to show up.

And a question occurred to the man who was visiting with him.

"Where's Sharon? At home?"

"I hope so," Sneva said. "But I hope she's not on the phone." ❖

Michael Andretti

August 3, 1987

BROOKLYN, Mich. — Auto racing is the strangest sport.

It's supposed to be about speed, but sometimes races are won when the car is moving only as fast as three men can push it.

That's what happened in the Marlboro 500 at Michigan International Speedway.

Michael Andretti drove the fastest 500-mile race in IndyCar history, averaging 171.490 miles an hour. He ran fast, and he ran smooth.

But in an afternoon that at first promised only one long yawn, then blended the ironic, bizarre and near-tragic, Andretti won not because of the speed of his car but because of the sweat of his crew.

What had begun as a free-for-all almost three hours earlier had been reduced to a three-car battle seven laps from the finish of the 250-lap race.

Andretti was in front. Behind him were Al Unser and Bobby Rahal, the only other drivers on the lead lap. Unser and Rahal had made their final pit stops, but Andretti could not finish without taking on another few gallons of fuel. So on Lap 243, he headed for the pits.

His lead was big.

All he had to do was get in, get gas and get out. That was all. But there was this problem, you see.

"We couldn't keep the engine running in the pits," Andretti said later. "We had trouble all day, and the crew had to keep kick-starting the car (by pushing it).... My hat's off to them."

So that was what was going through Michael Andretti's mind, and that's what was going through his crew members' minds, as he brought the car to a stop in his pit.

Five crewmen leaped into action, making sure he stopped in the right place, making sure the fuel hose matched up perfectly to the car's intake valve, making sure everything went right.

And listening to the engine.

Making sure they still heard it.

Andretti kept his eyes straight ahead, waiting for the signal to urge the car back to life.

One second passed, two, three, five … and they gave him the sign they were done.

Andretti put his foot on the throttle. And the car jerked. It sputtered. And it died.

For how long? For a moment? For a second? For a heartbeat?

Somewhere behind him, screaming down the track at 195 miles an hour, Al Unser and Bobby Rahal were making up ground at the rate of 286 feet a second.

It was a perfect time to panic. But there was too much to be done.

Skip Faul was one of those five men over the wall to help Andretti. On full pit stops, his job is to handle the tires on the right side. But this time Andretti took on only fuel, so Faul's job was to watch, not get in the way and to help if needed.

He was listening to the engine like everyone else. And when he heard it die, he leaped into action, falling in line with two of his mates at the rear wing of the car, pushing with all his might.

They pushed just a few steps, and the car caught, and they backed off. Then it died again — and with Unser and Rahal rushing ever closer — they were back at the wing, digging their feet into the hot asphalt until the veins in their necks bulged and sweat poured from their bodies.

Then they heard it. The engine caught again, and Andretti was off, smoke billowing off both rear tires as Faul, a rookie on this crew, thrust his fist triumphantly into the air.

"I was just glad the pig started," he said later. "You've just got to get the job done the best you can."

Andretti had gotten back on the track just ahead of Unser and Rahal, stayed ahead for the final 14 miles and won by 9.2 seconds.

It was a superb end to a race made deadly dull by the early dominance of Michael's dad, Mario, who had a two-lap lead over everyone when his car gave up on him after 156 laps.

And it was a happy ending to a race that brought the crowd of 68,000 to a hushed silence in the leaders' 184th lap when Danny Ongais and Ed Pimm hit the wall between Turns 3 and 4 and rescue crews took more than 10 minutes to remove Pimm — who suffered a broken right arm — from his wreckage.

It was an ending to a race that gave the younger Andretti his first 500-mile victory and answered his prayers, for while he was sitting in that car, eyes straight ahead, listening to the footfalls of his crew on the asphalt behind him, he was doing the only thing he knew how to do under the circumstances.

"I was praying: 'Please, God; please, God, let it catch.'

"And it did, or we would have lost it." ❖

Jim Crawford

May 30, 1988

INDIANAPOLIS — Do not believe the Indianapolis 500 is only about death.

Do not believe it is only about tragedy and a search for speed that ends only when blood is spilled and families are ripped apart and happiness is left only in memories and scrapbooks.

Do not believe it is just about crashes and fire and tears of despair and the drunks littering the infield.

It is also about heroism and courage and a driver named Jim Crawford, who walks with a cane, has a screw sticking out of his right ankle and must be helped in and out of his racing car.

Last May he was a newlywed, hoping for a competitive ride at Indianapolis after finishing 16th and 29th the previous years. He shoved the throttle to the floor in qualifying, and in one terrifying second, the machine slammed into the wall and Crawford's legs were shattered.

He did not see last year's race, he said, "because it was blacked out in

Indianapolis, and I was blacked out on morphine."

Jim Crawford did not race again until yesterday.

He started 18th in a year-old car powered by a Buick power plant that caused people to stifle laughter when they referred to it as a race engine.

It was a tribute to his courage and dedication that he made the field.

It was a triumph that he qualified 18th.

It was a miracle that he was in there when the command was given to fire the engines.

No more was expected.

No more was asked.

But on a sultry afternoon, hyphenated with 14 yellow flags, nine minor wrecks, a rabbit that had the misfortune to hop partway across the track, and post-race bickering about who did what, when, why and to whom, Jim Crawford's class and courage stood head and shoulders above the crowd.

The scoreboard showed him second when he flashed across the finish line. By day's end, a quick shuffle of the standings pushed him to sixth.

It does not matter.

Jim Crawford won.

There can be no greater triumph than over adversity and pain and the demons that claw at a man's soul.

Jim Crawford triumphed over them all, and Rick Mears, who also overcame severe leg injuries three years ago, paid tribute to him when it was over.

"What he's done today," said Mears, who won, "is probably good for about eight months' therapy. I take my hat off to him. He did a tremendous job."

Jim Crawford said, aw, it wasn't anything.

"A win would have been better, but I'm happy to come second. It gives me something to look forward to next year," he said before he knew his final standing was in jeopardy.

"After four years of trying, this is nice."

On an afternoon of mistakes and bad decisions and foolish gambles, Jim Crawford drove smart and strong, through the debris and the heat that hovered just above 100 degrees on the asphalt track.

He sized up his competition, then established a strategy and never deviated from it.

"I saw the Penske operation early on in the race, and there was nothing I could do about it, so there was no point in me doing anything silly," he said.

The legs? What about the legs? That's what everyone wanted to know. Did they hurt? Did you think about last year's crash?

Crawford seemed embarrassed that anyone even asked. He seemed not to want them as an excuse or as a reason to be singled out from the 32 men he raced.

"The legs did not hurt at all," he said. "They could have been hanging off, and I wouldn't have known it. All through the race, it never crossed my mind. It was just me, doing the best I could."

Sheila Crawford thought of it, though.

Sheila Crawford is expecting a baby — tomorrow.

For the better part of a year, she was her husband's private nurse. She drove him to the hospital six times for operations. She bathed him and rolled him around the house in a wheelchair. And she worried when the wounds became infected.

"Basically, I just waited on him hand-and-foot," she said.

In all those months of therapy and pain, Crawford's one question to his doctors was: When will I be able to get back into a race car?

And Sheila Crawford — who met her husband-to-be at a racetrack in Quebec — braced herself for Sunday's Indy 500. And all the Sundays that would follow.

"I knew what he was when I met him," she said. "You make the best of it and help him get back because he loves it so much. He just wouldn't be Jim without it."

Jim Crawford went to bed Sunday not really sure how he finished in his third Indianapolis 500.

He seemed for a long time not concerned about it.

He seemed removed. Stoic, almost. Oblivious to what he had done.

Was there more emotion inside? Was there joy looking for escape?

He looked up, sweat dripping into his eyes, his right leg resting on his wife's lap, and smiled. Just a little.

"Yeah," he said, "I'm going to go into the garage and scream and dance and yell."

He probably didn't.

But he should have because, for a moment, he made us understand the nobler side of the Indianapolis 500. ❖

Jim Hurtubise

January 24, 1989

A friend of mine died a couple of weeks ago.
You might have heard of him, Jim Hurtubise, who once upon a time was A.J. Foyt's greatest fear.
Early in the 1960s, he was the guy in Foyt's rearview mirror many a weekend afternoon.

He was young and fearless, a hothead with a lead foot from North Tonawanda, N.Y., who was determined to make a name for himself. Then, one Saturday afternoon in Milwaukee, his image filled Foyt's rearview mirror. And in one terrifying moment, their wheels touched and Hurtubise and his car became airborne, flying over Foyt before slamming into the wall and bursting into a horrifying ball of flame.

It was 1964, and I met Hurtubise a couple of weeks after that. I was a young sports writer in San Antonio, and he had been flown there to be treated at Ft. Sam Houston's Brooke Army Medical Center, one of the world's best burn treatment facilities.

Hurtubise was burned over 40 percent of his body, the tip of his nose was melted and the skin of his fingers webbed together by the flames. He had a punctured lung and three broken ribs.

When they loaded Jim Hurtubise onto the airplane for the ride from Milwaukee to San Antonio, one of the doctors told his wife, Jane: "If he can survive the trip, we'll try to get his hands in condition so he can do normal everyday work with them."

He had been rookie of the year at the Indianapolis 500 in 1960, going faster than anyone had ever gone there: 149.056 m.p.h. Along with Foyt and Parnelli Jones, he was the future of IndyCar racing a quarter of a century ago.

When I first saw him, though, he was broken and burned, and the doctors did not include auto racing in his future.

But Jim Hurtubise surprised them.

One day the doctors told him it was time to make a decision about his hands, stripped of nearly all their muscle by the fire. Surgery would be performed, they told him, which would leave the fingers in any position he wished. After surgery, he would be able to extend the fingers but would never be able to close them beyond the point at which the surgery left them.

Leave them almost closed, he told the doctors.

Leave them so they can grip a steering wheel.

And that is what they did.

Less than 10 months after his accident, Hurtubise returned to racing in a car named the Tombstone Life Insurance Special, and I wondered how his wife could stand it. Or the name of the car.

He was never an important factor in racing after that.

Some of his old friends say the accident left him embittered. I saw him as an idealist — hardheaded, stubborn and determined to prove (without a chance of succeeding) that he could still win, even with equipment considered obsolete.

He built his own cars — with the engines still in front of the driver, though technology had left that design far behind.

He was a front-engine man in a rear-engine era. He was leather helmet and goggles in a time of crash helmets and fire-retardant suits. He was a dinosaur — and damn proud of it.

He was a rebel whose cause was to fight the establishment. A 20th century Don Quixote, doing battle with windmills.

When Pepsi-Cola sponsored his car at Indy in 1968, he flew a Pepsi blimp over his garage, mocking the Goodyear blimp, until track officials threatened to shoot it down.

In 1972, when qualifying time ran out with his car still in line, he opened the cowl of the car and invited everyone over for a drink. There was no engine inside the car, only several cases of iced beer.

In 1978, though, he went too far. Denied an opportunity to qualify because he had been unable to get his car up to the required 180 m.p.h., he ran out on the track — on foot, not in a car — during a qualifying run by Jim Harkey.

The people who ran the track had treated his idiosyncrasies tenderly because of what he had been and what he had been through. But after 1978, he was not really welcomed.

"Who wants to go where they're not wanted?" he reasoned. And Hurtubise became a spectator.

He showed up at the track most Mays, told stories and shook hands with that gnarled, hard remnant of what used to be a right hand. One year, we worked on his biography until we became discouraged by a bunch of rejections from publishers who told us sports books do not sell very well and sports books about auto racers do not sell at all.

So he went to Port Arthur, Texas, where he could dip a fishing line into the Gulf of Mexico. On Jan. 6, at the age of 56, he died there of a heart attack.

His life deserved more than just a couple of lines in this newspaper.

He was not a genius or a saint.

He was not a hero or a forward thinker.

He was just a man who made his way through life the best way he knew.

And he was my friend. ❖

A.J.

June 15, 1991

A.J. Foyt said he loved it.

He looked like it was killing him.

In the middle of what is supposed to be his final season in IndyCar racing — but probably won't be — he decided to see how much pain he could stand without passing out. So he entered the Detroit Grand Prix, an excruciatingly slow road course with 17 turns on its 2.5-mile course beneath the city's skyscrapers.

Brake. Throttle. Change gears. Brake. Change gears. Throttle. Brake.

Slam your foot down. Over and over and over. For two hours or so.

Healthy feet ache when it's over.

A.J. Foyt's feet are a jigsaw puzzle.

The story has been told thousands of times in the past nine months about the mangled mess he made of his feet and legs in last September's wreck in Wisconsin. They put him back together, but still his feet don't look like a matched set.

When Foyt climbed out of his car after the first round of qualifying, he looked old and weary. Sweat dripped down his red face, and each step on the asphalt made his shoulders convulse in pain.

But half an hour later, relaxing in an air-conditioned room in his car hauler, he looked a little better. Felt a little better. But he admitted: "My feet are acting kind of retarded."

Foyt's fastest lap in the first round of qualifying was 80.326 miles an hour, 20th among the 26 cars that got onto the track. He did not come here expecting to win or even run with the leaders. He came here, he said, "for a therapy deal. I'm trying to learn the pedals again, to get oriented."

He looked more like a man who had sentenced himself to a weekend in purgatory.

He wasn't sure how many gear changes he went through in a lap. He thought it was about 20. Maybe 22.

Each time he has to clutch, and in many of the turns he has to brake.

And he goes home at night with aching feet.

No one really believes he can last two hours in this race. He probably questions it, too, but he won't allow himself to say it.

"I'll make myself do it," he said. And he looks you in the eye, and you believe this 56-year-old man, overweight once again, tired and worn but as competitive and combative as ever.

His feet are erratic. One day they are all but dead. Numb. And he has trouble feeling the pedals. He wears thin socks to enhance the feel. On other days, his feet feel as if every nerve ending is exposed.

"If somebody threw a $1,000 bill on the ground over there on the asphalt," he said, "I couldn't walk over to it barefooted. I'd cry like a baby."

In many ways, A.J. Foyt seems like a very confused man these days.

He is not having a lot of fun racing, but he fears he will have a worse time if he does not race.

He said he is here "because I love it. It's a challenge. A challenge you can't conquer. About the time you think you've got it, some guy you think is nobody blows your doors off.

"When you've had a wreck like I had, you don't forget it. I mean, if I didn't think I could run here, I wouldn't be here.

"But probably I shouldn't be here."

Everything is a contradiction.

He catches his breath after saying he shouldn't be here and the next words from his mouth are: "But that's not my type of racing. If you're a racer, you race. If you're not, you quit."

He had promised this would be his last go-round. His 34th Indianapolis 500 was supposed to be his last. But he was not certain. He was not at all sure retirement was what he wanted.

"But I'm tired — the wreck took a lot out of me — and I don't know if I'd campaign the whole circuit," he said.

One moment, he is a racer. The next, he is a retired racer.

One moment, the sport tugs at him. The next, age asks him to sit down and prop up his feet for a spell.

He sighed.

"You've got to call it quits sometime."

So there A.J. Foyt was, sitting in his car hauler, a man with one mangled foot in auto racing and the other one out, uncertain, it seemed, which way to go.

Pulled in both directions.

He has admitted pain, something he didn't do much in the past. He admitted his sport has hurt him and, to an extent, scared him. Somehow, though, it never occurred to him to throw in the towel.

So he'll be in the field, probably far back. He probably won't win the race. Jim Crawford, whose feet were severely injured in a wreck a few years ago, said: "I can't imagine why he's even trying it."

He's trying it, probably, because he's A.J. Foyt.

And if that doesn't explain it, nothing can.

Foyt started 19th and finished 23rd. ❖

King Richard

February 15, 1992

DAYTONA BEACH, Fla. — You want it to be the same as it was, for yourself, you suspect, as much as for him.

You want it to be the way it was when Richard Petty — and you — were young. When he spent sweltering summer Sundays looking at the rest of the world's auto racers in his rearview mirror.

They were specks. He was The King.

But the truth is nothing is the same. Richard Petty has aged, and so have you. He wears hearing aids in both ears, hasn't won a race since 1984, and tomorrow begins the final year of the most honored career in the history of racing.

He is calling it Richard Petty's 1992 Fan Appreciation Tour, and you have to wonder what that means. Kareem Abdul-Jabbar had a farewell tour. And so did Bill Shoemaker. And Magic Johnson put a perfect climax on his career at the NBA All-Star Game down the road in Orlando last week.

Those moments were in appreciation of the athlete, though. How, you wonder, will Petty's farewell be different? How will it honor the fan instead of the athlete? And then, in a couple of minutes on a hot afternoon, you understand.

Richard Petty's car was not working well. He will start 32nd in Sunday's 42-car Daytona 500. So Friday was not a good day for him. Not a happy day.

He wrecked one car Thursday and got only five minutes of practice in the new car Friday.

He sat in the balky car as an army of mechanics pored over the machine. They measured things and weighed things and aligned things, and Petty sat patiently in a car that was going nowhere.

A few fans tentatively stepped into the garage. Then more followed. And more. Many more. Eventually, it resembled a tour at Universal Studios.

There were men in caps made from material that looked as if it were taken from Hawaiian shirts, Nikons resting on ample bellies, women in double-knits and children in Richard Petty T-shirts.

Click! Click!

Click! Click!

And they were gone. And behind them were dozens more.

"Turn around, son," one man told a young boy, framing Petty's car in the background.

Click! Click!

Nobody told them to leave. Nobody ran them out. Nobody said they were in the way, that there was work going on.

"Hey," one visitor whispered to his buddy, "he's in the car! Gimme the camera!"

Click! Click!

They were Richard Petty's fans, though some surely never had seen him win a race. And he appreciated them as much as they appreciated him.

"I seen a bunch of 'em," Petty said later, shrugging off the notion that the crowd might have been bothersome or unwelcome in his garage.

"It would wear on me if I got out of the car and nobody was there. I expect it, and they do, too, so I do as much as I can.

"How would you feel if your hero was walking by and he didn't even look at you?"

The love affair between Richard Petty and his fans has endured the years and the aging and the long, painful drought that has seen him go without a victory since the Firecracker 400 at Daytona on July 4, 1984.

His fans are so loyal, they don't talk about it much.

Even the media is so enamored of Petty that they don't write about it much.

But at 54, he has faced the reality of it, and Friday he said what his best fans and his most friendly chroniclers have not.

"There are a lot of things I don't do as well," he said once he had left his garage. "Age took care of a lot of it, and circumstances and environment took care of the rest. I've not advanced in my races as much as some people have.

And long races are getting tougher and tougher. I get tired."

Sunday's race will be Petty's 1,157th Winston Cup start. When he made his 1,000th start — at Michigan International Speedway — in the summer of 1986, he said: "I have won a lot of races, and when the race was over, I did not feel satisfied inside because I felt like I could have done better. But I've run a lot of times when I run 10th or fifth or third and felt really, really good because I said: 'There ain't no human in the world that could have drove that car and done any better than I did.' "

He hasn't felt that way often lately. And it has bothered him.

"A lot of times I know I didn't do the car justice," he said. "The boys (in the crew) don't know that, 'cause I don't tell 'em. But when I go back home and go to bed, I think about it.

"Not winning races, not finishing races, not doing the things the team is capable of doing — all of it adds up. God may have given me 25 years of good luck, and I may be trying to stretch it to 35.

"But he gave me all the good times and everything I've got, and he's still letting me do something. He's took the wins away from me but not the racing or the fans or the enjoyment."

Despite disappointing losses, broken bones and frightening crashes, seldom has Petty left the track without feeling he enjoyed the whole experience. An exception was in 1965, when he tried drag racing.

One day his car lost control and plowed into some spectators.

"Something broke on the car, and we went out through the crowd of people and it killed a little boy and wounded some more people," Petty recalled. "It was really the blackest day. I don't never talk about it. It was really, really a bad day."

He told his father, Lee, he was quitting that day.

"I said we don't need to be doing this," Petty said. "I lost my enthusiasm for drag racing when that happened."

His father listened, but he told him he couldn't allow the accident to force him to change careers. Richard Petty thought about it, suffered over it and decided his father was right.

What followed was the greatest career in the history of racing: 200 victories, 10 in a row in 1967 and 27 wins in that 48-race season, and a legion of fans.

Quitting was not an easy decision.

The sport was his love. And racing with his son Kyle only enriched the experience.

Of racing, he once said: "When you get in the race car, there's no telephone.

There's no interviews. Your wife don't want you mowing the yard. You're totally by yourself, even though there's 39 other cars there."

And of racing against Kyle: "We kind of look out for each other and all, 'cause it'd be kind of hard for me to go home and explain to his mother that I done knocked him out of the race."

He has said: "I don't think I'll ever be remembered as the best race car driver there ever was or the most popular or any of that stuff. But the overall picture is that I want to leave a good impression, that I was somebody that done something, that done a pretty good job at it and enjoyed every dadgummed minute of it.

"Very few people came through life and have done as much they wanted to do as I did."

But time changes everything, and we are not who we were.

The present belongs to the young, but auto racing and its fans will be poorer the day Richard Petty steps out of his car for the final time. We have a summer to contemplate that, and to enjoy his final tour.

There will not be another like him. ❖

Death next door

May 22, 1992

INDIANAPOLIS — A large red auto hauler was parked outside Garage 9 in Gasoline Alley at Indianapolis Motor Speedway, and through its doors a silent parade of men passed, over and over again, carrying the supplies Euromotorsports had hoped to use in Sunday's Indianapolis 500.

There were auto parts and wrenches, fans and paint and decals, all intended for the use of Jovy Marcelo. But Jovy Marcelo is dead.

And a wilted red rose hangs from above the doorway to Garage 9.

And in Garage 8, Roberto Guerrero would rather be somewhere else.

Roberto Guerrero is 33, handsome and on the pole for the 76th Indianapolis 500.

In some ways, he is not typical of IndyCar drivers at all. He was born in Colombia. He came to the United States to learn English and went to England to learn racing. And in 1984, the first time he drove the Indianapolis Motor Speedway, he placed second to Rick Mears, the best finish by a rookie since

Graham Hill won 18 years earlier.

But in at least one respect, he is the most typical of drivers.

This track almost killed him, but it didn't scare him. And that makes him one in a long line of drivers who have left this track in ambulances and returned in racing cars.

Rick Mears' face was seriously burned at Indy in 1981. In 1990, he crashed during qualifying. A couple of weeks ago he crashed again, injuring his feet, which had been so broken in a previous crash that he said the doctors had to "string the bones together like beads."

He will start in the third row Sunday.

Jim Crawford spent six months in a wheelchair after crashing during a qualifying run in 1987. The next May he finished sixth, though he had to be lifted into and out of the car because of his still-healing leg injuries.

He will start in the seventh row Sunday.

Gary Bettenhausen has crashed at Indy. So has his brother Tony. His dad, Tony, was killed here in 1961.

Gary Bettenhausen will start in the second row Sunday.

Five years ago, Roberto Guerrero was testing tires at the track when his car hit the wall and the right front tire ripped loose and slammed into his helmet. When they took the first brain scans, the examining doctor confided that the outlook was bleak.

For 17 days, Guerrero was in a coma.

The first three days, the doctors did not know whether he would live. Once they became convinced he would, they began to prepare his wife, Katie, for what lay ahead.

They told her he might have to relearn how to eat. How to walk. How to talk. They told her that when he came out of the coma, he might be a different man than the one she had married.

"I remember thinking that if I stared (at him) hard enough, I could get him to get better," she recalled. "I wondered if I'd ever have my Roberto back. That was hard."

Gradually, he came out of the coma. And, almost miraculously, the injury was not as severe as the doctors feared.

Six weeks of rehabilitation left him almost as good as new. More than five hours a day he worked with computers to improve his mental retention, problem solving and hand-eye coordination.

And Dr. Steve Olvey, director of medical affairs for IndyCar — who long ago ceased to marvel at the phenomenon — said Guerrero's commitment is typical of what he has seen in other injured drivers.

"They love what they're doing and don't want to do anything else," Olvey said. "That makes them very compliant patients. I've never had a driver say after a serious injury: 'Boy, maybe that was a blessing. I'm not going to do this anymore.' With every single one of them, the only thing they can think about is how soon they can get back to racing."

Said Guerrero: "He hit it on the spot. Obviously, I wanted to get back really quick. Racing is my life."

Never did Guerrero and his wife, who was pregnant with their second child, discuss the possibility he might give up the sport.

"She never, even after the bad accident, said: 'I wish you didn't race.' She obviously gets a little nervous, but she understands. It's her life, too," he said. "Racing has been very good to us."

Always, though, there are concerns.

Drivers don't fear this track, but they have concerns: about drivers who might be too old, or too inexperienced. Or about speeds that put them always on the edge of disaster.

"The speeds are too fast," Guerrero said. "But what can we do about it? You have to treat these cars very gently at these speeds. I've always been comfortable on this track — from the first day I drove here — and I'm comfortable at these speeds, too, until something goes wrong."

Something clearly went wrong for Jovy Marcelo, the rookie from the Philippines who had occupied the garage space next to Guerrero. Marcelo went out for a practice run and never came back.

And they put a rose over his garage door.

And they took all the equipment that was supposed to get him around this track and loaded it in a truck and left.

And Roberto Guerrero, who has challenged the wall here and lived to challenge it again, has to look at that empty garage every day.

"It affects you, yes," he said. "But it's your job.

"Thank goodness when you're in the car driving, you've got time for nothing else at all. If you think about it in the car, that would be bad. Really bad." ❖

Kyle Petty

February 12, 1993

D AYTONA BEACH, Fla. — Kyle Petty isn't exactly sure when it happened — or where — but one day his father stopped being his benefactor on the racetrack and became his ward.

One day the son realized it was time to begin repaying all the lessons his father had taught and to use all the skills he had inherited. The King — winless since 1984 — was no longer king but he was still Kyle Petty's father, and there were times on hot and dangerous Sunday afternoons when he needed help.

"He used to be up here, and I was down there," the younger Petty said, leaning against a stack of tires and using his hands to illustrate his point. "But somewhere along the way we passed.

"And during the last three or four years, you didn't bump or bang him. I think all the guys felt the same way, kind of treated him with kid gloves. Nobody wanted to see him hurt.

"A lot of times when we were out there running and something would happen, you'd be a little concerned. And there were times when you know he's racing real hard, you slide a block in," Richard Petty's son confessed, a smile sliding across his face.

"But he's been in the middle of the pack the last few years. No matter how you sugarcoat it, that's the way it is."

Richard Petty has retired, and Kyle Petty has inherited a legacy.

A tradition three generations old.

Lee Petty won the first Daytona 500. Richard won seven more. And Kyle will sit on the pole for the 35th running at Daytona International Speedway. But he recognizes — at 32 — that there is some justification for those who believe he will never do the things his father and grandfather did.

"I've been fortunate to drive for teams that haven't put a lot of pressure on me, and I haven't put a lot of pressure on myself," he said. "But if I don't hurry up and start winning big races, I'll put pressure on to do what Richard Petty's done. I'm only 32, but I've been around so long people think I'm about 45."

He drove his first Winston Cup race in 1979 and ran 170 races — 10 years — before he took his first checkered flag.

Some questioned his dedication. Sometimes even his father did.

Kyle went through a phase when he felt he could mix a musical career with his driving. He let his hair grow. He seemed to be saying he was his own man: Kyle Petty, not just Richard Petty's son and Lee Petty's grandson.

But there was too much heredity to be denied. He kept the long hair, but as time went by, he became more comfortable with being the third generation of stock-car racing's most famous family.

"What has happened," Richard Petty said, "is Kyle has gotten focused. He has realized after the music and all that stuff that this is what he wants to do with his life."

And, gradually, he has become more successful at it.

Last season, the best of his career, Kyle won two races, finished fifth in the point standings and became the first Petty to win more than $1 million in a season.

"That's inflation for you," he said. "Everybody wants to talk about the money records, but the money records don't mean a thing. They're going to be broke. My grandfather was the first to win $50,000 a year, and that was probably worth three-fourths of what my million was worth."

The opportunity is there this year for Kyle Petty to become one of the wealthiest stock car drivers of all time.

Felix Sabates, owner of Petty's car, has put together an incentive package that will pay him $1 million each for wins in the Daytona 500, Coca-Cola 500, Mello Yello 500 and Winston Million. He can pick up another $1 million if he wins six or more races and another $1 million if he wins the Winston Cup points title.

Leaning against that stack of tires, though, his long hair flowing past his shoulders, Kyle Petty — on his own at last — seems more concerned with doing what Pettys have always done than with the prospect of becoming a millionaire.

"Daddy always raced and always won, and we always had money," he said. "But it was the 200 wins and the seven Daytonas that meant the most to him. When I walk into his house, I don't see the money. It's the same with me. We're looking for championships more than for the money."

Kyle Petty is not a copy of his father. Perhaps he is not the driver his father was. Perhaps he is not the competitor. But in some ways, the son is exactly like the father.

It was time to take his car out for practice, and Petty hurried from his transporter toward his garage 30 yards away. Halfway there, a man ran up to him, said something and threw his arm around Petty's shoulder.

The driver slowed and smiled into a camera so the fan could have a photographic record of their meeting. Then he hurried on to his car.

In the garage a young couple, wearing sweatshirts with Dale Earnhardt's name on them, waited. Spotting them, and making no reference to the fact they seemed to favor another driver, Petty motioned to the woman and posed for another picture before climbing into his car.

Always polite. Always accommodating. Just like daddy.

Then Kyle Petty drove onto the track — as he will in Sunday's Daytona 500 — carrying with him the tradition of three generations.

No longer is there anyone to look out for him. No longer is there anyone for him to protect.

It is his time.

But it wasn't his weekend; Kyle Petty finished 31st. ❖

Rick Mears

May 15, 1993

INDIANAPOLIS — You start by driving little cars on little tracks in little towns in California because you can't think of anything that's more fun.

You're a teenager, and racing is the biggest kick in the world.

Some people think there's nothing better than playing 18 holes of golf on a sunny day. Some think nothing is better than planting seeds in neat rows and waiting for their work to bear fruit. For others, perfection is a day in the woods, with the only sound coming from the wind blowing through the trees.

For Rick Mears it was racing.

It was never a business. It was only a hobby. Even when he quit the little cars and the little tracks in the little towns for the IndyCars.

Mears has never been a "Gee, aw shucks, this is great" kind of guy. But, inside, that was the emotion he was feeling. He felt it even after he won his first Indy 500 in 1979.

He became wealthy and famous, but mostly it was the thrill of his hobby that kept him coming back. The thrill was there when he won his second 500, and his third and in 1991 when he won his fourth, tying A.J. Foyt and Al Unser as the most successful drivers at this storied track.

But slowly, something changed within him.

He can't put a date on it or a reason. All he knows is the thrill of it all leaked out of his soul, and the hobby gradually became work. Work he didn't want to do anymore.

"I began to wonder if I should be out there, and I took that to be the first indication that I shouldn't — the fact that I'm thinking about it," Mears said on the eve of qualifying for the Indianapolis 500 — qualifying that would go on without him for the first time since 1976.

"I found myself taking it home at night, coming up with ideas about what we could do the next day that might make things better," Mears said. "I did other things than go home and think about the race car.

"I still enjoyed it, but not as much as before, and that's not fair to the team. I'd wake up in the morning and realize it was becoming a job."

Last fall, while recovering from a wrist injury, Mears watched from the pits as Paul Tracy, Roger Penske's newest prodigy, raced to a third-place finish in a 200-mile race in Nazareth, Pa.

"When I watched some of the things he did that day, it went through my mind that I used to want to do that more than I do now. The aggressive moves he was making, I wasn't ready to do that."

It wasn't fear that drove Mears from the driver's seat. But it might have been something similar. It might have been an awareness of his mortality and of the law of diminishing returns.

No longer were the rewards worth the risks.

"I've been there — I don't need to do it again," Mears said when talk turned to injuries. "I knew it could happen all along. You might want to call it 'a little older and a little wiser.' The way my feet are, I can't afford another one, and pretty soon the fun doesn't outweigh the other things, and that tips the scales."

So Mears quit last winter. At 41, he just called a press conference and said he didn't want to drive anymore.

He is here as an advisor for Penske's team, working with Tracy as the 24-year-old Canadian tries to fulfill the promise Penske sees in him. Some see it as an attempt to have Mears groom the youngster to fill his shoes.

Mears disagrees: "Paul Tracy has his own shoes. He doesn't need to fill anybody's shoes.

"And this is the perfect opportunity for him, the same way it was with me when I got the opportunity. There's a lot of similarities. It was one of those fairy tale stories."

To make his fairy tale come true, though, Mears had to learn to deal with this track and the things it can do to your body and mind.

"The pressure got to me, just as it gets to everybody," he said. "I just had to learn to control it. It's very relaxing being back in this role."

Mears wears a beard now, giving him an older and wiser look. It is, he said, only a sign that he got lazy one day when it came time to shave, then decided he liked the way the beard looked.

It is a new image for a man who is looking neither to the past nor very far into the future.

Mears has no urge to strike out on his own, he said, because "you do that if you think you can make something better. I think I'm with the best team in the business, so why would I want to do my own deal and still there's the best team in the business out there to compete against?"

And he doesn't expect to sit in a race car again, either.

Probably.

"You never say never, but I'm saying never to IndyCars," Mears insisted. "Maybe, if I get the itch, I might do some off-road racing or something like that just for the fun of it. But I don't know that I'll ever get that itch."

Maybe he'll never have that feeling he had once upon a time in a little car on a little track in a little town in California.

But it's been a heck of a ride, a fairy tale come true with a happy ending, because the hero knew when the story should stop. ❖

Ayrton Senna

May 2, 1994

I have begun to read the obituaries.

It started sometime after I passed my 52d birthday, I think, when a new ache would appear without warning. Sometimes in my back. Sometimes in my stomach. Sometimes in my head.

In the pages of my Free Press, I find them all the time. An attorney, dead at 55. A homemaker aged 49. An accountant, 52.

So it was really no surprise to hear the news about a race driver, dead at 34. Attorneys and homemakers and accountants think they will live to be 80. Think they will retire some day and relax. Think they will see their grandchildren graduate from high school.

Race drivers don't even give that a thought. Not even the best of them. And

Ayrton Senna was certainly that. But like every other driver, Monday's sunrise was always an iffy proposition.

The first time we met, he was barely 24. He hadn't yet won his first Formula One race, but he was young, and he was cocky, and he knew he would win. He knew he would win a lot.

Before he died Sunday in Imola, Italy, he had won three Formula One world championships and 41 races — three on the streets of Detroit.

And he was in front when he left this earth, leading the San Marino Grand Prix when he lost control of his Williams Renault on the seventh lap and slammed into a concrete wall with the car at full throttle.

By the time they pulled him out, a death certificate was a formality. The impact of the crash had crushed his skull. And at 34, Ayrton Senna had lived his last day on this Earth.

He had been a prodigy, so very skilled at an early age, that Formula One teams were courting him by the time he was 22 when he won the British and European Formula Ford titles, capturing 22 poles and winning 22 races.

Senna, though, wanted to know he was ready when he stepped up to Formula One. Wanted to know he was prepared. Because when he raced, he never held anything back, and though he was fast, he was never foolhardy.

The first Formula One race he finished — the Portuguese Grand Prix in 1985 — he won.

In his first Detroit Grand Prix, he hit both sides of the wall near the start-finish line in practice, was involved in a wreck at the start of the race and finally retired after hitting a wall 21 laps into the race.

It was a typical weekend.

He left the imprint of his tires on racetrack walls in every part of the world. Always he walked away, bruised, sore and smarter.

He and Nigel Mansell — now driving on the IndyCar tour — tangled time after time, each accusing the other of causing the accidents they found themselves in. Three years in a row, they started 1-2 in the Detroit Grand Prix.

"Put it this way," Senna said. "We are very competitive.... You are always open to have some good moments or bad moments."

He was fast and aggressive, but he was always aware, too, of what might lie beyond the next turn.

"On street courses," Senna said here one year, "you are always on the limit because if you make a mistake, you hit the barrier.... Sitting up front, you are safe from accidents at the start."

If he had not been arrogant before, winning made him that way. He was the best at what he did, and once that was proven, he could do pretty much as he pleased.

When he won here in 1986, Senna went directly from his pits to his hotel room in the Westin to watch Brazil's soccer team play a World Cup match. He had done what he came for; he had won the race. The photographers, the writers, the fans could do what they would like, and he would do what he liked. He would go watch television.

He won again in 1987 and '88, and after that last win, he said: "This is my time... ."

By the time he took his last green flag, he had won more Formula One races than Jackie Stewart. More than Niki Lauda. More than anyone except Alain Prost.

Here, we idolize Michael Jordan and Madonna and Billy Joel.

In his native Brazil, they idolized Ayrton Senna and Emerson Fittipaldi. Today will be one of mourning in Rio de Janeiro and Sao Paulo.

Reports from the track said Senna had been so shaken by rookie Roland Ratzenberger's death in a crash during qualifying that he did not get back into his car when qualifying resumed.

The Associated Press story quoted German driver Michael Schumacher, winner of Sunday's race, saying of Senna: "He looked nervous from the very first lap."

That was not Senna's character. Perhaps Ratzenberger's death had touched a spot in his soul. Perhaps the ever-present knowledge that racers were not meant to grow old grew even larger in him Sunday. Perhaps he had a premonition.

In the end, going into that treacherous turn for the seventh time, he was leading the San Marino Grand Prix. He was in front, where he had grown accustomed to being.

Until the last, he was young and fast. ❖

Golf

PAUL AZINGER

GARY PLAYER

ARNOLD PALMER

CHAPTER 6

Arnie

April 10, 1987

AUGUSTA, Ga. — It was the saddest thing I'd ever seen in sports.

I grew up watching the man on television, in awe of his skill and captivated by his style.

I remember how he used to stand over the ball and hitch up his pants with one hand. I remember how he would attack the golf ball with his whole body. I remember how he used to stride up the fairways, cocky and confident and waving to the crowd. And I remember those famous charges.

Arnold Palmer did more to popularize golf than any other man who ever lived. He was loved and idolized and imitated. He was the bridge from the era of Hogan and Snead to the era of Jack Nicklaus.

But the magic left with his youth, a lot of years ago, and Thursday, in his 33rd Masters tournament, he played like your next-door neighbor — the guy with the old set of mismatched clubs in his garage who plays the game in tennis shoes.

I followed him for nine holes; it was all I could bear to watch. He sprayed tee shots into the woods. He hit approach shots that did not reach the green. He hit putts that slid past the hole, then slid past again on his next try.

He was — on more occasions than one — a solitary figure standing in a mammoth sand trap, silhouetted by the rays of sunshine that leaked between the pines.

After nine holes, he was six strokes over par.

To the throng that dogged his footsteps or for the masses awaiting him at every green, it did not matter, though, whether he was six strokes over par or six under.

As he approached each green, the applause began. Not wild, uncontrolled, thunderous applause, but an applause that was somehow reverent. It was an applause given not for what he had done today but in appreciation of fond memories of other shots on other golf courses on other days.

There was something imperial in the process. Purposefully he strode, alone, toward each green, waving to the crowd as the applause washed over him.

The charisma is still there. But the stroke is gone.

"It's a shame," a woman whispered to her husband as Palmer missed a bogey putt on the sixth hole.

"Droppppppppppppp," a man begged softly as a Palmer putt rolled toward the cup on the eighth hole.

"Oooooooooohhh," moaned the gallery when it slid past.

On the press room scoreboard, I watched his round deteriorate even more on the back nine:

5 5 3   6 5 4   3 5 5   42 - 41 — 83.

I went out to watch the final hole.

When his second shot missed the 18th green, bouncing under a spectator sitting on a folding canvas stool, it caused only a murmur from the crowd. They knew the troubles he was having.

They had seen the scoreboard with Palmer's name and the figure 10, indicating the number of strokes he was over par.

But as he approached, they rose, first just a few, then dozens, then hundreds, and applauded him. He waved, shook hands with a young boy who had skipped school to be here and chatted with the spectators.

It took a mishit chip and two putts to finish the round — equaling the worst he has ever shot here.

People shook their heads and pressed their lips together. And as he walked toward the clubhouse, they reached out to him. They slapped him on the back, they stretched to touch him, they shouted encouragement.

He knows what he means to people in the gallery, and because of it, he said: "It makes me feel terrible when I play golf like I did today."

Perhaps Arnold Palmer needs the people as badly as the people need Arnold Palmer.

"Without that, it would be very easy to pack up and go home," he said of the affection the crowd lavished upon him. "The fact that they're there and they're rooting and they have been, no matter what, keeps me from packing up."

Watching Arnold Palmer play golf was like driving past an automobile wreck: You know you won't like what you see but can't keep from looking.

The man is 57 and his time is past.

Watching him play was like hearing Milton Berle tell a 30-year-old joke or Andres Segovia pluck on the wrong guitar strings.

Sad.

So sad.

I feel sorry for him.

I feel sorry for us.

Damn, but he was good, wasn't he? Once upon a time. ❖

Calvin Peete

April 11, 1987

A UGUSTA, Ga. — I used to call Chandler Park my home golf course, until a kid picked up my golf ball one day and ran off into the neighborhood.

Calvin Peete grew up not far from that neighborhood, but he never had a home course in Detroit.

Until he was 13, he lived on the east side. But golf courses were not a priority.

Eating was a priority. Making a living was one, too. Calvin Peete was one of his father's 19 children and, as a kid, he thought of becoming a professional golfer about as often as he thought of becoming a symbol of racial progress.

But he became both.

Calvin Peete was easy to pick out this weekend at Augusta National Golf Club. In the 51st Masters tournament, he and Jim Thorpe were the only black players in a field of 86.

Lee Elder was the only black to play in this tournament before Peete.

The Masters — above all else — is about tradition. Traditionally, the flowers here have been red and pink, the grounds and trees have been green, the players and spectators white and the caddies black.

With time, some of those traditions have slowly and reluctantly given way to progress, and Peete, who did not play his first round of golf until he was 23, avoided being drawn into conversations about past injustices.

He acknowledged: "I'm a historical figure just about anywhere I play."

But he would rather dwell on what he has accomplished than on what others did not.

It is improbable, but true, that Calvin Peete has won more money on the regular PGA Tour than Arnold Palmer ($2 million to $1.89 million through 1986). And it is improbable, too, that his name has shown up on the leader board through most of the first two rounds this weekend.

"I've never really thought about winning the Masters," he admitted before shooting a five-over-par 77 for a two-round 148. "I wasn't bred to win the Masters. I mean, I don't have a long line of golf history behind me.

"I'm happy winning anytime. I'll take the Milwaukee Opens and the Anheuser-Busch Classics, things like that. With my career starting so late, it means a lot for me to win anyplace."

Peete was a school dropout. Just when he dropped out is not clear — it may have been in high school. It may have been before he got that far along.

If he didn't get a diploma, though, he did get a driver's license. And before long, he was driving down rutted country roads from Florida to New York state, selling clothes and jewelry to migrant farm workers from the back of a beat-up station wagon.

Friends in Rochester, N.Y., tried to get Peete to take up golf, but he laughed at the suggestion. "I thought the game was silly," he said. "Who wants to chase a little ball around under the hot sun?"

About that time, though, Peete found out Jack Nicklaus was making more than $100,000 a year playing golf, and the sound of all that money made him realize there was life beyond being an itinerant clothing salesman.

He said he was hooked on the game from the day he first picked up a club, but it took him three tries to pass the PGA's tour qualifying school, and he didn't start playing the pro circuit until 1976 — when he was 33.

In 1980, he received his first invitation to the Masters. And he has been here every year since, rarely threatening to do what he threatened to do early in this tournament: become the first black with a chance to win the green jacket.

He has shot as high as 87 here. And as low as 66. But never has he finished better than 11th because his precision game is not suited to this course, which favors long hitters.

"It's hard to be confident coming to the Masters," he said. "But I think I've acquired the skills to win here.

"Nobody's ever told me I can't win here."

Imagine that.

Just a few years ago, not only would he have been told he couldn't win here, he would have been told he couldn't even play. ❖

The Diplo Club

August 14, 1991

H AVANA — Jorge Duque sat behind a small, simple, wooden desk, carefully examining his latest copy of Golf Digest.

"Come in," said one of Cuba's two golf pros. "Have a seat. We can talk, sure."

Jorge Duque has a lot of free time. At his course — Diplo Club — outside Havana, about 15 rounds of golf are played on a busy day, usually no more than 80 rounds in a week. The course is lush and green and beautiful. And it is not open to Cubans.

"It is not a part of our life, to play golf," Duque said. "It is more important to play baseball. You know it is really expensive to keep a golf course just for the locals, and we are not a rich country."

So the Diplo Club — golf course, restaurant, bars and two-lane bowling alley — is available to foreigners only, whether they are semipermanent residents of Cuba or visitors like the thousands here for the Pan American Games.

A round of golf costs $30 U.S. A pull-cart costs $10. And a caddie to pull the cart costs another $10.

Duque's job is good, the hours — 9 to 5:30 — reasonable. The course is his whenever he wants it, and when he doesn't care to work on his game, he can sit behind the wooden desk in the small air-conditioned office and read how Jack Nicklaus does it.

But a part of him is bothered that most of his countrymen seem to have so little desire and so little opportunity to play the game he has come to love.

There are 10 million Cubans and only two golf courses: Diplo Club and Varadero Club in the resort area where Mexicans and Germans and Canadians vacation.

Ten million Cubans and only two golfers, really, Duque and the man who is the pro at Varadero.

"I love this game because you're in touch with nature," Duque said. "It's a very healthy game.... . I hope maybe in 15 or 20 years we have golf courses here for the Cuban people."

Meanwhile, he is already encouraging one young Cuban to share his love for the game.

"My daughter, Claudia, is only 2 years old, but she has a plastic golf set. She's not playing yet, but she is going to play," insists Duque, who did not pick up a golf club until 1983, when he was 20.

When he finally did lift a club, he held it the way you would expect of a man who grew up in this baseball-crazed country.

"I held it like a baseball bat," he said. And he laughs at himself. He was a student at a sports school — expecting to become an instructor in water sports, surfing or water skiing or something like that — when a director from the Diplo Club visited the school in search of a golf pro.

"The pro here was 85 years old, and they were looking for new people to study golf," Duque said.

He and three others applied, and he got the job. He hasn't had a lesson since. He is a lean, handsome man, with dark hair and an easy laugh. And he laughs at the thought of being without a lesson for eight years.

Then he gives credit to the heritage of golf in his country.

"Here we have some very old caddies, and many of them have a very good eye. They sometimes give me little tips. The rest I take from the magazines or books or from watching tapes of golf tournaments that are televised. I slow it down and watch things completely."

If he shoots lower than 75, Duque is satisfied. His record score is 70, "par for this course," he said. "But I am trying to improve."

It is difficult to improve, though, with limited competition. He has never been to the United States, though he sometimes wonders what it would be like when he sees Augusta National or Oakland Hills on his television.

In his entire life, he has played just three courses: Diplo, Varadero and one in Merida, Mexico.

"All the time," he said, "I play here."

In the years before Fidel Castro took over as leader of Cuba, there were four golf courses in Havana. All but Diplo Club have disappeared, given over, Duque said, to the people.

"They were closed because the people who played them were rich people or people from other countries, and they left after 1959," he said. "The government built small communities on those spaces."

Like so many Cubans, Duque does not own a car. Having a car, he said, "makes you lazy." So he rides to work on a bus or on his bicycle. But he appreciates what he has and what he does.

Will you do this forever, I ask him? He slips a piece of paper into his Golf Digest to mark his place and sets it aside and looks at me with a smile.

"Maybe," he said. "Why not? It's not bad. But if you want to take my job, I will go to the beach."

I did not take his job.

And I suspect that this morning, Jorge Duque is not at the beach.

I suspect he is in his air-conditioned office, reading Golf Digest and waiting for a golfer to walk in. ❖

Mitch who?

April 9, 1992

A UGUSTA, Ga. — There was a commotion Wednesday around the 16th tee at Augusta National when CBS technicians wired a golfer for sound and fell in step behind him as he set off down the fairway.

"Who is that?" someone in the gallery asked his companion.

"Voges," replied the other, reading the name on the caddie's back. "Who's he?"

"Nobody," was the reply.

Nobody.

If you must be a celebrity to be somebody, the man in the gallery was right. If you must make a couple of million a year, he was on the mark.

But Mitch Voges definitely is somebody.

On the day Arthur Ashe told the world he contracted the AIDS virus through a blood transfusion, Mitch Voges, preparing for his first Masters, knocked on wood and gave thanks that the tainted blood he received seven years ago contained only hepatitis C.

"I can say I got jobbed on this deal," he said, sitting in the players' locker room, "or I can knock on wood and say I was lucky. I had to give myself shots of interferon every other day for six months. It's a nasty deal."

Mitch Voges thought, once upon a time, that he would be a professional golfer. He played at Brigham Young when Johnny Miller was there, but by the time Voges was 25, his back was screaming to him that he should give up the game. He played some, but not particularly well and not often.

"I'd look down at the ball and say: 'I don't want to swing at it. I know it's going to hurt.' "

So he quit golf instead of submitting to surgery.

Seven years ago, though, a couple of things happened that convinced him to have the operation.

"It got to the point where I couldn't have a pillow fight with my son. I couldn't lift my 2-year-old daughter and carry her around. So I had the operation — to be able to do things like that, not so I could play golf."

In 1990, Voges donated blood after a member of his church was hit by a drunken driver. Later, he received a letter from the Red Cross. "It was an angry letter," he said. "Basically what they told me was, 'Don't bring that stuff around here anymore.' "

And that is how he discovered that his blood was contaminated and that he had hepatitis C.

"Unwittingly, I'd probably spread that stuff around," he said, "because I'd donated blood lots of times."

The medication helped control his disease, but he was so weak last June that he shot an 86 in one round of the California State Amateur. A few weeks later, in the Southern California Amateur, he withdrew after nine holes because of fever and chills.

Weak and discouraged and 42 years old, he thought he would play just one more major tournament, then go back to his job as a carpet salesman in Simi Valley, Calif.

"The truth of the matter is, when I stood on the first tee at the United States Amateur last year, I wiped tears out of my eyes," Voges said. "I thought it would be the last big competition I played in. I thought I was pretty much done as a player."

Instead, he became the third-oldest man to win the event. And with the victory came the invitation to play in the Masters. And Voges doesn't care if the world thinks he is nobody because he is enjoying this week more than any other week of his life.

"Being a 42-year-old rookie, I don't look to have a long and storied history here," he said. "When you're young, you think you have eons of time. But as you get older, you realize you don't."

So he is doing things he thought he would never be able to do because he knows he will probably never do this again.

His clubs are encased in a tiny moon bag, so small that the putter must be carried separately because his caddie — his 13-year-old son Christian — could not carry the larger bag.

"I could probably save some shots if I had a club caddie," Voges said, "but this doesn't have anything to do with strokes. When else in my life am I going to have an opportunity to walk this course with my son?

"That's an emotional thing."

Wednesday afternoon, in the traditional nine-hole, par-three tournament, Voges switched caddies, asking his 67-year-old father, C.S., to carry his clubs.

On the final green, with the ball inches from the cup, the older man sidled up to his son and whispered in his ear: "Let me tap it in."

"I wish I had let him do it," Voges said later. "But I told him no. I didn't want to irritate anybody here."

His father will be on the other side of the ropes today when Voges plays the first round of the Masters with defending champion Ian Woosnam. So will his wife, their 9-year-old daughter Emily and his in-laws. This, for them, is a celebration, and it doesn't matter whether he shoots 68 or 86.

Mitch Voges is not nobody.

He has been blessed with a special moment and with the wisdom to understand that. And to enjoy it.

I wish all the selfish athletes in the world could see this, all the men and women who don't think the world does enough for them, who think $2 million isn't enough and that criticism is too harsh and road trips too long.

Mitch Voges has his priorities in place.

And that makes him somebody. ❖

Fred Couples

April 11, 1992

UGUSTA, Ga. — Anyone who has ever played golf knows how the game can destroy you.

Anybody can hit a ball 150 yards, but put a pond in front of a green and every Sunday player I know will hit the ball 140 yards. Drown it.

Throw a club.

Say things you would not say in front of your daughter.

I know someone who once hit a bad shot and said a four-letter word, and the twosome who had been playing along drove off in their cart and never came back. They were offended, I suppose.

If you hit one into the water, odds are you'll hit at least one more there.

None of us is exempt. Bill Laimbeer took a 14 on one hole in a celebrity tournament a year or so ago, and he'd like to try the pro tour when he's through with basketball.

The game gets into your head, eats at your brain like termites in an old log, makes you crazy.

It gets the pros, too.

Tsuneyuki Nakajima had a 13 on No. 13 at the Masters in 1978. And Tom Weiskopf shot a 13 on the par-three 12th at Augusta National two years later.

The game grabbed for Fred Couples yesterday. Grabbed and missed. It proved him human and more. Or less. For one gut-wrenching moment on the 14th hole, he played the game as the rest of us do.

If there is a better golfer in the world right now, nobody can name him. Since the first of the year, he is 130 strokes under par. In nine tournaments and half of this one, he has had just three over-par rounds.

After 13 holes, he was nine under for the tournament, six for the day and leading everybody — including those upstart foreigners, Ian Woosnam and Craig Parry, who finished the day atop the leader board.

Couples birdied five holes in a row — the sixth through the 10th — and on 13 he hit a driver, a six-iron, chipped to within a foot and made the birdie putt.

He was invincible, it seemed. In that groove where everything goes right. Where balls fly straight and true and putts roll along what seems to be a dotted line from the putter face to the bottom of the cup.

And then came the 14th hole, 404 yards of deceptive, wicked beauty.

He played it as I would. As a guy fighting for the third-flight consolation title at his club.

There was nothing wrong with his drive, but when he asked his caddie for the wedge, things began to go awry.

"It was 124 yards, and I never thought what happened would happen," he confessed later. "I thought I could get cute with a wedge and cut it in there, but when you try to get cute here, you pay for it."

His shot hit the front of the sloping green and rolled onto the fringe.

He tried to chip up from there, but he mishit the ball, and it rolled back at his feet. He was lying three on a par-four hole and still wasn't on the putting surface.

Nevertheless, he pulled out his putter and whacked the ball 12 feet past the hole. He two-putted from there for a double-bogey six, and when he next looked at the scoreboard, he was tied for second with Woosnam.

"You're up there thinking about making another birdie," he said, "and the next thing you know, you've made a score three strokes worse than that."

Termites in the brain.

Lumps in the throat.

Jelly in the knees.

Amateurs get those in such situations. And so do some pros.

Fred Couples didn't.

Some say he isn't really a champion yet because he hasn't won a major title. Some say he isn't hard enough. Not committed enough. Not ambitious enough.

Once, he said: "If I could play well and finish third, that's a good week for me."

That quote haunts him. He said that maybe people didn't understand what he meant, or that his outlook has changed or that it all depends upon how you look at things.

"You don't worry about who wins 60 games in basketball," he said Friday. "You worry about who wins the championship, and in our game that's the big tournaments. Consistency doesn't win the Masters — you need to do some great things. I need to do what I did today, tomorrow." What he did after that horrible hole was birdie the 15th, bogey the 16th, par No. 17 and finish with a difficult birdie — his ninth of the day — on the closing hole.

He shot a 67 despite the double bogey and was one shot behind the leaders, and it seemed appropriate to ask about the effect of that horrible hole. Did it unnerve him? Did he have to stand back and compose himself?

"No, I didn't," he said, and he was walking away. Quickly. "I've talked enough about the 14th."

Fred Couples was in a golf cart and gone.

Perhaps golf's termites did get to his mind.

But they didn't get to his game. And if he can keep them away for two more days, no one will ever again be able to deny he is a champion.

Couples fired 69-70 in the closing rounds, good for a 275 total and a two-stroke victory. ❖

Gary Player

June 12, 1992

I ordered a couple of eggs over easy, sausage patties, hash browns, coffee and toast. He ordered cereal, orange juice and decaf, please.

He wanted to talk golf. The Senior Players Championship.

But first he wanted to tell me about Laughing Harry.

"He worked in the gold mines," Gary Player said, sliding up the sleeve of his sports coat. "When I look at this gold watch, I always think of him. I remember going down to meet him at the mines when I was a boy, and as he came out, he'd pull off those big old rubber boots and pour the sweat out of them."

Laughing Harry was Gary Player's father, a jovial man who found time for fun and for golf despite having to raise his youngest son alone after his wife died when Gary was 8.

"I've got something in my head," Player said. "Something I want to do. I want to write a poem about him and have it framed so I can take it with me on the road and put it on my nightstand by the bed.

"It's amazing, you know," he said, looking around the elegant dining room of Dearborn's Ritz-Carlton hotel. "We were so poor. This is truly amazing."

He, of course, has not been poor for a long while now.

He has won $4.4 million playing golf, but that has been just the seed money for larger and more ambitious ventures, for a ranch outside Johannesburg, South Africa, for a stable of racehorses, for a string of golf courses stretching from Taiwan to Egypt, for a private school for 400 South African children, partially funded by Kellogg's.

For more than 30 years, he has been one of the most successful and recognizable men in professional golf.

He stands 5-feet-7 and his weight is up to 153 "because I've been doing extra weights," he said.

And all his life, he has had to measure up to the legends of Arnold Palmer and Jack Nicklaus, men bigger than him physically and made to seem even bigger by the measure of their accomplishments. "I grew up with Arnold and Jack, and from the beginning I knew I had to be fit if I was going to compete," he said.

It would be no surprise if Player had acquired a Napoleonic complex, if his size and his success had mixed into a combustible combination that would defy polite description.

A lot of our best athletes are like that. A lot take all they can get, then ask why there is not more.

Hey, look at me, they seem to say.

Look what I have done.

I'm entitled.

Gary Player, at 56, has earned $171,664 playing golf in the first five months of this year, but he remembers other times. Leaner times. And he can laugh about them. And feel blessed.

"It's different now," he said. "They have courtesy cars for you, and when you get to the locker room, there's four dozen new balls and four gloves and new shoes. They want to give you something every week. They ask: 'What can we do for you?' and they say: 'Thank you for coming.' They don't know I want to get down on my knees and fold my hands and thank them for what they have given us."

He is old-fashioned about a lot of things.

"I came into the hotel lobby the other day, and there was a man standing there with a golf cap on," he said. "Inside. I couldn't imagine. To me, that said something. Now if it was in a golf clubhouse or something, that would be different. But in a hotel lobby?"

Last Sunday, at the Senior Tour stop in Charlotte, N.C., he three-putted the final hole of the tournament. He was not happy about it. After all, he is still a competitor. But as he walked off the 18th green, young hands thrust programs in his direction, asking for autographs.

"We still get uptight," Player said, acknowledging that winning is still the objective. "But it's different. I signed those autographs when I walked off; I didn't just shove my way through."

Maybe that's the reason for the popularity of the Senior Tour.

Maybe there's more than just the game. Maybe it's the way the players conduct themselves, with class and style and courtesy.

Like human beings who don't allow their talents or their blessings or their wealth to blind them to the fact that they are not so different from the people who want to call their name and ask for nothing more than a wave or a wink or an autograph.

Player likes to summarize his youth by saying: "My dad was in the mines, my mother was dead and my brother was up north fighting in the Second World War."

It was a short youth.

He turned pro at 17, won his first tournament in Egypt a year later, got married at 21 and joined the PGA Tour the same year. Eventually, his entourage included his wife and six children.

"We had to get three rooms," he recalled. "And I had to tag 33 pieces of luggage. Can you imagine my wife doing that — at a time when there were no disposable diapers?

"I had to win just to break even."

He didn't always win, but when he did, it was usually in the big ones. He won the Masters and British Open three times each, the PGA Championship twice and the U.S. Open once. He has won the PGA Senior Championship three times, the U.S. Senior Open twice and Senior TPC once.

He has been a champion since the day he picked up a golf club.

He thinks his father had a lot to do with that.

Not long ago he named a colt — one he said had "the looks of a champion" — after his father.

He named it Laughing Harry. ❖

Paul Azinger

August 3, 1994

Y ou probably have to go through it to know exactly what Paul
Azinger is coming back from this week.

Unless you have sat in the cold sterility of a doctor's
examination room — at age 33 — and heard you have cancer,
you cannot know how that word slammed into his gut.

Unless you have experienced the aftermath of chemotherapy, you cannot
know how tidal waves of nausea sapped at his strength and his pride and his
will.

Unless you have sat and thought about it in the dark, alone, you cannot
know the clammy terror of facing a death that might be only months away.

"At age 33 and 34, I had to face the fact that I might die and I might die
pretty soon," Azinger said at Warwick Hills Golf and Country Club in Grand
Blanc, where he will test his recovery by playing in the Buick Open, his first
tournament since the cancer was discovered in early December.

"When I was sick, I didn't miss golf," he said. "I just wanted to live. Now
that I feel strong and healthy, my love for the game has returned. It's returned
tenfold."

There has always been something about the sight of a small white ball
cutting a perfect arc through the bright blue, early morning sky that has had a
grip on Paul Azinger.

Like each of us who swings a golf club, he knows a perfect shot when he
hits one. He hears it. He feels it. He holds the pose. He watches the flight of the
ball. Lately, he has had that feeling again.

"I made the decision to come back because I'm hitting the ball like I never
quit and because I don't have any more discomfort," he said. "They've been
going fairly straight, and I haven't needed to be a ball-beater because I've hit it
pretty solid."

The sun is shining, the birds are singing, the world is back on its axis, and
Paul Azinger is grateful.

"I love the sport. I love the game of golf. It's what I do best. It's a God-
given talent."

It is, though, a talent God bestowed in an unfinished form. Imperfect and
without a set of instructions.

When he was a senior in high school — a time when golf prodigies are breaking par — Azinger could not break 40 on nine.

He went to qualifying school to try to earn his tour card in 1981.

Sorry, they said. You flunked. Try us again.

He went back in 1983.

Sorry kid, you missed again. Maybe you should try another game.

On his third try, in 1984, Azinger finally earned his card. In 1985, his first full season on the tour, he won $81,179, barely enough to cover motels and airline tickets.

He was at the peak of his game last fall, though, when cancer struck. He had won the PGA Championship in a playoff with Greg Norman, and he had pocketed $1.4 million for less than a year's work on the tour. He had a wife and two daughters at home.

But he had a pain in his shoulder, too.

In early December, his doctor told him it was a lymphoma in his right shoulder blade.

Curable, doctors said.

It will just take time. And treatment: chemo and radiation.

To most of us, those are just words. Somebody else actually experiences them.

Chemo and radiation.

Azinger soon found what lay behind the words.

"I'd throw up for two or three days after the chemo treatment and be gaggy for another seven or 10 days, and the next 20 were pretty normal," he said. "After that, radiation was like a walk in the park. There were no side effects from radiation, except for a burn on my shoulder like a real bad sunburn.

"But if you've got to do chemo, brother, you know you're sick. I don't know how else to say it.

"Before my chemo treatments, I would look perfectly normal, other than for having no hair. But when I came back from them, I didn't want my friends to see me because I looked so sick. My parents almost cried every time they saw me because I looked so bad."

He lost all his hair and 20 pounds. There were days when, for a moment or two, he must have wondered whether it was worth the agony.

Six months of chemo took him into May. All that got him through it, he said, "was knowing there would be only two treatments after the fourth and only one after the fifth. And, of course, that the sixth one was the last.

"I didn't like it. I threw up *before* I did it, that's how much I hated it."

His doctors endorse his comeback. But don't overdo it, they tell him. Take it easy. A day at a time. A hole at a time. A stroke at a time.

"I join a long, long, long list of people who have survived cancer," said Azinger, who credits renewed religious conviction with putting his mind at ease through the ordeal. "I'm scared of dying just like anybody else, but I think I'm more at peace with it now. I feel like I've beaten this thing, (and) I'll be really excited on Thursday to get it all started again."

Since Thanksgiving, he has played just six rounds of golf. In five of those he rode a cart, so he's not sure what to expect this weekend, either from the fans — whose support makes him a bit self-conscious — or from his game, which hasn't been tested in eight months.

"My expectations are something I'm not ready to share, but I've always set high expectations for myself. I wouldn't be here if I didn't think I could be competitive, (but) if I shoot a 75 or a 78, I'm not going to be that volatile. I'm not going to get ahead of myself, and I'm going to enjoy the day."

Golf is still his favorite game. And competition still burns in his heart. But something about Paul Azinger will never be the same.

"I definitely walk a little slower, and I probably talk a little slower," he said. "I definitely appreciate every day I've got. I'd give up every nickel I have, every tournament I've ever won to be in good health.

"If you can wake up and do whatever you planned to do that day, you ought to be grateful because there are a lot of people who can't.

"I'm grateful for every day I feel good." ❖

Colleges & Preps

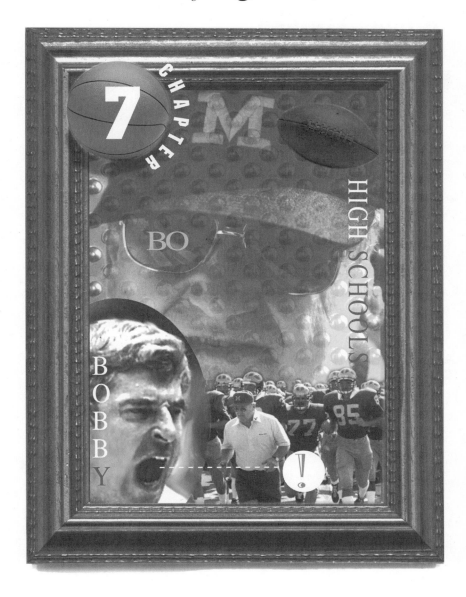

CHAPTER 7

M

BO

HIGH SCHOOLS

BOBBY

!

Muddy Waters

April 15, 1980

EAST LANSING — Muddy Waters cautiously steered the gleaming green-and-white Lincoln Continental into the University Club parking lot, his eye searching for a safe spot to park the symbol of his belated arrival to big-time college football.

"Opulent," he said. "Opulent. That's what I told Doug when he showed me this car and asked if I'd mind driving it. He told me he didn't think I knew the word, and I told him I'd just never had an opportunity to use it before," chuckled Waters, who began spring training with his first Michigan State football team.

"Doug" is Doug Weaver, the Spartans' new athletic director and the man who fulfilled Waters' 30-year dream by naming him to replace Darryl Rogers as MSU's head coach.

Waters, 57, has spent more than half his life coaching in relative obscurity, first in high schools, then at Hillsdale and Saginaw Valley colleges. His dream of returning to his alma mater, he thought, had passed him by.

But he sat in his opulent automobile on the campus of his university. And, as if to reassure himself it was real, he reached out and stroked a row of buttons in the center of the dashboard.

"Look at this," he said.

He pushed a button and the figures 12:31 flashed on a digital panel. "That's the time," he smiled, pushing another button. "Look, I can get my speed in miles … in kilometers … it'll tell me what my average gas mileage is, how much farther I can go before I run out of gas, my estimated time of arrival, anything I want."

He pushed each of the buttons, flashing a satisfied smile as the computer responded to every command.

"Before I came here," Muddy said, opening the door and stepping into the early spring sunshine, "I drove a Chevrolet."

Big Ten coaches, Waters has quickly discovered, drive cars more prestigious than that. They eat in private clubs. And they play a lot of golf.

"I've been invited to so many golf outings," he said after going through the University Club's buffet line, "that I had to go out and buy a set of golf clubs. I didn't even own a set, but when I'd tell people that, they seemed so disappointed that I figured I might as well go out and buy some. Now they're just going to have to put up with the way I play."

Waters, in years past, has had to prepare his teams to play Adrian, Olivet and Wayne State. Next fall, he will find more formidable names on the schedule: Michigan, Notre Dame and Ohio State. But the job, he insisted, is the same. Only the tools at his disposal have changed.

"Sure it's different," he said. "It's a helluva lot different. You feel more appreciated — that's as good a word as I can come up with. Here, I have all the things to work with that I've dreamed about but couldn't justify with a super-tight budget. Saginaw Valley was exceptionally wicked because those people are fighting for their existence. Every dollar that comes in has 1,000 places to go.

"But people who downplay small colleges just don't understand. Those kids put out just as much as these. These are just a little bigger, a little quicker, a little more talented, and maybe a little meaner."

From 1949, when Waters completed his eligibility as a Michigan State football player, until he was named head coach, he was on the East Lansing campus only as a visitor. He was like the thousands of aging men who walked the tree-lined campus on Saturday mornings, hoarding memories, treasuring remembrances, reliving accomplishments achieved in a less complicated day. But wherever he coached during those 30 years, he carried Michigan State with him.

"I'm a sentimental guy in many ways," he said, pulling a card from his wallet. "This," he said, holding up the card, "is a pass to Michigan State's spring training in 1952. You can just barely make out Biggie Munn's signature.

"I remember when they were first building this golf course," he said, looking out the University Club windows at the Fred Akers course. "I came down to visit Biggie, and he showed me the course and told me how much money they had spent on seed. It was more than my whole budget at Hillsdale. He just laughed and said: 'Oh, I had it hidden away in one of my budgets.' "

A waiter brought Waters back to the present by dropping the bill on the table in front of him.

Once again Waters went to his wallet, pulling out another card.

"When I joined this club," he said, "I wanted to use my old Michigan State uniform number as my membership number, but it was already taken. They were real nice, though — they gave me my old high school number, 7, and my MSU number, 43 — 743."

Though Waters is one of their own, MSU supporters did not universally hail his appointment. Nor was it popular with some segments of the media.

"People were saying: 'How come a small-time coach is gonna take a job of this caliber?' They really cut me up," he recalled. "But a couple of days later, I was introduced at a basketball game, and the kids gave me a standing ovation. I damn near cried.

"Now people ask for my autograph. A couple of months ago, I was at Saginaw Valley, and nobody knew me. I haven't won a game — all I did was get a job."

It was the job he has coveted for a lifetime, though. For dozens of years, Waters has been able to picture a scene in his mind's eye: Across the field stands Bo Schembechler or Dan Devine or Earle Bruce mapping strategy to counteract his, while a sea of faces encircles them, chanting "Go Green! Go White!"

This fall, those dreams will become reality, and Waters admitted: "I'm gonna be overawed, I really know I am. It's going to be very thrilling to me."

But Tuesday is the day he is really looking forward to.

"It's going to be a special day. The first day I'll see 'em in uniform, especially to see the green," he said quietly. "I haven't been around green for a long time. I can identify with every kid out there. I've got a lump in my throat already."

Muddy Waters has finally made it to the big time.

His stay was brief. Waters compiled a 10-23 mark in three seasons. ❖

Annie Hall and Bo

October 15, 1985

NN ARBOR — In the movie "Annie Hall," Woody Allen and Diane Keaton — lovers-to-be who have just met — stand on a rooftop and make small talk. As they speak, subtitles tell the audience what they really mean, what they'd really like to be saying to each other.

That's the way it is in the real world sometimes, too.

You get the feeling that's the way it is when Bo Schembechler meets the press, as he did at his weekly luncheon at Weber's on the outskirts of Ann Arbor. It went something like this:

Press: "USA Today has you ranked No. 1. What do you think of that?"

(Will you finally admit, Bo, that your team is the best in the country?)

Schembechler: "I don't get that paper."

(I don't read what any of you guys write.)

Press: "Do you get the New York Times? It has you ranked No. 1, too."

(Come on, Bo, admit it. Michigan is the best team in the country.)

Schembechler: "No. They have us No. 1? I wonder what all the criteria are. It would be interesting to see what they use."

(How could someone in New York, who hasn't seen us play in the past two weeks, possibly have any idea how good we are compared to everybody else in the country? How presumptuous can you be?)

Press: "Saturday's game against Iowa is being billed as the unstoppable offense against the immovable defense. How do you look at it?

(You don't really believe Iowa can score on your defense, do you, Bo?)

Schembechler: "The games we've played against Iowa lately haven't been high-scoring games, but their offense generates a lot of yardage and a lot of points."

(I don't think they can score enough to beat us, but I'll be darned if I'm going to be quoted as saying so and give Hayden Fry something to put up on their locker-room bulletin board.)

Press: "Does Iowa have more first-round pro prospects than anyone else in the Big Ten?"

(OK, Bo, if you want to say nice things about Iowa, we'll give you a chance, then we'll try to sneak in a hard question later.)

Schembechler: "Well, there's Chuck Long, Ronnie Harmon and Larry Station, if somebody wants to take a chance on a 5-foot-11 linebacker.... There's three pretty good players right there."

(Everybody says Long, Harmon and Station are studs. They haven't played us yet. Ask how good they are after we're through with them.)

Press: "Would you rather see Harmon as a receiver or as a runner?"

(Bo, give this guy some credit. He's gained 512 yards in five games and caught 249 yards in passes.)

Schembechler: "I'd rather see him as a blocker."

(I'd rather see him flat on his back with 11 of our guys on top of him.)

Press: "When was the last time you played an opponent this good?"

(Do you really think this Iowa team is in the class with some of those great Ohio State teams?)

Schembechler: "Well, last year's Iowa team was pretty good when we played 'em. They're good this year. But I wonder who's going to win this thing. Ohio State and Illinois, Purdue, Iowa, Michigan, Minnesota and maybe Indiana are still in there."

(We've got six games left, guys — Ohio State, Illinois, Purdue, Iowa, Minnesota and Indiana — and I'm not going to offend any of them by writing them off. If any of them beat us, I'll be surprised and mortified, but I'm sure not going to say that for the record.)

Press: "Does it make this team special that they weren't supposed to win anything but seem to want it more than some other teams?"

(Are you enjoying stuffing our preseason predictions that Michigan wouldn't be very good down our throats?)

Schembechler: "I suspect so. I read the Iowa papers before the season began that said it was a good thing that their big games came late in the season: against Illinois and Ohio State. Nobody thought we could play. That's what makes this so gratifying."

(You bet I'm enjoying stuffing it down your throats.)

Press: "What's this week going to be like for you?"

(Some people have written that you never win the big games. Can you handle this week?)

Schembechler: "You know the last few times we've been up against the No. 1 team, we've played pretty good. We beat Miami last year and Notre Dame a couple of years ago.... OK, guys? You got enough to write?"

(Geez, what a dumb question. I've wasted enough time with you guys. I've got a football team to coach. See you next Monday.)

Actions speak louder than words — final score: Iowa 12, Michigan 10. ❖

Bessemer Speedboys

December 1, 1985

They came 568 miles and 13 weeks and countless bumps and bruises to get here.

From the farthest corner of the Upper Peninsula, the Bessemer Speedboys bused over the Mackinac Bridge and down I-75 to the Silverdome, towing behind them the hopes and dreams of 2,000 souls.

One victory from the state Class D football championship, they were typical of every football team from every village and hamlet in Michigan. The pride and lifeblood of withering towns. The hope for the future.

On autumn Friday evenings the citizenry of Bessemer makes the pilgrimage to Massie Field to watch the youth of the community grow toward manhood. Coming of age in rural America is done on the football field.

And this season, the Speedboys had grown and prospered better than any Bessemer football team before them.

They had won 12 straight games and had not given up a point in the playoffs. They awoke at their hotel in Troy yesterday positive they would win again.

They didn't.

Battle Creek St. Philip beat them soundly, 31-8. The Tigers scored five touchdowns before Bessemer scored one in the fourth quarter. St. Philip found big holes in the Speedboys' defense, stopped Bessemer in its tracks and gradually, but steadily, sapped the Speedboys' confidence.

With each score, the mood on the field changed. Both teams had come here cocky and proud, sure they were better than the team across the field. Soon, though, there was no question Bessemer was overmatched and out of its element.

Not only were they far from home, the Speedboys — accustomed to the muck and mire and mud of the UP in autumn — were indoors, where the turf was dry and the footing perfect. St. Philip's quick backs cut and dodged, leaving Bessemer defenders empty-handed, sprawled on their faces on the Silverdome turf.

"There's not much cutting like that up there because of the weather conditions," said Bessemer's Mike Contratto. "Our defense has never faced anything close to that."

Contratto quarterbacked Bessemer to what was — until yesterday — a perfect season. And when the other team had the ball, he threw his 5-foot-9, 170-pound body into the defensive effort, playing cornerback.

He epitomized the Speedboys' success. And he epitomized their frustration. And their class.

He threw for Bessemer's only touchdown but completed only three of nine passes for 22 yards before the winners went up, 31-0. He was responsible for St. Philip's last touchdown, losing a fumble in the end zone. And he was left in the wake of Mike Reece, whose 51-yard reception set up St. Philip's first TD.

"Every time we got high because we stopped them, they'd make a big play and bring us back down," he said. "It was an emotional tug-of-war."

Have you ever tried to make a tackle with tears in your eyes? With a lump the size of a grapefruit in your throat? With the knowledge that all you've worked for, all your little town had talked about at the coffee shop for the past month, has slipped out of your grasp? For good.

That's the way Bessemer played the second half.

"I told them I was very, very proud of them," said Bessemer coach Pat Gallinagh. "I told them to hold their heads up high. Maybe another day, at another time, it might have been a little different. Today there was no argument about who was the better team."

Sometimes we snicker at the idea of sport being a character-builder, as coaches tell us it is. Times when coaches curse officials, when players lose their composure and their tempers and their respect for their opponents fuel those feelings.

But cynics would have cringed at the Silverdome.

Beaten, their dream of a perfect season and a state championship dashed, the Speedboys stood at midfield and watched St. Philip celebrate when the game ended.

Helmets in hand, they watched two dozen other young men do what they came here to do: grinning, hugging their cheerleaders, thrusting a single finger into the air.

Then — the celebration over — they lined up to shake the hands of the Class D state champions. Mike Contratto was first, extending his hand to St. Philip's Brad Morgan.

And when St. Philip was presented the championship trophy, the Speedboys applauded.

Bessemer could not be prouder if the Speedboys had won.

Neither could football. ❖

South Bend Saturdays

November 15, 1986

SOUTH BEND, Ind. — I walked where Knute Rockne walked. I stood on the sidelines where George Gipp stood. I talked with Roger Valdiserri, who convinced Joe Theismann to change the pronunciation of his name from These-man to Thighs-man so it would rhyme with Heisman.

I saw the glint of the late fall sun on the golden dome.

And I was as moved as I was the first time I came here, 15 years ago. It didn't exactly bring a lump to my throat or a tear to my eye, but it made me feel the way I always feel when I come here — like I'm in a one-of-a-kind place.

Francis Scott Key got emotional over a tattered flag still waving over a fort in the first light of dawn.

Some people break out in goose bumps at the sight of the Beach Boys in concert.

Some find the most delightful sight in the world to be a dividend check.

I feel like that about Notre Dame's campus, even though I know it's corny and I wish I didn't feel that way.

It is, I think, because it is one of life's promises that did not disappoint.

My first knowledge of Notre Dame was by word of mouth, from the guys who broadcast the Fighting Irish's football games in the late 1940s. Was it Ted Husing? Or Mel Allen? Or Bill Stern? I don't remember, but I remember the word pictures of the campus and the atmosphere on those crisp football Saturdays. And overriding their words every now and then would be the sound of music: "Cheer, cheer for old Notre Dame, wake up the echoes cheering her name... ."

In those days before television, I could conjure it all up in my mind's eye.

I didn't see it for myself until 25 years later, but it was exactly what they described.

To me, it is the most beautiful college campus in America. The smell of hot dogs and hamburgers roasting over open fires on the quadrangle, music drifting out from dorm windows, thousands of people promenading in the crisp air and a modest, 59,000-seat stadium that has stood unchanged for half a century.

I can't tell you just why I feel the way I do about it. I know today that Gipp hung around pool halls, that Notre Dame hasn't finished in the Top Ten since

1980 and that the school is looking for a way out of some of its football contracts, including the one with Michigan State.

I don't care.

I brought my youngest son here one summer when he was in his early teens. Some of my feeling for the campus, I thought, might rub off. I never entertained any ideas of going to school at Notre Dame — my family could not afford that — but I thought maybe my son would want to go to school here someday.

He wasn't impressed.

Instead, he went to Wayne State and Southwest Texas State.

But I get back every couple of years, usually to cover something like what's going to happen in that old brick stadium this afternoon.

And if this campus and this school and this football program are not something a little different than any other, please tell me why ABC is televising a game between the No. 3 team in the nation and a team with a 4-4 record.

And why did the oddsmakers make the No. 3 team only a five-point favorite? Outcome doesn't matter.

On paper, the difference is far greater. Even Blue & Gold Illustrated, a weekly newspaper published for fans of the Fighting Irish, rated Notre Dame inferior to the No. 3 team in 45 of 47 categories this week.

"Realistically," noted the paper, "Penn State is the clear-cut favorite … (but) do not count Notre Dame out. These are the kinds of games that the Irish … have thrived on throughout their history."

But I do not care who wins here this afternoon. The outcome will not make me richer or poorer, happy or sad, disappointed or satisfied, will not change my life at all.

Sitting in on it will be enough, though I realize that's an emotion that isn't universally shared.

The Penn State Nittany Lions got here yesterday.

They walked the same ground I did.

Today they'll play where Rockne and Gipp and Johnny Lujack played.

And you know something? I bet not a one of them feels the way I do about the place.

The Irish, under first-year coach Lou Holtz, lost to Penn State, 24-19. ❖

Ethics 101

August 20, 1988

W e've all seen Bo Schembechler grow evangelical about ethics.

He gestures.

He points.

His voice rises, and he sticks his chin out in defiance and calls for thunder and lightning to strike down the frauds and cheats in college sports.

He sometimes comes across as a combination of Elmer Gantry and Woody Hayes, college football's conscience, preaching against drugs and agents and recruiting violations.

"Why then," someone on the telephone wanted to know, "did he sign an endorsement with a shoe company? And do his players have to wear that company's shoe, too?"

It's true.

If Schembechler has feet of clay, they are encased in Nike shoes.

He signed a contract with that company for an undisclosed amount — believed to be about $40,000 a year. And when the University of Michigan football team ran into Michigan Stadium yesterday morning for press day, every one of the players was shod in Nikes.

Conflict of interest?

A payoff?

Money over integrity?

Schembechler said not.

"I don't get one red cent of it," he insisted. "I did not decide on Nikes because they offered me the money. I was going to use Nike shoes anyway, because I liked them. We had for our assistant coaches here no setup whereby they could get any break for tuition or any kind of scholarship for their children to go to college.

"I would feel offended to take the money, (so) I said if they could work it out where it goes into a coaches' scholarship trust and we can distribute the money to be used for their children, I'd accept it. I do not and never have taken 10 cents.

"And don't think it's not a benefit to the athletic department, too. We get an awful lot of shoes for nothing."

Before going any further, I have to admit I am not impartial here. I respect Schembechler. I think he is a hard man with tunnel vision that allows him to see little that goes on beyond the end zones, and sometimes he goes around with this chip on his shoulder.

But if I were laying odds, I'd say the chances of him cheating are about the same as the odds on Los Angeles slipping into the Atlantic Ocean tomorrow.

Call me naive, but I believe this man practices what he preaches.

This is not Jimmy Swaggart.

This man doesn't have as much hair. And doesn't dress as well. But if you ever find him in a New Orleans motel room, it will probably be with a movie projector and a dozen reels of football films.

He gets nervous at the mere mention of wrongdoing because he recognizes the vulnerability of a program the size of Michigan's. And he likes to tell the story of how he almost got the Wolverines put on probation a few years back.

"We were at the Rose Bowl one year," he recalled, "and I was eating lunch, and this old gentleman I never met before introduced himself and says: 'Look, I've got a kid I'd like you to meet.' So I went out and shook his hand, and he told me he was a quarterback, and they asked if I'd put my arm around the kid for pictures.

"I told them when we got back (to Ann Arbor) we'd get some film on him. He was from Las Vegas. When we checked the kid out, he was a pretty danged good quarterback, but he was interested in Nebraska and never even visited here.

"The only contact by anybody at Michigan was me standing in the courtyard of the hotel with my arm around him for those pictures. Well, the kid goes to Nebraska — his name is David Humm — and the NCAA investigates Nebraska. And Nebraska says: 'What are you on us for? Michigan took him to the Rose Bowl.'

"Well, the NCAA goes to this old guy... . He's an old Michigan guy, and he's a pilot. He threw them out. He told them: 'If I want to fly him to the Rose Bowl, I'll fly him to the Rose Bowl.'

"The long and short of it is this guy flew this kid to the Rose Bowl. He saw us play. That's a direct violation of NCAA rules, beyond question. Our faculty rep had to fly down and plead our case, and the case was simple fact: Ignorance. When I'm out there in the courtyard, I don't know David Humm from Adam."

There is a faction at Michigan, though, that raises questions about Schembechler, about the power he wields, about the autonomy of the athletic department and about what they see as lack of accountability.

It is true. If he cannot put his finger on it, if he cannot reach out and grab it, if he is not in complete control of it, Schembechler is a little uneasy about it.

He gets upset when the NCAA writes to ask why an assistant coach showed up at a recruit's home on signing day at 7:45 a.m. instead of the prescribed 8 a.m.

He deplores the use of steroids and tells parents of recruits he will randomly test their sons for drugs while they are on campus.

He does not care to hear about the ACLU. About invasion of privacy. About statutes and legal questions.

"It is," he said, "in their best interest. We've had some (tests) come back positive. Absolutely. Maybe two or three a year, maybe one, some years none. We handle it ourselves, and nobody ever knows about it."

He is starting his 20th season as Michigan's head football coach — two decades of success without sacrificing ideals and without probation in a world that seems, to some, more tempting every day.

"There's a lot more negative influences on the athlete than there was 20 years ago," he said. "When I first came here, we didn't have the agent problem, and I don't believe we had the steroid problem that we must address today.

"But as long as we keep writing about it and enough guys out there are talking about it, the majority of people are going to do it the way it's supposed to be done."

He is honest, he said. And it is apparent it bothers him that anyone would question that.

But he said he is not unique in his honesty.

"Hell, no!" he bleated, when asked if he's different from most coaches. "I'm not a special guy at all. Ninety percent of them out there are like me.

"I know guys that got fired because they wouldn't (cheat). They could have won, but it wasn't their nature. It's happened to a lot of my friends. It happened to Gary Moeller.

"There's probably only about 10 percent that cheat, and they're the same ones who'll be doing it 10 years from now or 20 years from now."

And even though he endorses Nike shoes, that 10 percent doesn't include Bo Schembechler. ❖

Jenison Field House

March 12, 1989

EAST LANSING — He was probably 20 and probably a student. He was sucking a soft drink through a straw, standing in the corner of Jenison Field House at halftime while an announcer was introducing Spartans past to the crowd of 10,004.

"From the Spartan squad of 1941 and '42, Bill Burk.... All the way from Marshfield, Massachusetts, Bob Brannum, from the Class of '48.... Now living in Adrian, a letterman in '50, '51 and '52 and captain in 1952, Sonny Means."

"Say," the young man, sucking on the pop, said to a man nearby, "do you recognize any of these names?"

The older man nodded and the litany went on.

Bill Eckstrom.

Al Ferrari.

Pat Wilson.

And "a three-year letterman, the most valuable player in 1958 and 1959, an All-American in 1959 and a 14-year veteran of the NBA, Jumpin' Johnny Green!"

Leaning in to be heard over the approving roar of the crowd, the youngster with the pop had a one-word question.

"Who?"

Michigan State played its final regular-season game in Jenison Field House, and it was a time for memories and some tears.

It was a time for recalling what used to be, and for trying to recall what used to be.

"My favorite memory," said Nick Kerbawy, who was sports information director at MSU from 1944 to 1948, "was us beating Kentucky in here. That was before the Detroit newspapers sent reporters out here, and I could not make them believe we had beaten Kentucky when I called.

"One of them insulted me. He accused me of being drunk. Kentucky was the king of basketball then, and they couldn't believe we had done it. I don't remember the year, '45, I think.

"Then a couple of years later, it came out that those Kentucky ballclubs had been shaving points, and some of them went to jail, and it turned out our game was one of those they shaved, and it got out of hand, and not only did Kentucky not cover the points, but they lost the game."

But MSU's media guide shows the Spartans losing twice to Kentucky in 1945 and splitting in '44, with the win in Lexington.

Memories are imperfect things, subject to the passage of time, to age and the way we want to remember things.

Pete Gent played on the great Dallas Cowboys teams when Tom Landry was undergoing the transformation from mortal to legend, and when he retired, Pete Gent dressed up those days just a little, changed names and wrote "North Dallas Forty." He played basketball for Michigan State University in the early 1960s, but his favorite memory of this old barn is his first.

"I was a kid from Bangor, and this place was huge to me. We beat Grand Rapids (Wyoming) Lee for the state championship here. I had a wonderful time at this place."

Gus Ganakas was the victim of the biggest tragedy that ever happened under this old metal roof. He was the coach when black players walked out one day in 1975.

But he remembers good times here.

"The first game I coached in here, as high school coach at East Lansing, and we beat River Rouge and Lofton Greene to climax a 24-0 season.... My first game as an assistant to John Benington because I was an alumnus ... and my first game as head coach. Those are my best memories.

"After that, I didn't have a lot of pleasant memories."

Memories.

And names from the past.

Fred Thomann.

Pat Miller.

Gregory Kelser.

Kevin Smith.

Carlton Valentine.

When they had introduced them all, the MSU band played Auld Lang Syne, and the former players waved at the crowd, and the crowd waved back, and a tear was shed here and there.

But what is historical to some is merely old to others.

Those who are legends to some are unknown to others. Old-timers.

Few in the crowd could tell you Frederick Cowles Jenison was a former MSU engineering student who died a millionaire and left his fortune to his alma mater. Someday, few here will be able to tell you who Jack Breslin was.

Time goes on, and it passes men by, and it passes buildings by, too.

A place must be made for the young and for the new.

Pete Gent, Nick Kerbawy and John Green are part of Michigan State's past.

And now Jenison Field House is, too.

They are memories.

Now it is time for Matt Steigenga and Steve Smith and Ken Redfield.

Now it is time for the Jack Breslin Student Events Center.

That is the way of things.

We are no one, and then — if we are lucky — we are someone for a while, then we are no one again.

Memories.

Old-timers.

Names from the past.

A time will come, in another century and recorded by another sports writer, when old men named Steigenga and Smith and Redfield will be introduced to a crowded arena, and a young man sipping soda through a straw will turn to someone near him and ask:

"Have you ever heard of any of those guys?" ❖

Bob Calihan

September 26, 1989

I can't honestly say I remember the first time I met Bob Calihan.

But I'm sure he was smiling.

He always was.

If you had come to Detroit in the past 10 years or so — or if you have never had any interest in the University of Detroit's athletic programs — you might not know Bob Calihan or who he was. That is your loss.

He died Friday.

I got the news in the Rose Bowl press box Saturday afternoon when I opened a copy of the Free Press, thoughtfully delivered by a late arrival for the Michigan-UCLA football game. Heart failure and pneumonia, the story said, had ended Calihan's life at 71.

And suddenly, to me at least, the things that would be happening with athletes the next few days were not very important. We get caught up in ourselves and in the things that happen with athletes and athletics. We get caught up in the flash and dazzle of sport, in promoting athletes and ourselves. And, in reality, I guess, there is nothing wrong with that.

Frivolity has a place in life.

Frivolity is a necessary counterpoint to reality. It is a balm for drudgery.

Sport and all the pseudo-importance we attach to it provide an escape. For a while, we can forget that "boss" even spelled backward is double-s-o-b. We can forget bills are due. We can make believe it matters how much Raghib (The Rocket) Ismail scores or how much Tony (The Racket) Mandarich talks.

But death is the ultimate reality, and when it strikes close to you, all that fluff of sport shrivels like so much cotton candy left too long on a damp day.

Bob Calihan's lifetime work was sports — basketball specifically — but he never took himself very seriously.

He was the University of Detroit's first All-America. He coached the school's basketball team for 21 years, then was athletic director. And long before his time was up on this planet, the people he had worked with for so long acknowledged his contribution to the school and their love for Bob Calihan by naming the university's field house after him.

He was the stereotypical Irishman: open, friendly, convivial, always with a smile and a handshake and a clap on the back. Always with a story.

He was, simply put, a fine man. He was buried at Holy Sepulchre Cemetery in Southfield.

When I first met him — in the winter of 1970 — he had just left coaching, turning that job over to Jim Harding, a man with a personality as stable as nitroglycerine.

Calihan sat in his office, just a few steps from the basketball floor where he had coached All-Americas Dorie Murrey and Norm Swanson and Guy Sparrow and Bill Ebben, and stayed out of Harding's way. He did the same a few years later when bombastic Dick Vitale came to town and took the Titans basketball team to even greater heights than Calihan had.

His office was filled with mementos of his achievements, but the two furnishings I remember best were the small refrigerator, always stocked with liquid Irish hospitality, and above it Calihan's favorite picture, of Dave DeBusschere guarding Spencer Haywood when both were stars in the NBA.

They were his foremost achievements as a coach, two young men who grew into manhood under his coaching at Detroit and went on to greatness in the NBA.

Over the years, I lost contact with Bob Calihan. He retired. I covered events at the University of Detroit less and less frequently.

We would bump into each other only every couple of years. But he always reacted as if he had missed me. Always a smile would split his face, and he would pump my hand and ask how I was doing, though it was he who was beyond retirement age and gamely getting along on arthritic limbs fitted with artificial joints.

Bob Calihan died the same day as Irving Berlin, and over the weekend every newspaper in the country ran an obituary of America's greatest songwriter. And at the two football games I attended on the West Coast over the weekend, I waited in vain for the bands to pay tribute to Berlin in the most obvious way — by substituting for the national anthem his stirring creation, "God Bless America."

Neither did.

But God has blessed America in many ways. We were all blessed in being touched by Berlin's music, and those of us who knew Calihan were blessed in being touched by his charm, his wit and his friendship.

God bless Irving Berlin.

God bless Bob Calihan. ❖

Bobby Knight

February 27, 1990

T his is personal, so I hope you will indulge me.

In the years since 1958 — when as a skinny, recently graduated-from-high-school 18-year-old I got my first newspaper job — I have interviewed thousands of pleasant, intelligent, articulate and helpful people and a few sour jerks. Men and women. Boys and girls. Black, white, brown. Baseball players and basketball coaches, archers, Olympians, football players and swimmers.

Some were professionals, some were amateurs.

Some were successful, some were trying to be.

Some had just won, some were drying tears of defeat.

Some were at the beginning of their careers, some were past the end.

Darryl Dawkins, Darrell Evans, Darryl Rogers and Darrell Royal.

Joe Morgan, Joe Dumars, Joe Namath and Jo Jo White.

Bubba Paris and Refrigerator Perry and Andre the Giant.

A.J. Foyt and O.J. Simpson and J.R. Reid.

Some had seen better days than the one on which I approached them.

Some did not want to be interviewed.

Some let me know it.

It goes with the territory, I always figured.

The readers of this newspaper don't care to hear my problems. You get out of bed every morning, too, and go to jobs that have to be a lot more demanding than this cushy thing I call a job.

So I always figured there was no call to share the trials of my day with you. That is a cross only my wife had to bear.

Today, I break my rule.

Today — if you read one word more — you will have to listen to the problems I have had with one man: Bobby Knight, basketball coach of the Indiana Hoosiers.

Every time I have been in his presence, he has gone out of his way to insult and demean the people around him, frequently his players, and always the media.

I am not sure I can even define the difference between profanity, vulgarity, cuss words and curse words. But I think Knight has used all of them in referring to the media. And he does it to our faces. And, make no mistake, he does not do it in the good-natured tone of buddies popping each other with towels and calling each other names in the locker room.

I have stood with amassed media in Indianapolis, Bloomington, Ann Arbor, East Lansing and in Los Angeles during the 1984 Olympics and suffered silently while he called us names.

I doubt he knows who I am, and that makes it even worse.

I am only one of those sons of bitches. And that is the most flattering thing he calls us.

Over the years, I have become more angry with myself and with the other people in my business who have done nothing to challenge this man than I am with him. He calls us names, and we giggle nervously.

We are afraid to confront him, I guess. I guess we think he is too intimidating, too strong, too defiant to challenge.

We would rather stand there and be sons of bitches.

Who gave him the right to call us that?

Who gave him the authority?

Being one of the best college coaches in the history of the game does not give him that power.

We gave him the power by standing there before him and nervously shuffling our feet, acting like gutless wimps, cowered by the power of his presence.

He called us SOBs again after Michigan State beat Indiana at the Breslin Center. I am ashamed to say we all cleared our throats nervously once again. We looked at our notepads, and not one of us said: Where do you get off with that?

Not one of us rose to say: I'm not going to listen to that from you anymore.

He had been asked whether the officiating hurt his team, and he replied: "The officiating didn't hurt anybody, and I'd like you sons of bitches to use that answer just once. If the question was important enough to ask, then use the answer."

Knight suffered an injured left thumb early in the game, wildly gesturing after he thought an official had missed a Michigan State foul. Joe Falls of the News asked Knight whether he had hurt the thumb.

Knight ignored the question. He did not look at Falls. He did not answer. He stood there before us collected sons of bitches in his imperial silence, daring the next person to speak.

"Can we use that answer, too, Bobby?" I asked.

He turned toward where I was standing, near the exit, and glowered, a black cloud of disapproval covering his face. "I don't have to take this," he said, leaving the podium and walking toward the door, keeping me fixed in his angry scowl all the while.

Probably he'll know this SOB on sight next time.

I think I have made a commitment now that will never allow me to stand silently again when he insults me individually or in a group.

That does not make me big or brave.

It just restores my pride. ❖

Eddie Robinson

September 6, 1990

Where everybody is somebody.
— Grambling State University motto

GRAMBLING, La. — Eddie Robinson does not want to recall the bad days, when he had to find a separate water fountain, a separate rest room, a separate restaurant.

Eddie Robinson has a philosophy that more militant men might argue with, but he has lived by it, and it has served him well.

"Anything is possible in our society if people are willing to pay the price," he said, running a weary hand through thinning hair. "Nobody's gonna give you anything. Oh, maybe they'll give you a free lunch, but you've got to stand in line.

"It's competition, whether you want to compete or not."

It is nearly 11 p.m., and the Grambling campus, nestled among a stand of northern Louisiana pines, is growing still, but Robinson, 71, is fervently preaching the doctrine he first espoused when he took over as football coach here in the fall of 1941.

He had been in California the day before to see Colorado play Tennessee in the 1990 opener and to receive another award. He flew through the night to Shreveport, held a noon press conference, drove 90 minutes east to Grambling and coached his football team in 100-degree heat, the nearest cloud hovering somewhere over Arkansas. He met with his coaches, went home to eat and wound up a day like so many others over the past 50 years.

Eddie Robinson has won more games than any other coach in the history of college football. And he is one of the most durable men in his sport. When he came to Grambling from a feed mill — the only job he could find when he graduated from Leland College in Baker, La. — black men and white men did not play football against each other. In some parts of the South, they did not speak to each other. Certainly they did not mingle more than necessary.

"I have feelings," he said, "but I'd rather say good things than bad things."

And that is as much as he will say about the days when racial injustice was accepted as a way of life in our land.

"I am not a Martin Luther King," he said. "I couldn't operate like that."

And he would not approve a couple of days later when Doug Williams — his most successful project, the first black quarterback to become an established starter in the NFL — was quoted in newspapers across North America as saying racism was still rampant in pro football.

Robinson has sent scores of players to the NFL, including Ernie Ladd, Buck Buchanan, Tank Younger, Charlie Joiner and Willie Davis. And he has taught thousands to play football. But he has tried to teach them more.

"Just being a football player isn't enough," he said, sitting in an office cluttered with trophies and awards. "You're a football player, but you're a man, and you're a citizen, and you owe as much as anybody else. To whom much is given, much is expected.

"I don't want a kid to walk away from here and say: 'All Eddie wanted was for me to play ball.' I want every one of them to be a better man and to get a degree."

Eddie Robinson, it seems, was born to coach. And to teach.

He was the first of his family to finish elementary school, and by the time he was in the fourth grade, he said, he knew he wanted to coach.

"I didn't have a choice about going to school," he said. "My daddy had the quickest belt in Baton Rouge. And he didn't just whip you, he'd talk to you. He'd say: 'I want you to be a good person.' And then whoop! 'You can grow up and do things on the street, and they'll put you in prison.' And there'd be another 'whoop!' "And I'd say, 'Well, just go ahead and whip me and don't talk to me.' And he'd say: 'Nooo.' And he'd whip awhile and talk awhile."

And you can see the pride and the appreciation and the love in his eyes.

He had never coached a down of football when Grambling hired him, so included in his first contract was a trip to a coaching clinic in Chicago, where the 22-year-old black coach approached Pappy Waldorf, one of college coaching's best of all time.

"He told me: 'You've got to get yourself a system. Take the plays you liked from the school where you went to college and the best plays from the schools you played against and put them in a binder and put your school's name on it and that's your system.'

"Boy, that train couldn't run fast enough to get me back to Grambling."

Success wasn't instant, though.

Grambling was 3-5 in Robinson's first season. But in 1942, the Tigers were undefeated in eight games, and Robinson has had only three losing seasons since.

Last Saturday's 42-13 victory over Alcorn State ran his record to 359-125-15.

But when you ask about successes, he will tell you about Willie Davis, who — after a Grambling counselor told him he did not have the mentality for business school — earned a master's degree in business from the University of Chicago. Or of the man who approached him at a Burger King in Ruston, La., a few weeks ago and thanked him for talking him into returning to school three times.

"When people feel you have been instrumental in them becoming somebody, that's what keeps your motor going," he said.

"You've got to tell them what is really happening. You've got to compete for jobs. You've got to be able to do the job. The guy's got to be prepared.

"I want them to know what's out there, if they're willing to pay the price. Sooner or later, you've got to decide if you're a part of this great nation or if you're holding back because you're black. I'm a part ... and I'm going to enjoy all the good things. I'm getting all the benefits. Hell, if you start talking about Americans, you've got to talk about Eddie Robinson because none of them are going to be better than I am. And none of them are going to love what we're all about more than I do.

"Everybody around the world ain't living the way we are. Everybody around the world ain't got the same rights we do. Everybody ain't employed the way we are. I talk this to my football team. I tell 'em the best thing that ever happened to them was to be born here.

"I don't believe any coach, whether he's white or black, can out-American me."

And there seems no reason to argue.

He has met Ronald Reagan and Gerald Ford, and after shaking Ford's hand, he refused to wash his right hand until he returned to Grambling.

He is proud of what he has achieved on a football field, but he has his own perspective on his accomplishments.

"When I got up to 300 wins," he said, "I got tired of looking at myself in the Shreveport and Monroe newspapers, not on the sports page but on the front page. Well, football is important and all that, but they didn't have to put me on the front page."

He teaches by example and by discipline. He finds nothing unusual in having his trainer count towels in the locker room before a road game — and after — to make sure none of his players is stealing. And on the field, his strongest words are hell and damn.

"I tell my players: 'You're going to school, you can find another word for those things,' " he said.

If, going into his 50th year of coaching, he has a concern, it is that his hands-on style of coaching has become antiquated.

He has half a dozen assistants now, but he paces the field, clipboard in hand, trying to oversee every phase of the game. Just like the old days.

"My style of coaching is past," he said. "There won't be many more people like me in football as head coach. I've got to know what the offense is going to do, what the defense is going to do, be a part of all of it, planning it. I've got to know what the play is. I've got to know what the defense is. I've got to know what coverage we're in."

You wonder if this man ever thinks of retirement, and he laughs in the night and says sure.

"Doris and I have had talks of retirement over 20 or more years," he said, referring to his wife. "We agreed that if I can continue to compete with the young coaches, I'll continue to coach. And I'm gonna work like hell not to let those people beat me so I can go on coaching.

"It's just been so much fun. I've been paid to play. I pity the guy who has a job that he doesn't enjoy doing.

"I'm happy as long as somebody gives me a team to coach." ❖

Bill Frieder

March 21, 1991

PHOENIX, Ariz. — More than anyone else I know, Bill Frieder has the world neatly divided into two camps: Those who are for him and those who are against him.

His friends and his enemies. You are one, or you are the other.

In Arizona, where he came to escape a lot of people who were becoming enemies back in Michigan, everyone is his friend.

Two seasons as Arizona State basketball coach have yielded an invitation to the National Invitation Tournament, one to the NCAA tournament and a growing number of adoring fans for the man who has revived a team once given up for dead. Bill Frieder, a man who loves to be loved, has found a new home.

"It's been a honeymoon," he said the other night at his 65-year-old remodeled adobe home in suburban Paradise Valley. "There has not been one thing negative in two years. The people here are so excited. It's all been terrific."

And for a man who felt unappreciated in his final years at the University of Michigan, the best feeling of all came last weekend in Atlanta, where the Sun Devils beat Rutgers before losing to Arkansas in the NCAA Southeast Regional.

It was in Atlanta that Frieder's world came apart two years ago, when he accepted Arizona State's coaching job before the NCAA tournament began and Michigan athletic director Bo Schembechler told him he could not coach the Wolverines in the tournament.

"I thought it was ironic that on the same day I resigned and was told I couldn't coach there, two years later to the day, March 15, I'm coaching there," Frieder said with the clear sound of satisfaction in his voice.

Schembechler, you see, is near the top of the list of people Frieder considers members of the enemy camp.

"Let's give Bo credit," Frieder said, with a sarcastic edge to his voice. "He did his situation a lot better than I did. He resigned just as football coach and got his new football man in there before he resigned as AD. So give him credit. He deceived and was a hero. I was honest and acted up-front and I was a jerk."

High on the list of foes, too, is much of the Detroit media, which he said wrote lies about him and implied he used negative recruiting tactics against U-M the past two years.

"I resent that. I have never, ever said anything negative about Michigan. I would never do that. I love the place too much. And that irritates me because I don't want those people to think that. They've been too good to me."

Some members of the U-M administration are on the enemies list, too, because Frieder saw them as obstructionists when it came to building a basketball team.

"You make enemies because you fight so hard for your program. I had to go over a lot of heads to get Terry Mills and Rumeal Robinson into school, and that made me some enemies. But the funny thing is when we won, those people were the ones out there on the floor hugging them and patting them on the back."

Suggest that it seems there is a clear line drawn between friend and foe and Frieder will concede: "Yeah, I've got that divided up pretty clearly."

And when you ask if it is possible to move from the enemies list to the friendly side, his wife, Janice, breaks in with the information: "It's difficult."

Frieder's us-versus-them mentality so permeates those around him that his 11-year-old daughter Laura, overhearing us talking about a Detroit sports writer, interrupted to ask: "Is he one of the good guys or is he a bad guy?"

At Arizona State, Bill Frieder is a savior, raising the Sun Devils' home attendance average from 3,700 to a record 8,588 this winter.

ASU basketball information director Mark Brand said more than 2,000 fans waited in the stands for an hour after the final home game for Frieder to return and address them.

"Never in 16 years at Michigan did I see anything like that," Frieder said, obviously pleased. "It was incredible. These people have been terrific."

In nine seasons as Michigan coach, Frieder won 191 games and took his team to five consecutive NCAA tournaments. But always it seemed there was criticism in the media and dissatisfaction in the stands.

"The negativism, whoever created it or how it happened, they were not satisfied with Bill Frieder, and we did a great job. They can't question that," he said. "So as a basketball coach, it was time to leave Michigan.

"Here, there hasn't been one negative thing in the media. Three of them have written, the last line has been, 'Thank you, Bo.' "

At the top of Frieder's list of friends is the man who hired him — Schembechler's predecessor as U-M athletic director — Don Canham.

"I love Canham," Frieder said. "I thrive on loyalty — that's why I love him. He's great. He hired me. He stayed with me early when we weren't doing well. He's a good man. I talk with him all the time."

By no means, though, is Canham the only Michigander on Frieder's friends list.

"Al Renfrew (U-M's assistant director of tickets) and Rockey Ross (a longtime U-M basketball supporter) are good people. We had more people in Atlanta from Michigan than we did from Arizona State. See, Arizona State is just learning. They haven't learned yet you drop travel plans, spring vacation and go to Atlanta and see the team. But all my Michigan people that used to go when I was the coach were there."

He is proudest, though, that some of his former players keep in touch.

"Rumeal Robinson came up to the hotel after we lost in Atlanta, and Gary Grant just called to say hello. Those things are nice."

On more precarious ground is his relationship with his former assistant coach, Steve Fisher, who succeeded him at U- M.

"Our relationship is good," Frieder said, "but I haven't talked to Steve a lot. But he's a great guy."

And though Frieder said he has "talked from time to time" with highly recruited Chris Webber of Birmingham Detroit Country Day, he said he "decided when I took the job, because of my friendship with Fisher, I didn't even want to recruit Michigan."

Now Texas and California are his primary recruiting areas, and Frieder hopes his old friends in Michigan understand when he says: "I'm a lot happier out here."

"They had 10 years of nothing here. I mean 10 years of a joke. I'm glad I did it, and people back there, I think, get the wrong idea. I love Michigan. It's a great university. It's been a part of my life half of my life. I went to more Michigan football games than Bo Schembechler because I went when I was a kid."

Frieder just finished the second year of a four-year contract, and Arizona State probably will offer a three-year extension during the summer. But he remembers Michigan, and he knows honeymoons do not last forever.

"If we build a monster here and they're booing me five years from now," he said, "I'm gonna shag out of here. I mean it's as simple as that. There's no reason not to be happy. Life is too short."

For now, he is happy in the Valley of the Sun. Ann Arbor and the University of Michigan are parts of his past. But he hasn't forgotten either.

And he hasn't forgotten his friends there.

Or his enemies. ❖

Higher education

September 19, 1992

The rain had beaten down upon the bus for half an hour, and the windows were left steamy and streaked, but if they looked hard, the 35 young men huddled inside that bus could see, on the other side of the football field, Harry B. Keidan Elementary School.

It was locked, filled only with classrooms of chairs stacked on top of empty desks.

Like all public schools in Detroit, it sat unused two weeks into what should be a new year of learning.

The halls were silent.

Grass grew tall on the lawn.

There were no children to disobey the sign on the front of the building: No Ball Playing.

But inside, the bus parked at McCabe Field on Detroit's west side, the young men in red jerseys and white pants were ready to represent Northern High School, though they hadn't seen the inside of a classroom since June.

Hadn't opened a school book in three months. Hadn't done a minute of homework.

While the Detroit school system is on strike, the Public School League is playing.

There is no science or geometry or literature, but there is golf and cross-country, football and girls basketball because the teachers union and the Detroit school board gave their blessing to sports while they continue to work on a new contract.

So John Dean and others like him have been preparing their football teams since Aug. 10.

"Sports supplies motivation to a lot of them," Dean said of the young men sharing the crowded bus with him. He is athletic director and football coach at Northern. He has been there since 1967, and he said: "If I spent as much time trying to make money as I've spent with these kids, I'd be close to a millionaire. But you've got to do what satisfies you as an individual."

Coaching young people satisfies Dean.

"We've worked them out a couple of hours every day," he said. He is proud that most of his players are not problems and several are honor students. But he acknowledges that too much free time could have been a problem to "a few of the kids we have."

"This," he said, "is something they can identify with, and we try to teach them not just football but the important lessons of life, too. We try to present a family front, and we teach them that we're all in this together. We teach them time management and how to act in public.

"But the only thing we've talked to them about in relation to the strike is that when they get back into the classroom, they've got to bear down. I tell the kids they have to work hard for a scholarship and extra hard to maintain it."

Dean is not a big man, but you sensed from the moment you stepped onto the bus that he is a man who has the respect and attention of the young men who play for him.

The field was turned into a swamp by the downpour, but when it was time to play, Dean stood and softly addressed his team.

"OK, we came over here for a business trip. Let's take care of business and get back home."

The response, from the 35 in unison, shook the bus.

"YES, SIR!!"

"Let's jump on them real fast and see if we can have them out of it by halftime."

"YES, SIR!!"

"Let's go out and play the best we can play and be the best we can be."

"YES, SIR!!"

"Now let's say a prayer. Our Father... ."

"OUR FATHER ... !!"

Dean has been through Detroit school strikes before. He's not exactly sure how many. "Four maybe," he said, wagging his head. "You just have to keep the faith."

If you're not an athlete or a coach or a parent, Public School League sports don't seem to count for much. Northern beat Northwestern, 31-8, in the rain and the mud and the slop of McCabe Field, but when I counted, there were just 43 people in the stands — and 12 were cheerleaders.

A few of the players will get a college education because of their football abilities. Dean said maybe eight of his 35 will play at some level in college.

But there is an unanswered question here: What does it say that the Detroit school system has its athletic programs in place but not its academic ones?

Dean laughed, his teeth flashed and, beneath the bill of the baseball cap he wore, his eyes twinkled mischievously.

"I wouldn't touch that one with a 10-foot pole," he said. "You can't get me to answer that one."

I'm not sure what it means, either.

I don't think it means the Detroit school system values athletics over academics. I hope it means it thinks the young people of the city deserve more than another month on the streets, another month with too much free time, another month without being able to prepare for their future.

Thousands of young people don't care enough to go to school here.

Thousands drop out and hang around on the streets and get into trouble, and we read about them not on the sports pages but in the crime reports or on the obituary page.

So it's neat that the people who run Detroit's schools are allowing their resources to be used for the good of their athletes. It's neat that their spare time and energy can be exhausted on the football fields.

But what about the student who just wants an education?

And what about the little kids who should be in class at Harry B. Keidan Elementary? ❖

The Tide turns

December 30, 1992

N EW ORLEANS — When they talk of their football team and their university, they talk of tradition. Of how Alabama has been a name to be reckoned with in sports for 100 years.

I know about Alabama tradition. My father played freshman football there and lettered in basketball, and on the Christmas before he died, I bought him a crimson sweatshirt with a big white ALABAMA across the chest, and he smiled at the memory of days long gone.

I knew about his pride in his home state and his school. When he enrolled in 1923, it seemed the natural thing to do. He had gone to Simpson High in Birmingham and led his team to two national high school basketball tournament appearances in Chicago. He had fit right in with the rest of Alabama's Roaring '20s athletes — hair slicked down and parted in the middle, all fiery-eyed and clean-cut and muscled.

They had another thing in common, too.

They were all white.

There would not be a black football player at the University of Alabama for another 48 years.

Legend says that changed on a September afternoon in 1970 when Paul (Bear) Bryant's Crimson Tide lost to Southern California in Birmingham, 42-21, because of the running of a brilliant black back named Sam Cunningham. The story goes that Bryant vowed to his assistant coaches that day: "I'll never lose again to a team because they have Negro players and I don't."

And in 1971, John Mitchell, a defensive end, became the first black to play football at Alabama.

By that time James Teague was starting a family, Robert Penchion was playing at Alcorn State, and Eddie Hall had given up the dream of playing football after high school.

When Alabama was voted national champion by United Press International in 1973, 13 blacks were in the team picture. Six years later, there were 20.

Of the 63 players pictured in Alabama's Sugar Bowl media guide this season, 34 are black, including the sons of James Teague and Eddie Hall and the nephew of Robert Penchion.

George Teague is Alabama's starting free safety and intercepted six passes this season. Lemanski Hall is a linebacker who led the team in tackles. Antonio Langham is a cornerback who matched Teague's six interceptions.

They are first-generation members of the Crimson Tide. The tradition they draw from is of recent vintage. It is not the tradition of Harry Gilmer and Joe Namath and Lee Roy Jordan and Slick Vincent.

Alabama blacks didn't pay much attention to college football at the "white schools" then.

"When Coach Bryant was there, I don't think blacks were tuned in to the tradition of Alabama football like they are now," Langham said. "Back then, they didn't realize what the tradition was. They might have known about Alabama football, but they didn't think much about it."

Alabama tradition to the black athlete is barely 20 years old. It is the tradition of Siran Stacy and Ozzie Newsome and Bobby Humphrey, athletes who — had they been born a few years sooner — would not have been a part of the school's football history.

Lemanski Hall's father was a running back at an all-black high school. Hall, a 6-foot-1, 220-pound linebacker, said: "I was recruited by Auburn, but once I made my visit to Alabama, that's where I wanted to go. I fell in love with the Alabama tradition when I visited there.

"My parents call me Shun. We talk about the past sometimes. They've told me: 'Shun, we're so proud of you. Back then we never had the opportunity you've got, and it's important that you do well with it, in the classroom and on the field.' "

Antonio Langham grew up in Town Creek, Ala., a wide spot in the road where he is such a celebrity that the manager of a Red Lobster restaurant once got on the public address system and announced Langham's presence to everyone there.

Robert Penchion is his uncle. Penchion was talented enough to play guard for the Buffalo Bills for a couple of seasons in the early '70s, but when he graduated from high school, no "white" university in Alabama was interested.

"We don't talk about that much, though, when we get together," Langham said. "We talk mostly about what things are like in the NFL and the things I need to work on."

It is history. The past. Why dwell on it — on unpleasantness?

George Teague doesn't know much about his father's football career. Or about what happened long, long ago, in 1970.

"He just did what all the kids he knew did back then," Teague said. "He went into the service."

Gene Stallings has re-created the tradition of the Bear Bryant years. The winning. Then pride. The competitiveness.

And in a lot of ways, he is the reflection of his old coach.

When Stallings took his first head-coaching job, rebuilding a troubled team at Texas A&M in 1965 — just as integration was beginning in the Southwest Conference — he said he would not pursue black athletes.

"I have nothing against the Negro athlete," he said. "But I don't believe he fits into our plans here at A&M right now. What we need is a team that will work and pull and fight together and really get a feeling of oneness. We need to be a complete unit. I don't think we could accomplish this with a Negro on the squad."

Times change, and people do, too.

The wheels of justice grind. ❖

Wide World of Sports

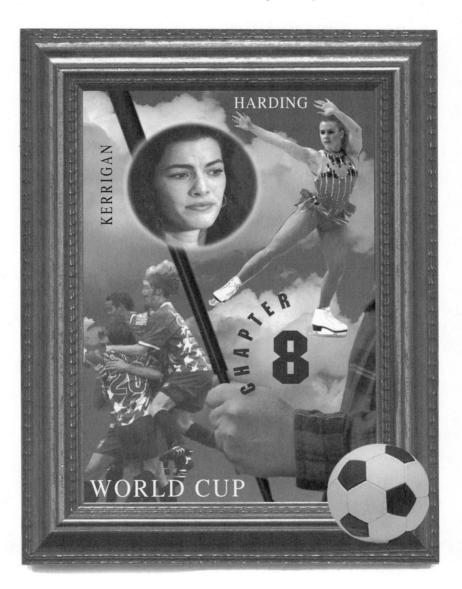

KERRIGAN

HARDING

CHAPTER

8

WORLD CUP

Five-ring circus

January 13, 1980

L AKE PLACID, N.Y. — Joe Pacitti hoisted his ample body onto the stool at the end of the Woodshed Tavern bar and ordered a couple of brandies.

He toyed with the tips of his walrus-sized mustache, lifted a glass to his lips and sighed as the warming liquid began to counteract the effects of the Lake Placid winter.

"It's all fake, chicanery to a degree," he began, describing his job as technical chief of the Winter Olympics ceremonies and awards presentations. "It's all false, more or less, because we've programmed it. We have this, that and the other thing — like we know how to make the elephant disappear."

Pacitti's job is to make goose bumps rise on your arms as you watch the opening ceremonies of the XIII Winter Olympic Games.

"It's pretty much a seven-day-a-week job," he said. So when he isn't in his office overlooking Mirror Lake, he can be found at the end of the bar in the Woodshed — within arm's length of the pay phone he uses as an auxiliary office.

Pacitti knows to the second what is supposed to happen in the Olympic Stadium. And he was beginning to get a few butterflies because his presentation was likely to be witnessed by the largest television audience in history.

"Nine hundred million — maybe even a billion with the Chinese coming," he estimated. "It will be the world's largest single watched event until that time, but it will probably be broken by the Summer Olympics."

Pacitti has the whole thing programmed in his head. He has pictured how it will happen over and over during the past year. Still, he knows there will be a flaw here, a mistake there, that could potentially detract from the drama.

"I know something won't come off the way we have it on paper," he conceded, sipping on the brandy. "But we'll come up with something at the last minute if we have to. Then, when it's over, we'll sit down and say: 'Gee, if we'd have done this, it would have been so great!' "

What they have planned is an ambitious undertaking, calculated to get the Winter Olympic Games off to a rousing start.

"It's like a mini-story," he said. "It's got a beginning, middle and an end — in an hour and ten minutes, it's over."

The tableau parades through his mind, and he tries to paint it in words.

"First there is the entry of the dignitaries. Lord Killanin (president of the International Olympic Committee), Rev. Bernie Feld (president of the Lake Placid Olympic Organizing Committee) and President Carter, if he can be here.

"There'll be a welcome. They'll say: 'How are you?' and this and that and the other thing, and then there'll be the parade of nations.

"Greece will be the first, followed by the other nations in alphabetical order, with the exception of the host country, which always enters last. As each nation enters the stadium, the first thing you will see is that country's flag, followed by the placard carrier, carrying the nation's name.

"With the mountains behind, it's as natural a setting as you can get with 22,000 people there.

"Then we bring in the International Olympic Committee flag, carried by 12 boy scouts and escorted by 12 champions from both the Winter and Summer Olympics, like Art Devlin and Sheila Young Ochowicz. While that is going on, the 120-piece orchestra and 450-voice choir from the Crane School of Music in Potsdam (N.Y.) will sing and play the Olympic Hymn.

"Then comes the person picked out of the 52 flame carriers who will run into the stadium carrying the Olympic flame. He will circle the stadium, then — walking between an honor guard formed by the other torch bearers — will ascend the steps and walk to the caldron.

"The caldron slowly rises to the top of its 45-foot tower, and when it gets to the top, we will release 2,000 pigeons with the message: 'The XIII Olympic Games in Lake Placid, N.Y., have begun.'

"They will circle the field, braving wind and rain and hawks — they have a bit of trouble with hawks — and return to their homes.

"Next comes the Olympic oath by an athlete and official of the host nation. They will grasp a corner of the American flag, and the athlete will say he's going to compete in the spirit of the Games, and the official will say he's going to be impartial and so on and so on and so on.

"Then we exchange the Olympic flag, which first flew in Oslo. The mayor of Innsbruck, where the flag has been since the 1976 Games, will come on the field accompanied by a Tyrolean band, and he will present the flag to Robert Peacock, mayor of Lake Placid, who will be accompanied by the Fort Ticonderoga Fife and Drum Corps.

"They'll drink a little schnapps while there's a little ice ballet going on in the middle of the grounds.

"That's about it, except for the grand finale, when we send up 40 hot air balloons, each trailing a banner of a competing country."

Through every second of the 70-minute ceremony, Pacitti will be backstage, holding his breath and crossing his fingers.

And to Pacitti, who served as director of the Julliard School of Music's stage department for eight years, the brief spectacle will be every bit as thrilling as it is to the millions for whom he prepared it.

"The feeling that is created there, I don't think it will ever leave," he said, draining the brandy glass. "I could get real romantic about it if I'd like." ❖

Linda Fratianne

February 12, 1980

LAKE PLACID, N.Y. — The scene was bizarre.

A perfectly sculpted 19-year-old girl, clutching a white fur coat and a Dior handbag, was surrounded in the stairwell of the Olympic cafeteria in the basement of Lake Placid High.

The mob of reporters pushed and shoved around her, at times teetering on the steps with only a toehold, while she cooly flashed a toothy smile.

This is what Linda Fratianne has been programmed for. During the past four years, she has been constructed piece-by-piece.

Dick Button, the onetime Olympic skating champion, called her flashing dark eyes, "the most beautiful in America." Her thoroughly Italian nose was bobbed to enhance her appearance. Her coach, Frank Carroll, dictated her hairstyle and selects outfits he feels best show her 5-foot-1, 97-pound physique.

Now the day is at hand.

Through most of her teenage years, her life has been devoted to winning the gold medal in women's figure skating in the XIII Olympic Games.

Carroll and Linda's mother, Virginia, have supervised the creation of an ice skating goddess, and, in the process, her father, Robert, was made to feel left out, useless and unnecessary in both their lives.

Last spring, he moved out of their Northridge, Calif., home, a casualty of Linda's success.

Before every competition, though, he still sends her a bouquet of roses and a card.

"I went through a hard time," Linda said. "I thought things like this only happened to other people. We were supposed to be the All-American family, you know? I went through this big guilt thing. I just went really crazy, totally out of it.

"I cried myself to sleep every night. I went to someone about it, and she showed me that it wasn't my fault at all. I don't cry about it anymore. I haven't cried in a long time, and it won't affect me in the Olympics. It's past."

There have been other casualties along the way, too. Lisa-Marie Allen went to school with Linda at Valley Professional School in Los Angeles. She was the valedictorian of their five-student class, and she is the second-best women's singles skater in the United States.

When they speak, though, it is not a pleasant exchange. They make no secret of their dislike for each other, though Linda will say nothing more than: "I was taught that if you don't have something nice to say about someone, don't say anything at all."

Nothing — certainly not a rivalry with an old classmate — is as important as the Olympic gold.

Four years ago, Fratianne was eighth in the Innsbruck Games. But she was world champion in 1977 and again last year, and there is little doubt that she will reach her ultimate goal next week.

She has to.

She does not regret devoting herself singularly to the quest for the Olympic championship. But she doubts she could go through another four years of nearly monastic existence.

"At the top, they expect so much of you," she said with only a hint of uneasiness.

"This Olympics is something I've aspired for all my life. When the day comes, I'll just put everything into it.

"But this last four years has been very difficult. It's one road, one path, and I've just stayed on it as best I can. The '80 Olympics is something I've set aside. My mind is so geared for it.

"But it would be very difficult to push myself another four years."

If she has to push herself the next four years, she will not do it for free. She will follow in the footsteps of Dorothy Hamill and Peggy Fleming — skating for dollars. Big dollars.

She doesn't want to get ahead of herself and talk about that. Not until she holds the gold in her hand.

But she is very aware of what she has to do. And she is very aware that she has been given all the tools to reach her goal.

The poise, the composure, the bobbed hair and nose, the flashing smile, the costumes.

"Appearance is part of it," she conceded. "If you go out in a not-so-pretty dress and you skate well, you won't score as well as someone with confidence, who knows she's good.

"If I'm skating well, you see me smile."

Next week, when the spotlight catches her at the center of the Olympic Arena ice and the television cameras follow every movement, the crowd will be with her.

The smile will come. And with it the gold.

And somewhere Robert Fratianne will feel a rush of pride.

Fratianne won the silver medal, finishing behind Anett Potzcsh of East Germany. ❖

The competition

March 11, 1987

C INCINNATI — I was 14, I think, an eighth-grader who loved sports and believed that some day — if I worked hard enough — I could be a good athlete.

When we had to run laps in phys ed classes, I was always near the front of the pack. I didn't know most of the kids thought it was a chore to be shrugged off with a curse and a weak effort.

So in the misguided belief that I was fast, I went out for the track team. I ran the quarter-mile. I ran it very slowly. Most of my athletic career is a fogged memory. It was, after all, more than three decades ago, when the four-minute mile was about to be broken, television was black-and-white and people still talked about the Korean War.

But I remember one Saturday afternoon well.

We were getting plastered in a little meet — it seems three or four schools were in it — and I was just passing the time until my event was called, when I happened to walk up behind my coach, just as he began speaking to the host coach:

"Do you mind if we make a switch in the 440?" I heard him say. "I've got a sure last place entered, and I'd like to make a change."

When he turned and saw me standing there, he got this strange look on his face, and I realized he was talking about me. I hadn't known I was a "sure last place." I thought I could beat some of those people.

Of course, I never found out. I watched from the infield as the guy who replaced me finished last. Sure last place?

I don't remember much more about that track season. I don't know if I ever beat anybody. Maybe I was last in every race I ran.

But I do remember trying. I remember wanting to compete. I remember wanting to have a chance.

And I remember feeling anger and hurt and embarrassment that somebody thought I wasn't even good enough to have a chance.

That's why I have a soft place in my heart this week for Chi-Man Wong.

He is a 30-year-old fashion designer from Hong Kong.

And if there is such a thing as a sure last place in the men's competition at the World Figure Skating Championships this week, he is it.

When the 27 competitors for the men's championship were asked to do three sets of compulsory figures earlier this week, he finished 27th in each. He was last again, scoring 0.4s and 0.5s, in his short routine while the rest were routinely in the 4s and 5s.

This is the first international meet Chi-Man Wong has entered.

When he was 16, he saw a figure-skating competition on television and fell in love with the artistry and gracefulness of the sport.

But then, as now, Hong Kong had no figure-skating coach. And there is only one skating rink, a cozy 30-by-70-foot affair, where the ice sometimes gets slushy and the Zamboni works only occasionally.

So Chi-Man Wong taught himself, with little more than the television pictures he had seen as a guide. For years he skated alone because there were no figure-skating competitions in his part of the world.

"Because Hong Kong's weather is so hot in the summer," he said, "sometimes the rink is more like a pool. The ice is not perfect like it is here."

I talked to him after a practice. Skaters practice in groups here, and among his group is Brian Orser, the Canadian who is one of three skaters given a chance to win the world championship.

The other skaters practiced double and triple spins; Chi-Man Wong began with a half-revolution.

Other skaters leaped into the air; Chi-Man Wong's skates barely left the ice.

And when he finally did attempt a complete spin, he fell. And when he tried it a second time, he fell again, then picked himself up and dusted the ice shavings off the seat of his pants.

He skated for only about 30 of the 45 minutes allotted, then leaned against a railing and watched the others do things he cannot. And when Orser finished practicing his four-minute free-skating routine, Chi-Man Wong joined the spectators in applauding his ability.

"He is very good," Chi-Man Wong said. "Every other competitor started out at an early time, seven or 10, and has his coach a long time with him. That is very common.

"I started too late. In my case, we just have to get experience here, because for everything there is a first time."

Being here is a triumph for Chi-Man Wong. Being here means he has a chance.

Wouldn't it be neat if he could beat just one person? ❖

Jill Trenary

March 14, 1987

CINCINNATI — CBS will televise the women's World Figure Skating Championships tonight.

There will be beauty in it, and a certain amount of drama. But it cannot rival the mighty documentary of human emotion CBS could have captured had it kept its cameras with Jill Trenary the past few days.

Trenary is an 18-year-old high school senior from Minnesota who last month unexpectedly won the United States women's championship and came here floating on a cloud.

In 1985, she was told she would never again walk without a limp, the result of a midair collision with another skater that left her left calf slashed to the bone.

With hard work and patience and more hard work, she overcame that and last month won the U.S. championship from Debi Thomas.

And now she is acknowledged as one of the best figure skaters in the world. Roll the cameras.

Trenary steps onto the ice at Sabin Convention Center. The exercise is compulsory figures, the tracing in the ice of precise loops while a panel of eight judges watches.

Soon after she begins, Trenary's skate slips and she misses her mark. She misses not by a millimeter or a eyelash. She misses by six inches.

At this level of competition, that single mistake determines that she will not win the world championship. And in front of the judges and a few hundred fans, all the bravado runs out of Jill Trenary, like a burst bag of salt.

Zoom in for a close-up.

Tears well up in her eyes and — after finishing the worst set of figures in her career — she walks as fast as her skates will carry her to the dressing room, ignoring the autograph-seekers, pens and programs in their outstretched hands.

Fade to black and hear only the sound of sobs coming from the dressing room.

Twice more she had to return to the ice and trace different sets of figures. Twice more the judges came with their pads and their pencils and looked for her mistakes. Each time they looked as if they were seeing what your neighbor's dog leaves on your lawn.

Of 27 contestants, the American champion placed 12th on the first figure, sixth on the second, 11th on the third and was hopelessly behind long before she got into the spotlight of Riverside Coliseum, where tonight's finals will be held.

Suddenly, she was yesterday's news. Last month's champion. History.

Roll the cameras again.

Bundled in the Navy jacket that is standard winter gear of the U.S. figure skating team, Jill Trenary walks quickly down the steps of Sabin Convention Center, into the afternoon sunlight, her father's protective arm around her shoulder. She is trying not to cry anymore. But she is 18, and she has failed. And she can't help herself.

As shoppers stride by on the crowded sidewalk, she buries her head on her father's shoulder and lets the tears come.

"Would you look at this," a man says to a woman.

"Oh, poor thing," says an elderly woman walking by.

Fade out.

Now Jill Trenary is concluding her short program before 14,000 in the Riverside Coliseum.

She has skated well enough to move up to eighth, but even as the waves of applause wash over her and she skates off the ice, she knows there will be no medal for her.

Roll 'em.

"I'm really pleased with the way I skated, being I was so down," she tells a half-dozen reporters who gather around her. "I had a lot of talking done to me in the last couple of days. Because I won national a month ago, it's hard being 11th in figures.

"I went through one phase this morning when I thought, 'Oh, God, I have nothing to lose.' Then I broke down before we came. But the more I cried, the better I felt."

She's not smiling, but she's trying.

"I just wanted to show them today I can skate. It's good to lose, I guess; it builds character. You have to prove to other people and to yourself that you're tough."

Keep the camera on her as she walks toward the ice tonight for her four minutes in the spotlight.

And at the bottom of the screen put the words:

To be continued.

Trenary stayed with it and finished fourth at the 1988 Winter Olympics. ❖

Greg Louganis

July 17, 1987

DURHAM, N.C. — The price of success and fame is exacting enough on the body. It demands work and sacrifice and sweat and, sometimes, blood.

But what it demands of the mind can be measured only in fitful nights and sweaty palms and sometimes-irrational thoughts tumbling over one another because it is in the mind where the awful fear of failure resides.

Success carries with it the insatiable need to succeed again. And again. And again.

Succeed or be called a failure.

Greg Louganis has been a performer since he was 3 and one of the world's best divers for the past 11 years.

He has won 41 national titles and five world championships.

He has stood on the diving board, surrounded by the deafening silence of worshipful fans, and heard voices inside his head asking whether he really was good at what he was doing.

He has climbed, dripping wet, from pools around the world and heard cheers that most can only imagine. And he has retreated into the security blanket of cigarettes and alcohol and teddy bears.

There were times when his success brought less joy than anxiety. Was he really an outstanding diver? Could he stay that good? What if he messed up?

What if somebody beat him? What if he let people down?

"So many times, once I get to the end of the platform, I'm more afraid of failure than anything else," Louganis said before the U.S. Olympic Festival three-meter springboard diving preliminaries in Raleigh. He then made four perfect dives and outdistanced his nearest competitor by more than 60 points.

"I worry that I'm going to do a cannonball or something like that. The last thing I tell myself is, 'No matter what happens, my mother is still going to love me.'

"And knowing somebody is going to be there, no matter what, makes it easier."

Greg Louganis is 27, his hair is flecked with gray. The younger divers call him "Grandpa." This is his seventh Olympic Festival, a stepping-stone to what he hopes will be his third Olympics.

Gone, he said, are many of the demons that nipped at his soul. It has been four years since he quit leaning on smoking and drinking to reduce his self-doubts. And he has given his friend and confidant, Garfield the teddy bear, to a boy in a California children's hospital.

But the memories are still there. And the pressure to succeed has not really diminished.

It is the price he pays for the rest of it.

He tells of a "sweet older couple" who attend meets around the country. "The older gentleman came up to me at one meet and said: 'I hope you're going to dive better today. In the last meet you were getting 7.5s, and I was so disgusted that I left.' "

He tells of how in 1984, when he won two gold medals in the Los Angeles Olympics, "Gar (the teddy bear) gave me a lot of strength" to overcome doubts and fears.

He tells of days when he wanted to walk away from it all. Of days when he just "didn't want to get wet." And of standing on a diving board in Syracuse one day and realizing: "I didn't want to be there."

He has come to terms with that, he said. He has stepped back from his sport just enough to realize he can enjoy it, if he does not allow it to suffocate him.

"Diving isn't my life," he said. "It isn't everything. It used to be. I was so obsessed with diving, if I had a good workout, I had a good day. If I had a bad workout, I had a bad day.

"Now I've found other things to feel good about myself about."

Those things are dancing and acting.

He made one film, a yet-to-be-released comedy called "Dirty Laundry," in which he said he plays "a beach bum womanizer." He smiles at the disparity between that role and his image.

In October, he will make his professional dancing debut, in Indianapolis, an event to which he looks forward with obvious delight.

It will be a new stage for Louganis, who, it seems, has always been on a stage of one sort or another. Singing and dancing when he was only 3; a gymnast by the time he was 7 and a diver when he became a teenager.

He is, he said, more performer than athlete. "I had to learn to compete, and I learned that from Bruce Kimball," Louganis said of the Ann Arbor diver who won an Olympic silver medal in Los Angeles.

If you listen to Greg Louganis, the performer, long enough, you wonder whether — despite the purging of the cigarettes, the alcohol and the teddy bear — he has come to grips with the pressures of competition.

They rattled about in his soul last winter when he failed to win any of the three U.S. national indoor diving championships.

"I was second in the one-meter, and I told myself: 'It's no big deal. It doesn't count.' But it bothered me more than I allowed myself to believe. I started to have doubts: 'Oh, my god, am I too old for this?' I started not believing in myself, and it had an adverse effect on my performance throughout the meet. It really tested my commitment to continue to dive."

A week later, in the World Cup championships in the Netherlands, he found himself almost hopelessly behind a Chinese diver with one dive remaining. "I was, basically, up a creek," he said. But he made what he calls one of the best dives of his career, won the title and, for another day at least, put the demons behind him.

This is, it seems, a trial he must put himself through. A ritual to test his worthiness. His manhood, maybe, or his spirit. Or his heart. Or his soul.

"You test your own strength," he said. "You test your own mental toughness. It's something a lot of people never do.

"That's exciting."

And tough. Very, very tough.

Louganis won two gold medals at the '88 Olympics, and in 1993 he starred Off-Broadway as a gay chorus boy dying of AIDS in the award-winning play "Jeffrey." ❖

Debi Thomas

January 13, 1990

Eleven years they had been together, and when they split up, it was, the man said, "kind of like a divorce."

He was older than she. Much older.

And though the split might have seemed like a divorce to him, there was never anything personal between the two.

He was her teacher. Her maestro. Her chaperon.

He began when she was 9 years old. He strapped skates on her feet. He took her arms and moved them first into this position, then into that. He glided across the ice with her in dark and cold ice arenas. Together they worked. And, year by year, she got better. Year by year, more and more people said their names.

He was Alex McGowan.

She was Debi Thomas.

Together, they were to win the gold medal in ladies figure skating at the 1988 Olympics in Calgary. That was the plan.

They disagreed before they got there, though. And they argued almost as the spotlight sought her out on the glistening ice.

So when it was over and Debi Thomas and Alex McGowan had to settle for third place in their one and only Olympics together, they split up.

And today — two years later — they still have only nasty things to say about each other.

"He never, ever knew me," Thomas said on her way to Detroit for tonight's Stars On Ice show at Joe Louis Arena. "He never knew what made me tick, what my goals were or what I wanted to accomplish with my skating.

"He wanted to win the gold medal more than I did."

McGowan now is figure skating director at Fraser Skating Club, but he won't see Thomas skate in Detroit. He is at the Midwest figure skating regionals in Minneapolis with a new group of teenage protegees, looking for a new Debi Thomas.

"I sent her a Christmas card and wrote her twice," McGowan said of their post-Olympic breakup, "but there was never any communication, so I stopped writing.

"I gave her lots of money, and I was never repaid or even thanked. She has made close to $1 million, and I got nothing. I taught her from age 9 through 21, and when it ended, it was kind of like a divorce."

Thomas was America's darling two years ago, the young woman from the broken home and the modest background who had overcome every obstacle except Katarina Witt, the great East German.

Thomas had won the national and world championships at 18, had slipped some the next year because of tendinitis in both ankles, but recaptured the national title six weeks before the Olympics.

Mikhail Baryshnikov had helped her achieve more grace. But always it seemed there was, somewhere deep within her, doubt.

Discouraged with her progress, she tore up her application for the nationals in 1986. But her mother, Janice, consoled her, comforted her, encouraged her, then taped the shredded entry form back together, ironed it smooth and sent it in. That was the year Thomas won her first national title. And her only world championship.

Once McGowan scolded her: "If you train as much as other skaters, you will be unbeatable."

"But," she responded, "then I wouldn't be happy. I need balance in my life."

That was a disagreement they never resolved.

Once he accused her of skating like a jelly bean and a wimp.

He asked her to be a tigress on the ice. And, she said, she tried.

But it was not her.

"I had a hard time sticking with it," she said. "It was almost too much. Like I was sick of it. That's probably one of the problems I had at the Olympics.

"It would have been nice to have been excited about the whole thing. I felt comfortable with myself and how I trained, but Mr. McGowan didn't agree. We spent more time arguing than working on the routine. I needed someone to be supportive. I got sick of him telling me what was wrong with my figures when I already knew what was wrong."

An 11-year relationship was unraveling as the big night in Calgary approached.

McGowan demanded more work.

"I trained her to the best of my ability," he said. "And it was good enough to win two nationals and one world."

But Thomas, a 20-year-old left unjaded by years of traveling the world for competitions, wanted to enjoy the time in Calgary.

"I wanted to enjoy the Olympics, to feel like I was a part of it," she said. "But we went from Calgary back to Colorado to train, and then back to

Calgary. He wanted extra ice time and, in the end, we did it his way."

On the night they had worked 11 years to achieve, Debi Thomas caught her toe on the ice early in her routine, and a single thought engulfed her mind.

"It took all the spirit out of me," she said. "It was like: 'Can I start over?' That's what I always did in training. There was no use."

She was overtrained, she said.

He said: "She didn't skate well, and she looked for excuses."

All marriages do not work out.

And all American dreams do not come true.

It is sad.

But it is life. And life, despite the setbacks, does go on. ❖

Road game

June 18, 1990

F ERNETTI, Italy — It was several hours past closing time at the little bar high in the mountains above Trieste. But Leo had found an accordion, the wine was still pouring from the tap behind the bar and their singing could be heard across the Yugoslavian border a few hundred yards away.

Leo pumped the bellows faster and faster, and his friends — Franco and George, Horst and Dieter, Robert and Walter, Joe and Klaus, Dieter and Lothar, Manfred and George and John — wrapped their arms around each others' waists and danced and sang the night away.

They had come a great length for this — from Sterling Heights and Lathrup Village and Orchard Lake and Mount Clemens and Royal Oak, 14 friends gone to the World Cup, but gone, too, to do it one better.

They are all members of Sports Club 24, an organization founded 66 years ago in Detroit to bind new Americans — primarily from Germany. And the glue that binds these people, each born in Europe just before or during World War II, is soccer.

They are not young. Even they will admit that.

The oldest is 57, the youngest, 47. And tonight they sing and drink and let the night slip into the tomorrow when they play soccer.

Saturday is for partying.

Sunday is for sport.

True sport.

The way sport was supposed to be before the Yankee dollar and the Italian lira and the German mark turned it into something else.

Who knows what thoughts were in their heads when they lay them on their pillows in Sunday's early morning hours?

Perhaps they slept a peaceful sleep.

Perhaps they dreamed only of the game that would be played in the afternoon's searing heat, on a gravel field at a boys home in Opicina — another of Trieste's hillside suburbs — against Sant'Andrea Football Club.

Perhaps they dreamed of their childhoods — of bombs bursting in their neighborhoods.

Perhaps John Benesch dreamed of what he had seen for the first time just a few days before: the grave of his father, a German soldier, who was killed when he was 5 years old.

Perhaps Manfred Nitsche was dreaming of his first day in Detroit, when — understanding only a few words of English — he picked up a copy of the Free Press and began to walk away with it "just to look at the pictures" and was grabbed by an angry newsstand vendor and told the Free Press was not free.

Perhaps Franco Pertot, born just down the mountain in Trieste — here to see his ailing mother as well as to play soccer — dreamed of the day 31 years ago when as an adventurous 19-year-old he left this sliver of Italy, clinging by its fingernails to the coastline between Yugoslavia and the Gulf of Venice, singing as the train pulled out of the station and tears ran down his mother's face.

One-by-one, refugees of one kind or another, they came to America's shores. And to Detroit.

George Sepetys was first, leaving Lithuania as a 14-year-old in 1950.

For each, soccer was an anchor, a link to his heritage, a place where they could feel at home in a strange land.

"Soccer," said Dieter Dittmar, "is my psychiatrist."

They came to Italy 10 days ago to watch World Cup matches in Milan. But they were more ambitious than that, and more interested in sport. So they found teams to play near Trieste and in Rorschach, Switzerland, near where George Wohlwend grew up, and in Oelbronn, Germany, near where Horst Lehrer was born.

They looked for teams of players like themselves — whose game skills had waned, but whose love for the game had not.

They are here for fun and friendship and all those things that sport is supposed to be.

What I saw on that hot and hard little field in the hills above Trieste was not the World Cup.

That's exactly what I was counting on. It was, instead, sport the way sport was meant to be.

Eleven people sat in the stands.

For two hours, the teams ran up and down and sweat poured off players competing not for a dollar but because they loved to play. And, in a way, they loved each other.

Klaus Menzel explained it best when he said: "You cannot buy a situation like this for a million dollars."

Sport Club 24 scored its only goal when Leo Sklena — the accordionist and a native of Yugoslavia — dribbled past two defenders and sent a shot by the Sant'Andrea goalkeeper.

The final score was 1-1, but it was not a tie — it was a 1-1 win. For everyone.

And when it was over, 28 weary players exchanged sweaty handshakes and smiles on the rock-hard field where each had given his best to be better than the other.

They trudged 100 yards, and speaking English and German and Italian — but understanding little except the goodwill they felt — settled beneath a giant shade tree and exchanged gifts.

They opened beer and wine and cut raisin bread and laughed together — and shared a moment few professional athletes will ever know. ❖

East meets West

July 6, 1990

EAST BERLIN — Chunk!
Chunk!
Clang!
Chunk!
Clang!

It was in the distance, a noise that almost defied description.

It was joyous destruction in the midday sun.

It was the sound of metal on metal and metal on concrete. Hammer on chisel and chisel on a damnable wall.

I was a couple of hundred yards to the east of where Checkpoint Charlie used to stand when I first heard it. It was obvious that demolition was in progress, but I had to get much closer to realize what kind of demolition.

Next to those portions of the Berlin Wall still standing, enterprising capitalists rent a hammer and chisel for 15 minutes. The price is about $3.30 American, and you are free to do your part for democracy and capitalism and pocket a piece of history in the process.

I bought 15 minutes' worth.

Breaking down a wall is hard work. I left with only a few chips in my pocket. But they were the most coveted kind — colored with flecks of paint from the graffiti that grew on the wall over the years, like a fungus of protest.

I thought that was great — an official piece of the Berlin Wall, tinged with an official paint fragment of graffiti.

Then I smelled something. I looked around, and behind me was one of the enterprising capitalist hammer-and-chisel renters spray-painting a portion of blank wall.

Capitalism has just arrived in the eastern part of this reunited city, but it is easy to learn. Give people what they want? No. Sell people what they want.

I do not know what it was like in East Berlin a year ago or five or 20. I only know what I have read and heard and the pictures I have seen.

But I know what is there today.

Last weekend, the two Germanys unified their currency. Then all passport and identification checks at the old borders ceased.

Centrum Department Store on Alexanderplatz, several miles into the East, began selling Western-style goods for the first time, and shoppers I saw stood in awe of the variety before them. In huge groups they gathered before the shelves of unfamiliar merchandise, picked it up, fingered it, felt it, read the labels, looked at the price. Some bought, some only looked.

The only shortage I saw was in shopping carts. I saw people lined up outside a grocery and did not know why until I saw the woman at the head of the line pounce on a cart deposited at the doorstep by a departing shopper.

All along the streets are stands selling fresh fruit: peaches and bananas, strawberries and pineapples.

The other day, I got on a train in the center of West Berlin and rode it right into Alexanderplatz.

For 29 years, nobody could do that.

For 29 years, the train and subway system that serpentines over and under the streets of this city was severed at the Wall.

Then one day it changed.

Overnight.

Capitalism and maybe even democracy rushed into the East through gaps in that damnable wall, breached by a determined people.

In Alexanderplatz you can buy a shish kebab, sausage, beer and Coke for about $4.65 American — but only after the vendors discuss the charge for a moment, still unsure of values just days after their currency had disappeared and been replaced with the money of the West.

Young men who grew up under the Eastern system, influenced by the Soviets for so many years, now open folding tables in the shadow of the Brandenburg Gate and spread out — for sale — Soviet military hats and fur caps.

In the heart of East Berlin is a shop that sells nothing but Lacoste clothing. A few miles away, apparently not influenced by the changes, is a storefront bearing the utilitarian name: Boutique No. 140.

Travel agencies are promoting travel to Paris and London and Rome, cities off-limits to East Germans eight months ago.

Freedom has come to East Berlin, but freedom comes in many forms.

I happened across a protest march — organized by the Committee for Social Defense — outside the U.S. embassy in East Berlin the other day.

The young man in charge explained they were protesting because "in Pennsylvania there is a black journalist who has been on death row since 1982."

The young man and 20 or so followers paraded with protest signs around an intersection beside the embassy, under the watchful eye of the police and a muzzled guard dog or two.

"We strive for political justice in Germany and the whole of capitalistic countries," the young man told me.

He sounded misled but sincere.

And he, as much as anyone, is the story of what has happened here.

Never stop fighting city hall.

Never say your voice and your vote don't count.

Never say there is nothing you can do to change the things you find objectionable.

Here the people never abandoned hope.

And they brought a wall tumbling down. ❖

Parade of nations

July 25, 1992

B ARCELONA, Spain — Everybody has a reason for being here for the Olympics.

Some come for the fame. Some for the camaraderie. Some for the gold.

Some come because they can.

And some come because it is different, because they will stand beneath a flag different from the one they stood under before.

Some come, too, because they can make a difference.

Sarunas Marciulionis already has won an Olympic gold medal, as a member of the Soviet basketball team in Seoul. He is marginally an American, spending half the year as a member of the Golden State Warriors. But he spends the other half in Lithuania, where he grew up a citizen of the Soviet Union but with the heart of a Lithuanian.

After the Soviets won the gold medal in Seoul, Marciulionis posed with the entire squad for a photograph. But when the ceremonies were over, he and three other Lithuanian players went into another room and had another picture taken.

They called it their team picture. Lithuanians only.

In 1988, he could not have dreamed what has happened since. He could not have imagined the breakup of the Soviet Union. He could not have imagined that Lithuania would be in these Games as an independent nation, under its own flag and anthem and in uniforms with his country's name spelled out in letters larger than those of any other country competing here.

But all of that has happened. And he is here because time, money and fame have not changed who he is.

"When I see that enormous panoramic view of San Francisco Bay," he told a New York Times reporter, "it is beautiful. But it is like a picture to me. It is not real because it is not mine. I don't feel I could belong to that city, but when I see something beautiful (in Lithuania), it may not be as spectacular, but it is mine."

In the Olympic village, policemen patrol with big walkie-talkies and little guns. Sometimes vice versa.

And we're reminded here every day how quickly things can change. How quickly two countries can become one or one country can become two. Barcelona is a beautiful old city in the region of Spain known as Catalonia. When Francisco Franco was dictator, he banned the area's native language, Catalan. Now people here speak it more often than Spanish, and many would like to be independent of Spain.

Mirsada Buric became a worldwide symbol of what is happening in the former Yugoslavia after an Associated Press photographer pictured her running through the rubble in Sarajevo last month, training to represent Bosnia-Herzegovina here.

She was a teenager when the Winter Olympics were held in Sarajevo in 1984. The city was festooned with flags. Strangers were so welcome that one journalist, attempting to flag down a cab, was picked up by a Yugoslavian who didn't tell the writer he wasn't a cab driver. He just wanted to help a stranger in need.

Today Sarajevo is a battlefield. And it isn't in Yugoslavia anymore because Bosnia-Herzegovina isn't in Yugoslavia anymore. And survival is a daily job.

Buric is a symbol of the changing times, a solitary figure loping down paths littered with concrete chunks blasted from buildings, around burned-out cars, past families decimated by war.

The International Olympic Committee didn't know what to do with her. Or with her country. Or with her former country.

Finally, Bosnia-Herzegovina was officially invited to come here. And so were athletes from the remaining Yugoslav states — but only if they compete individually as Independent Olympic Athletes and salute no flag and honor no anthem.

They will come — Bosnians and Yugoslavs, running and jumping and throwing — because they are competitors.

Because they are athletes.

Because they have prepared for this, and they want to be here, for an old country, a new country or no country at all.

Hassiba Boulmerka of Algeria comes because she is a modern Muslim woman, 23 years old and looking to the future. That scares some Muslims to death. And it makes them angry.

When she won the 1,500 meters in the world championships in Tokyo a year ago, she became the first Arab woman and the first African woman to win a world championship in track and field. Thousands of youngsters in Arab lands looked at her and wondered what was wrong with what she was doing.

Wondered whether some day they could be like her.

Fundamentalist Muslims fear her as a symbol to the young, an Arabic translation of "You've come a long way, baby."

She wears shorts and runs in front of strangers; more traditional Algerian women cover their bodies and heads with black dresses and veils. In parts of Algeria, Boulmerka's actions are condemned as scandalous, and she has stopped training in forests for fear of "fundamentalist delinquents."

But Boulmerka's mother remembers the old days. Not the good old days; the bad old days.

She lived them. She was not allowed to go to school. It was not a girl's place to get an education. It was not a girl's place to compete — with men or in sports.

All change doesn't always have to come from the barrel of a rifle, or in the aftermath of a mortar shell.

Some change comes because young athletes have the courage to do what no one else has done before.

Some change comes from sport.

And from people such as Hassiba Boulmerka. ❖

Bull session

August 3, 1992

BARCELONA, Spain — The man's name was Jesuline Bazan — Jesuline de Ubrique to his fans.

We never learned the bull's name.

The bull was not long in the Plaza de Toros Monumental. He arrived exactly at 6:30 — galloping haughtily through a red door into the sandy arena, without even a glance at the thousands sitting in the seats above him in the late afternoon sun — unaware that he had 15 minutes to live.

He was big and strong and muscled and as the toreadors taunted him with their hot pink and yellow capes, called veronicas, his eyes widened and his nostrils flared.

And when he charged, they would retreat behind wooded barricades.

But then they began to stick things into his back.

First came a man — on an armored horse with ears plugged and eyes covered so he could not see or hear the danger he faced — to jab a lance squarely between the bull's shoulders.

Then three other men on foot pierced his neck with brightly colored banderillas, hooked darts that flop around, imbedded into him for the rest of his life.

Finally Bazan appeared, a lean and handsome 18-year-old with a smile that could kill, and thousands cheered as he stood in the dust at the center of the arena in his skin-tight suit of gold and white.

Spanish ladies fanned themselves, trying to beat back the oppressive August heat. A 16-piece band played brassy Spanish music. Vendors hawked potato chips and popcorn and beer. And a little girl in front of me — doing what she saw older people do — applauded the handsome man with the red cape and the deadly sword.

It was the scene exactly as it is portrayed on posters. There was splendor. And beauty. And romance.

And soon there would be death.

By now there is blood running down the nameless bull's back, and as he wheels to follow Bazan's flowing red cape, his legs sometimes buckle and he falls to his knees.

The band plays, a signal the end is near, and Bazan lifts his sword and buries it to the hilt on the bull's back, then stands back to admire his work. And a moment later, he reaches over the bull's horns and extracts the sword.

The bull cannot comprehend what is happening. But everyone else knows. He is dying.

The matador stands before him, reaches out and touches the horns. The bull's stomach heaves, his knees wobble and he falls into a heap.

Bazan waves to the crowd. Cheers pour down upon him from the fans who filled only a quarter of the arena, and a team of horses quickly enters, is hooked to the lifeless bull and drags him from the ring, to be delivered immediately to a slaughter room beneath the stands.

I had heard the grisly stories of bullfighting and heard the advice not to go. But Sunday afternoon in Spain means bullfights as surely as Sunday morning in Spain means going to mass.

You wonder why some find it so mesmerizing and others find it so repugnant. You wonder how a child can decide to become a bullfighter.

Bazan was born in the industrial town of Ubrique and fought his first bull when he was 13. He has been awarded 247 ears, in recognition of fights well done.

Matadors, I am sure, must be brave. But until the Dream Team came to Barcelona, they were the biggest cinches in town. There is a path worn in the concrete leading from the interior of the arena to the slaughter room, left by the carcasses of thousands of freshly killed bulls.

It is near the chapel, where matadors pray before facing the bulls, and near the souvenir stand, where they sell the little stuffed bulls with swords sticking in their backs that 5-year-old Chris Balfoure wants to take home.

His family is from Connecticut, and they are here for the Olympics, but Sunday they went to the bullfight. Neither of his parents liked it much, but Chris was enthralled.

"The bull is bad," he said. "They have to kill it. Maybe when I grow up, I'll be a bullfighter."

They killed five more bulls Sunday in the brick arena, decorated with blue and white tiles in Moorish patterns. Some were quick and efficient. Some were done poorly and booed and jeered and whistled at in Spanish derision.

By nine o'clock, it was all over, the fans streamed from the stadium, onto Gran Via, one of Barcelona's biggest streets.

A few feet away — in the slaughter room — a nameless bull, big and strong and fearless in the hot Spanish sun, hung on meat hooks as the evening grew cool. ❖

Tonya and Nancy

February 2, 1994

Ron Hoevet convicted Tonya Harding.

He stood before microphones and television cameras in Portland, Ore., and said she agreed to the assault on Nancy Kerrigan at Cobo Arena and that she participated in the cover-up.

Ron Hoevet was convincing.

But he is not a policeman. Nor is he with the FBI. Nor is he a prosecutor or a district attorney.

He is Jeff Gillooly's attorney, and in the past three weeks, he has become convinced that his client — who pleaded guilty to racketeering — is a truthful man. He thinks his client is contrite. He thinks Gillooly is interested only in justice when he says his ex-wife should be barred from skating in the Olympics in three weeks.

Hoevet said just a week or so ago that Gillooly was "prepared to fall on the sword for Tonya." Now, though, Gillooly and Hoevet want to throw Harding on that same sword. Both think it will be an injustice if she is allowed to skate in Lillehammer.

"When you hear the truth, she can't skate on the Olympic team, and Jeff believes that as well," Hoevet said. "It would be unconscionable for Nancy Kerrigan and Tonya Harding to be on the same team."

It is imperative that U.S. Olympic officials find a way to keep Harding from skating, Hoevet said, because "no trial or disposition" of the case will be made before that.

"Participating in the cover-up ought to be unsportsmanlike, don't you think?" he asked.

"We know beyond any doubt that she absolutely participated in the cover-up... . I demand that the United States Skating Federation and the Olympic committee figure out a way to give her due process so this 13-year-old girl (Michelle Kwan) can skate on the Olympic team with Nancy Kerrigan."

In half an hour on television, Ron Hoevet served not only as Gillooly's attorney, but as judge, jury and character assassin for Tonya Harding.

The facts are there, he said, to substantiate everything he claimed.

The FBI tailed Harding and Gillooly. Watched them drive by Shawn

Eckardt's house in an attempt to monitor his meeting with the FBI. Watched them make phone calls.

"Denial," Hoevet said grandly, "is no longer plausible."

But the FBI has charged nothing.

The FBI, I suspect, is interested in justice. Jeff Gillooly seems interested in vengeance. And so does his attorney, who, incidentally, refused to say whether his client had submitted to a lie-detector test.

We know one thing: Harding failed to run to authorities when she learned — after the fact — about the conspiracy. We might suspect more. The FBI might, too. But suspicion is one thing and proof another, and no police department, no federal agency, no legal body has accused Tonya Harding of a crime.

The impatience of the U.S. Olympic Committee and U.S. Figure Skating Association is showing, though. They have put their heads together in hopes of finding some plausible reason for kicking Harding off the team.

It is a witch-hunt they should abandon, not escalate, as Hoevet would hope. When they get involved in law and order and crime and punishment, they are moving too far from their area of expertise.

Based on history, some even contend Harding should skate regardless of any evidence against her. A reader called a few days ago to say all the fuss over this case is misguided.

"The Olympics are not about who is the best person," he reasoned. "They are about who is the best athlete. The first Olympics were held when the countries were at war. They suspended the war long enough to compete in games. That's what the Olympics are supposed to be about: Who is strongest and fastest and the best at what they do. It has nothing to do with how good a person you are."

I don't subscribe to that theory.

I don't think villainy should be rewarded. I don't think it is OK to cripple your opponent to enrich yourself.

But Harding should be dealt with only when, and if, proof surfaces that is more credible than the word of her abusive ex-husband. And certainly there is precedent for retroactive judgment.

Jim Thorpe was one of the greatest athletes of the first half of this century. He won the 1912 Olympic decathlon and pentathlon. But after it was discovered he had played professional baseball before his Olympic appearances, his medals were repossessed.

The same can be done to Harding if she is proved guilty of involvement in the assault. The medals can be taken away, and she can be locked away, as criminals should be.

But none of that should be done without proof of wrongdoing.

Do I think Tonya Harding is innocent? It doesn't matter what I think. It matters what the authorities can prove.

And Ron Hoevet, attorney for a confessed felon with an ax to grind against his ex-wife, does not qualify as an authority in my book.

Harding was allowed to skate but did not win a medal at the '94 Olympics. One month later, she pleaded guilty to conspiring to hinder the prosecution of those involved in the attack on Kerrigan, and she resigned from the U.S. Figure Skating Association. ❖

U-S-A 2, Colombia 1

June 23, 1994

PASADENA, Calif. — Soccer learned a new language.

For decades, the game has spoken German, Italian, Spanish and Portuguese.

Occasionally, it even spoke English.

Now the game must learn American.

The game has arrived on our shores, borne by a bunch of young men who may as well have been Tom, Dick and Harry — or even Larry, Curly and Moe — a week ago, but who seem certain to be household names before World Cup '94 is finished.

In an improbable victory that recalled the 1980 Miracle on Ice, the United States stunned Colombia, 2-1, before 93,194 in the Rose Bowl — the largest crowd ever to see the U.S. national team play in this country — and all but assured itself of advancing to the second round.

It was the United States' first victory in a World Cup match since its stunning win over England 44 years ago, and when it was over in the early evening Southern California sunshine, no one left the stadium, except the bedraggled Colombian team, which faces the prospect of returning home to an angry nation.

As the American team danced around the field, Alexi Lalas' shoulders were draped with a flowing American flag, reminiscent of goalie Jim Craig's tour around the Lake Placid ice in that historic hockey upset 14 years ago.

In the stands, the Americans screamed and stamped and waved flags and chanted the familiar U-S-A! U-S-A! U-S-A! Meanwhile, Colombian supporters sat in disbelief.

The Americans came to this tournament on a free pass as hosts — just another team, a lot of people figured, to be knocked off by the teams that really deserved to be here. Colombia, on the other hand — oh, Colombia!

Colombia has carried an awful label for so many years: Drug Producing Capital of the World. C stands for Colombia — C stands for cocaine.

Suddenly, in the last year its people had something else. They had a soccer team to make them proud. One of the world's best, everyone said, in the tradition of the great Argentine and Brazilian squads.

So they came to the United States, the Colombian team and its fans, proud to wave their flag, proud to call themselves Colombians because their soccer team gave them reason to hold their heads up high.

Pobre Colombia.

Poor Colombia.

They flew first into the face of an inspired Romanian team last week, then they were dominated by a U.S. team determined not to leave its own tournament with a whimper.

The Americans, the supposed lightweights in this match, were the aggressors from the first minute. Eric Wynalda and Ernie Stewart threatened before the game was three minutes old. In the 29th minute, Wynalda hit the goalpost.

Stewart, Tab Ramos and Marcelo Balboa all threatened from inside the box but were turned away.

Always, though, the Americans kept the pressure on, and in the 35th minute that pressure forced the Colombians into a disastrous mistake. John Harkes brought the ball up the left flank and sent a crossing pass toward Stewart, racing down the right side.

Colombia defender Andres Escobar got to the ball first and tried to poke it away from Stewart. But instead, he sent it into his own net, past his stunned goalie, Oscar Cordoba, who could only fall on his back in despair.

It's not the way you score in most sports, but it happens so frequently in soccer that they have a name for it: an own goal. The goal doubled the Americans' confidence, and as the game wore on, they played aggressively on defense, too.

Fernando Clavijo, making a rare start, saved one goal by kicking the ball from the goalmouth after it had eluded goalkeeper Tony Meola, who performed flawlessly after making the mistake that allowed Switzerland its goal in the 1-1 tie at the Silverdome last week.

The Colombians, on the other hand, were disorganized and quiet, and when they had a goal opportunity, invariably the shot was wide or high or directed right at Meola with all the threat of paper wad.

Stewart, who hadn't scored a goal since August, made it 2-0 early in the second half, beating Cordoba after a pass from Ramos. And Colombia's goal came in the 90th minute, long after the U.S. celebration had begun in the stands.

Alan Rothenberg, president of the United States Soccer Federation, called the victory "the biggest so far in the history of soccer in the United States — with all due respect to the win over the English in 1950. We've only begun. It's great to be where we are, and unless some absolute mathematical fluke occurs, we're in the second round."

It was the day soccer learned to speak American.

And the day it had to feel a little sorry for those who speak Spanish.

"Our participation has been a disaster," Colombia coach Francisco Maturana conceded. "This is not what people expected of us. I don't think even if we tried to play bad on purpose we could have played as badly as we have.

"Unfortunately, the rules allow us only to make two substitutions. The ideal situation at that time would have been to make 11 substitutions."

The compassion in me forces me to say: Pobre Colombia.

The American in me responds: U-S-A! U-S-A! U-S-A!

Team USA advanced to the second round but was eliminated by eventual champion Brazil, 1-0. Escobar was murdered in Colombia less than a week later. ❖

Boxing

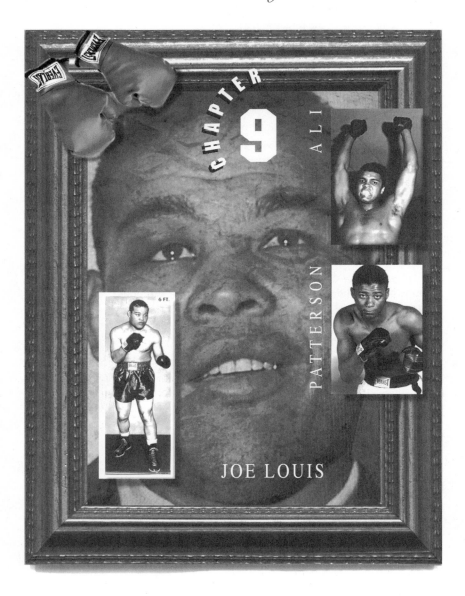

CHAPTER **9**

ALI

PATTERSON

JOE LOUIS

Harold Weston, somebody

July 9, 1980

T he voice came cracking over the telephone lines from midtown Manhattan. In the background were the barely audible sounds of feet skipping lightly on a plain wooden floor, the staccato beat of leather against leather and an occasional shout of encouragement.

"If it hadn't happened, man, if it hadn't happened, I'd be fighting Pipino Cuevas instead of Thomas Hearns because he'd have one loss," said Harold Weston, speaking from the Times Square Boxing Club, where he is trying to put his career back together after eye surgery 13 months ago.

"Pipino Cuevas can wipe out Roberto Duran, and he can wipe out Sugar Ray Leonard. There's only two he can't wipe out, and that's me and Thomas Hearns. I wish Tommy all the luck in the world when he fights for the title. Maybe after he wins it, he'll give me a shot."

That's what Harold Weston lives for these days, the chance to be Harold Weston, welterweight champion. Harold Weston, a man with a lot of folding green in his pocket. Harold Weston, somebody.

Hearns and Weston crossed paths just once, on May 20, 1979, in Las Vegas. When the fight was over — stopped in the sixth round — Weston had become the 19th of 28 victims on Hearns' path to his title fight against Cuevas.

He had become half blind.

The punch that ended the fight left Weston with a detached retina in his right eye. Doctors looked at it and shook their heads. His boxing career was over, they said.

Delicate surgery put the eye back together and, at 28, Weston can see as well as ever. One more punch, though, the doctors cautioned him, and he could lose his sight permanently.

He was not listening.

"Five specialists have seen the eye, and they all advise me not to fight," Weston said. "But you take a risk. When you go into the ring, you don't know if you'll be alive when you come out. But you don't think about it. You can't think about it. Does a cop think every day that he might be killed?"

So Harold Weston, who has not had a fight since that night in Las Vegas, was looking for an opponent.

During the past year, he kept body and soul together by doing some modeling, trying his hand at matchmaking and handling one fighter.

But only through fighting, he believes, can he become somebody important.

He was close, he thought, to being somebody when Thomas Hearns jabbed his fist in his eye that night in Las Vegas. "I was coming back," he said. "I would have won the fight if things hadn't happened the way they did."

It was a thumb, not a fist, Weston insisted, that turned his dream to a nightmare, and it is that unfulfilled dream that drives him despite the risks.

Had it not been for that ill stroke of luck, Weston believes it would be him, not Thomas Hearns, fighting for half a million dollars and the championship on Aug. 2.

"If you don't have anything, and you have all the health in the world, you don't have a thing," he said. "But if you have something — if I have the world championship — then people will recognize me.

"It was just turning into some money, and all of a sudden this happened.

"I had set a standard of living. Now I've had to change that some. I had to cut some of the women loose — they're expensive. Now I just have one major lady. I have 20 pairs of shoes, but I haven't bought any new ones in the last year. I just make sure these get to the shop to be taken care of."

The New York State Boxing Commission refused to give Weston a license to fight, siding with the doctors who said it is far too risky. So he went across the Hudson River to New Jersey and is waiting for the match that will revive his dreams of being somebody.

"I don't have anything definite set up yet. I'm biding my time, taking it slow," he said.

"But I'll be back. I'll be back in action."

Then he hung up, dreams of fame and fortune and foxy ladies bouncing happily around in his head.

Weston returned to boxing — as a promoter. ❖

Joe Louis

April 14, 1981

L AS VEGAS — He was just lying there, resting on his right side and looking up at me from the bed where he spent most of his last days.

Joe Louis.

The man who destroyed everyone who had the nerve to step into the ring with him during the 1940s looked up through helpless eyes and tried to speak.

His lips moved slightly, but only incoherent sounds came from between them. They were the sounds of a man condemned by fate and illness to live out the final months of his life in an eerie loneliness, surrounded by the people who loved and cared for him but unable to be a part of their world — the world that once proclaimed him king.

In the final years before his death two days ago, Louis' world consisted mostly of a single room in the rambling house at 3333 Seminole Circle, a cul-de-sac a mile east of America's most tawdry piece of real estate — the Las Vegas Strip.

In that room he spent the majority of his time, sleeping or lying there, thinking thoughts he could transmit to no one else.

An aneurysm, followed quickly by a stroke, ended his public career late in 1977 and left him virtually helpless.

Only on rare occasions after that did he venture from the security of his home. Several times he had to fly to Houston's Methodist Hospital for a checkup. Three nights ago, he was taken in his wheelchair to the Larry Holmes-Trevor Berbick heavyweight championship fight in Las Vegas, where he received a long standing ovation.

Two years ago, Louis had planned to attend a fight between Mike Rossman and Victor Galindez in Las Vegas. In preparation, he conserved his strength for days and marked the occasion by having his nurse give him one of his infrequent shaves.

But at the last minute, the fight was postponed and the site shifted.

"When the fight fell through, I felt sorrier for Joe than for anybody," recalled his wife, Martha, whose singular devotion to her husband of 23 years sapped her strength, too, in the final days.

Martha Louis, a successful attorney in Beverly Hills, abandoned her practice to attend to Joe's needs. She had all the steps in their home replaced with ramps so he could maneuver his wheelchair. She had the doors to the bathrooms widened so he could wheel his chair to the toilet.

Friends say his physical condition improved slightly in recent months after doctors implanted a pacemaker in his chest. It could not, however, conquer the forces in his body that slowly but inexorably eroded the man who once seemed much more than mortal.

It was a sunny, warm afternoon in March 1979 when I walked into his bedroom, cluttered with wheelchairs paid for by Caesars Palace, the Las Vegas casino that employed him as a greeter until the day his heart decreed he would never work again.

He lay there, beneath an ornately carved headboard, and extended his left hand. The hand, firm and muscular, felt as though it could still strike a blow for freedom, like it did that night in 1938 when it crushed German Max Schmeling in less than a round.

But beneath the sheets were almost useless legs, and the messages from his brain to tongue were hopelessly garbled.

A therapist made 11 trips to Louis' home every week, arriving twice a day Monday through Friday and again on Saturday morning.

Exercise bars stood in the living room, where Louis would painstakingly attempt a few steps on his stronger days. There were wheelchairs, manual and motorized, and a Jacuzzi. Outside was a private pool, seldom used since the Louises' adopted infant daughter fell into it in 1977, narrowly escaping death but leaving her a lifelong invalid.

Beside his bed, high on a chest of drawers, were rows and rows of medicine bottles — dozens of containers of pills and medication to make his final days less painful.

"He has good days and bad days," Martha Louis said. "Some days I can't even understand him, but on other days he's just fine. We try to make things as pleasant as possible, but it's not easy.

"Some of the doctors suggested I put him in a home, but I wouldn't do that to a dog. We'll keep him right here at home. That's where he should be."

During his years as an invalid, she drew strength and hope from every minor improvement in his condition.

"Of course, he can't go anyplace by himself," she said. "But he can get in and out of a car with hardly any help at all. The doctors say the therapy is not just to maintain him at this level — he has gotten better."

His condition never improved enough, though, to allow him to take part in the daily routine of family life that went on around him. His wife, their four adopted children, the nurse and the housekeeper all went about their chores — and though their efforts were frequently intended solely for his benefit, often it was possible to forget he was even in the house.

Cards and letters from admirers never stopped arriving, but visitors came to the house less and less frequently.

Even before his last illness, Louis had no financial resources. The deathwatch required mountains of money, money that had to come from friends. They say Frank Sinatra paid a lot of the bills, and Caesars Palace picked up more.

In Louis' case, though, charity did not seem exactly the right word.

An employee of the Stardust Hotel might have said it best:

"Why shouldn't his bills be paid? He's an American institution."

And Louis was that until the very end. Neither time nor his personal tragedies could diminish the magnitude of the man and the things he represented.

I only wish he could have stood when I met him. I wish he could have said "Hello." ❖

Floyd Patterson

July 18, 1987

DURHAM, N.C. — So call me a sissy.
Or a pacifist.
Or some sort of pinko anti-American because I want to shut my eyes when I go to boxing matches.
The only "Rocky" movie I've ever seen was about a raccoon.

I've been at ringside, because it was my job, and I've cringed at the savagery of the sport and at its hunger for blood. And I've felt guilty about being there.

I wouldn't want my sons doing that for a living. But a father told me the other day how happy he is that boxing is his son's chosen work.

The father was here to accept induction into the U.S. Olympic Hall of Fame.

His name is Floyd Patterson. And in a sport too often populated by crooks, liars and fakes, he is a beacon of what can be right about boxing.

He was 17 when he won the Olympic middleweight championship in Helsinki, Finland, 35 years ago.

A month before his 22nd birthday, he won the world heavyweight championship from Archie Moore.

And by the time he was 24, he had lost the title to Ingemar Johansson, a defeat so traumatic that he left the arena alone that night — in a fake mustache and beard.

"Defeats are always based on people," Patterson said. "If I had been defeated and no one was really interested, it wouldn't bother me at all.

"The fact that so many people depended on me and I go out there and I lose the crown, not only did I lose it, but I lost it to another country. I felt very much ashamed, so I put the mustache and beard on. I felt I'd let the country down.

"Back then I was unable to take it, but now as a grown-up I would feel just as ashamed. One thing I've learned is not to be ashamed of being ashamed."

By the time he was 25, Floyd Patterson avenged that defeat, becoming the first to win back the heavyweight championship.

Now his 22-year-old, 126-pound adopted son Tracy is undefeated in 19 professional bouts as a featherweight. And the father, who spent part of his childhood as a runaway-delinquent on the streets of Brooklyn, said that makes him happy.

"I know what boxing did for me," Floyd Patterson said of whether he had doubts about his son following in his footsteps. "Had it not been for boxing, I would probably be speaking to whoever would listen to me from behind bars. The slums were that bad. Boxing gave me a whole new life."

One of 11 children, Floyd Patterson ran away from home because, "There were too many of us. I felt like a parasite. I felt it would be better if I just left. They would have one less mouth to feed."

So he lived on the streets of Brooklyn for a while, occasionally stealing milk from the back of a truck and sneaking it into the Patterson family refrigerator while the others slept.

Cus D'Amato, he said, put him on the path that would straighten out his life. Soft-spoken, thoughtful, seemingly gentle, Floyd Patterson is a defender of boxing and its principles.

"When I got into the ring, I didn't think in terms of trying to kill my opponent or knock him out or anything like that. It was to hit and not get hit. To outbox him and outthink him. Not to hurt him in the process."

But what about Muhammad Ali, his speech and coordination destroyed by too many punches?

"That's really sad," he said. "In my opinion, outside of Joe Louis, who was my idol, he was the most popular fighter there ever was.

"But he's only one. One out of hundreds, perhaps out of thousands. And I'm not really surprised. I'd never seen anyone as able to take a punch as he. He'd let guys hit him, not realizing the damage. There's a lot of fighters out there who never make the newspaper, walking around as normal as you and I."

Which gets us back to Tracy.

He was 11 when he first showed up at Patterson's gymnasium.

He hung around awhile. Just watching. And when the other kids left, he was still there.

"Whaddaya want, kid?" Patterson asked.

"Oh, nothing," he said.

"You wanna work out?"

"OK."

That's how it started. Like out of a movie. Or like out of Floyd Patterson's life 30 years earlier.

Only this time Patterson was playing the role of D'Amato. And Tracy was the young Patterson.

"Tracy was sort of living with his mother, but he was basically on his own," Patterson recalled. "I took to him rapidly because he reminded me so much of myself. The difference was he didn't have a father, and I did."

When the other boxers left, Tracy would linger until Patterson, convinced "there was something wrong with this kid," asked whether he would like to help work around the yard.

And a little while later, he offered Tracy a place to sleep in the gym.

"Two weeks later, I came back from a trip, and he was still in the gym. That's when I realized there must be even more of a problem, so we started feeding him at our place, and he started staying there.

"I found his life was very similar to mine."

When Tracy's mother moved to the South two years later, she allowed Patterson to become his guardian. Three years later, the former heavyweight champion adopted him.

I still don't like boxing.

I wouldn't want any of my kids to earn their living that way.

But the next time someone says "boxing" to me, I won't immediately think of the men whose lives have been ruined by the sport.

I'll think of Floyd Patterson, too.

And of Tracy Harris Patterson.

And I'll know the sport has saved some lives, too. ❖

Ali

August 5, 1989

T hey said he was not giving interviews.

Sorry, the young lady said.

But there he sat just a few feet away — Muhammad Ali — beyond a velvet rope, seated at a brass-and-glass table, hardly ever looking up but methodically scratching out for each man, woman and child his autograph on a card bearing the logo of his new brand of cologne.

If I was to get even a word with the man whose face was once the most recognizable in the world, I had to do what everyone else was doing at Hudson's Fairlane store.

So I got in line.

Ron Samarian was just ahead of me.

"I shook his hand in 1968," he said. "He was here for an exhibition against Blue Lewis. And when I shook his hand, he said: 'You shook the hand that shook the world.' "

Once upon a time, Ali was the most loquacious athlete on the face of the earth. He said: "I am the greatest!" He said: "I am the prettiest!" He said: "Them Viet Cong ain't done nothing to me," and he refused to go fight in Asia.

That was long, long ago.

He doesn't talk like that any more.

In public, he hardly talks at all.

And none of the people in line held any grudges about that long-ago decision to object to a war most of the country came to object to.

"He objected because of his religion," said Michael Schroeder, who took time off from his job at a sporting goods store to get Ali's autograph. Ali was stripped of his title because he objected to the war. Schroeder, who is white, said: "If he was a white man, it never would have happened to him."

What happened to Ali when he was reinstated, though, is even sadder.

Oh, he won his title back. And by the time he was done in 1981, he had fought professionally for 22 years, 61 fights and 43 exhibitions — 682 rounds.

He had won a fortune and fame and ensured that never in this century — and probably not in the next — will what he did in the ring be forgotten.

But something is wrong with Muhammad Ali.

Some say it was caused by the accumulation of all those years, all those fights, all those rounds. Some say it is something else entirely.

Whatever the cause, the effect is plain. As he sat there, there were times he looked almost like a mannequin, barely moving, his face frozen, eyes blank as he scrawled his name.

"It's like a temple here," said Jesse Nyikon, who like all the others could quote dates and opponents and highlights from a career that meant so much to so many in the 1960s and 70s.

John S. Garner was in line behind me with his children Johnathan, Johnette, Johnletta and K.C.

K.C., at 9 the oldest of his children, was a baby when Ali retired, "but all of them know him because we've got films of his fights at home," Garner said.

The line was moving quickly, and my turn was next. In 10 seconds, what could I ask, and what kind of response could I expect?

"Do you really use this cologne?" I asked.

"Hrmppft," he said, his eyes looking up, his lips hardly moving.

Dumb question.

Sad answer.

Muhammad Ali was once so sleek, so quick, so glib, so cool.

And there were moments Friday when he recaptured that for a moment. Invariably, it was when he looked up and saw a child.

He kissed them and smiled at them. And when Faz Husain sent his 6-year-old, Ali, to the table in boxing gloves, Muhammad Ali posed for a picture with the child planting a left on his chin.

Samarian looked me up later, too, to tell me what Ali had said to him.

"I hit him with that," Samarian said, "told him what he had said to me, and he looked up and said: 'White T-shirt and blue jeans.' I swear, that's what I had on. Of course, that's what everybody wore then. I know he didn't really remember me, but he was pretty quick. I've got to give him credit for that."

Most did not attempt to speak to Ali.

Most stood reverently before him, their hands clasped before them or their arms at their sides.

It was like an audience, which he repeated later at Northland and will repeat again today at Eastland.

The purpose is to sell Muhammad Ali cologne and aftershave at $25 and $35 a bottle.

When Schroeder and Nyikon left, though, they left empty-handed. No cologne? No aftershave?

"No," they said, almost in unison. And Nyikon added: "I'm not that stupid."

Then he added one more thing.

"This is so depressing."

"He was," Schroeder said sadly, "an incredible man. It's sad to see people in a condition like that."

I am not sure why these hundreds of people were here.

Maybe some came to recapture the past.

Maybe some came just to say they shared a few moments with a man who once upon a time was the greatest boxer on Earth.

Mostly, I think, they came to say: "Thanks for the memories."

When Ali stood to leave, a tape played in the background, a tape he requested. It was George Benson singing "The Greatest."

And as Muhammad Ali slowly made his way down the aisles, the crowd applauded. ❖

Martha Louis

December 5, 1989

The frail little lady in the plain, blue-flowered frock and imitation pearl beads did not remember me. She had no real reason to.

I hadn't seen her since 1979. That's when her husband, Joe Louis — once the epitome of strength and might and the American way — lay, weakened by strokes and angina, withering away in the back bedroom of their Las Vegas home.

She strained to remember, though, when I introduced myself. Her brow furrowed, and she gripped tightly the sides of her wheelchair.

But she looked at me blankly. I was a visitor welcomed not because she knew me, but because any visitor is better than none at all.

Martha Louis, the first black woman to practice law in California, turned 77 about three weeks ago. She celebrated the birthday as she celebrates most days now, alone except for the company of fellow patients and the staff at Farmington Nursing Home.

I had lost track of her because she wasn't news anymore, and that is the unfortunate nature of my business. If you are news, we will find you, seek you out, ask you questions you would rather not answer, ring your doorbell, hound your footsteps, put your name in the paper.

When you are no longer news, we forget you.

That's just the way it works.

But Martha Louis had been good to me. She welcomed me into her home 10 years ago, though she was struggling with the physical and mental strain of caring for her husband and for their adopted 2-year-old daughter Janet, who had been left an invalid after falling into a backyard swimming pool and remaining submerged for several minutes.

I wanted to meet her husband. Do a story. Talk to her. Talk to him. She welcomed the stranger from Detroit, and I never forgot it.

For 23 years, she was married to the man who was probably the best boxer of all time. But Joe Louis did not handle money well. He died broke, a charity case, supported in his final years by his friends in Las Vegas.

And he left Martha Louis broke, too.

The wheelchair she sat in was borrowed. She can no longer walk, but she can't afford a wheelchair of her own, either.

She needs false teeth. And new glasses. But there is no money for any of those things.

Medicaid pays for part of her care. The nursing home writes off the rest.

And most of her clothes are donated by members of the staff.

She has diabetes, and sometimes — when asked about the misty, long-ago past — she became confused. She is no longer sure of the ages of her four adopted children: 21-year-old Joe, 18-year-old Johnny, 15-year-old Joyce and Janet, 12, who she said are living with friends in Las Vegas.

When asked for special memories of her years with Joe Louis, her mouth became a tight line. Her eyes closed, the lids fluttering softly. For a long time she did not answer. When she did, she said: "I can't think of anything that stands out in my mind."

But when someone — knowing she had no love for boxing — suggested she "didn't care for a boxer, you cared for Joe Louis," a broad smile creased her face.

She knew her birthday was Nov. 9 but either didn't know or didn't care to confirm her age.

"When you're past 70," she said, "it doesn't make much difference."

She has no plans for Christmas.

"I just take it a day at a time," she said. "Holidays now are just like any other day to me. It wasn't that way when I was married and had the kids. They always had a nice Christmas."

That, though, was then.

How about now?

"Last Christmas?" I began to ask Linda Mlynarck, administrator of the nursing home, wanting to know whether Martha Louis had visitors over the holidays.

But before I could finish, she shook her head left to right.

"No," she said. "No visitors."

There have been occasional phone calls from the children, and last week there was a check from a boxing organization that helps indigent fighters and their families.

Usually, though, her days are filled only with soap operas and the companionship of those who share her predicament.

There are charities, it seems, on every corner. There are the Old Newsboys and the United Fund and the Leukemia Society of America and dozens of others.

There are drives to raise money for the public school athletic program and to send a junior high band to a parade in another state and to buy a dialysis machine for someone who will die without it.

So this is not a plea to send Martha Louis money. This is a reminder to be thankful for what you have this Christmas season. For love and family and health and for enough money to heat the house and feed the kids.

Someone will always have more.

But so many will always have less.

God bless Martha Louis. And God help her, too.

Martha Louis died in 1991. She was 78. ❖

Etc.

FOOTBALL

WAYNE FONTES

5

RACING

CHAPTER 10

Billie Jean

May 6, 1981

BOSTON — On a bedroom wall in my apartment — surrounded by dozens of others reflecting the growing-up years of children — is a picture of three brightly smiling people.

Two are my daughters, at the time in their early teens. They have on their faces the ecstatic and giddy look of young girls who have just met their idol, for standing beside them, sweaty and red-faced after a match at Cobo Arena, is Billie Jean King.

To them and to a generation of young women, Billie Jean King has been a heroine. A bit larger than life, a woman of grit and determination and certainly of a mind all her own.

Now the tsk-tsking begins.

Billie Jean King has admitted to an act beneath heroines and idols, a homosexual affair with her former secretary.

Lesbianism is not something we all talk about around the dinner table. It's a subject that is dealt with, if at all, in whispers.

It has been widely suspected, though, that lesbianism is not uncommon among female athletes. One Big Ten tennis coach told some of her players that she left the pro tour because it was rampant.

But never has the issue been held up for scrutiny, not until Billie Jean King, president of the Women's Tennis Association, winner of nearly two dozen Wimbledon titles, the best-known nave in the sport, sat before a bank of microphones and television cameras late last week.

You could almost hear the shrieks of righteous indignation from millions of people who felt she had somehow betrayed them.

Once we get over our initial attack of the "ooohs" and "ahhhs," once we revive all those who refuse to admit such things do, indeed, go on, we may discover a couple of things.

One: The only people who should be directly affected by King's confession are the parents of teenage prodigies such as Grosse Pointe Shores' Susie Mascarin, who will have to sit down and decide whether this changes their conviction that the pro tennis tour is the place for their 16-year-old.

Two: We seem never to learn the lesson that athletes are merely people who are skilled in one sporting endeavor or another. We never seem to learn that it is our fault — the fault of parents and the fault of the media — that these athletes are often elevated to superhuman levels in the eyes of the young and in the minds of those who seek escape from the workaday routine by equating athletic heroics with nobility.

There are some — feminists mainly, I suspect — who may say her confession makes Billie Jean King an even bigger person, one unafraid to admit a transgression. There were those who said the same thing a decade ago when she was one of the first female athletes to admit having an abortion.

I disagree. Her confessions neither enhance nor decrease her.

They emphasize only the mistake we make in deluding the young.

We give them Santa Claus and the Easter Bunny. The tooth fairy and Billie Jean King.

We give them fantasy instead of reality.

Our grandfathers made Shoeless Joe Jackson a giant among men, and when he betrayed his team in the 1919 Black Sox scandal, a nation pleaded: "Say it ain't so, Joe!"

We create Babe Ruth and Joe Louis and Denny McLain. And when they all prove human, we say the fault is theirs.

Because some men can hit a baseball or throw a football or make a dunk, we send our children in search of their autographs, an apparently harmless exercise. But are we not also telling those children that if the autograph is worth pursuing, the individual must be worth emulating?

Must this not be a person a cut above the rest of us?

Billie Jean King is merely a woman who, in her prime, was one damn good tennis player. And as far as I know, that's all she ever claimed to be.

She never set herself up as an example of morality. She has merely been what she is.

She said she was wrong in engaging in an affair with Marilyn Barnett, and she asked the understanding and compassion of her fans.

I think that plea is unnecessary.

If we ever looked upon her as anything other than an outstanding tennis player, as someone better than your run-of-the-mill human being, someone to be singled out for adulation, then the fault was ours.

The mistake of a parent.

The mistake of the media.

For Billie Jean King is fallible, as we all are. To think anything else of a human being is folly.

To teach anything else to a child is a crime. ❖

Row your boat

September 22, 1981

O N THE PLATTE RIVER — The first thing you notice is that canoeing isn't really difficult.

The prospect of paddling 7½ miles, from the point where Michigan Route 22 crosses the Platte River to where it empties into Lake Michigan, had made sweat break out on the brow of this city boy. It sounded like an intimidating chore, and into the mind flashed visions of the canoe going around and around in endless circles while I struggled to right it.

That's what happened the only other time I attempted such a thing.

It was on a lake at a Boy Scout camp about 30 years ago. After watching me and an equally inept companion thrash about aimlessly for 15 minutes, a camp supervisor rowed out and towed us back to the safety of shore.

Since that day, I'd never been in a motorless boat.

My fears were unwarranted, though, thanks in no small part to the presence of John Russell, who served as my photographer, guide and helmsman.

As the canoe entered the river, his expertise complemented the gentle flowing current of the shallow river, and we were under way. The paddles cut easily through the water and the canoe moved away from civilization.

Five hundred yards from the livery, we were alone.

Such is not always the case. The pleasure of canoeing is no longer a secret in Michigan. No one knows how many there are statewide, but one Sunday in August, the National Parks Service counted 217 canoes on the Platte River alone.

On this day, there was no such traffic jam. There were no people. No noise.

The birch trees closed in on the narrow river, dangling their limbs over the cool water. The silence was so complete that the chirping of a solitary cricket cut cleanly through the afternoon air.

The river, seldom more than 30 yards wide, meandered through Sleeping Bear Dunes National Park. The water was so clear, you could see the trout, clam shells and fallen trees resting on the bottom.

After a couple of miles of solitude, the river suddenly opened into Loon Lake, a wide but shallow expense of water, and — trying to keep away from the middle of the lake — John and I paddled ourselves onto a sandbar where the water is no more than 10 inches deep. John told me I'm on my own.

So while he pulled out his camera to capture the excitement of the moment, I tugged off my boots and stepped into the lake, pulling the canoe (including my 200-pound photographer and all his equipment) free of the sand.

Soon, John and I were under way again. We navigated through the narrow weir where the Department of Natural Resources captures young fish for areas that require stocking. My notes fell in the water, but nimble John retrieved them before they joined the clam shells and submerged trees.

The tranquillity was broken only by occasional noises such as from a blue heron, startled by the lapping of our paddles, soaring skyward from his marshy resting place.

In the stillness I could almost imagine, just beyond those trees that blotted out everything but the sliver of water we were on, a log cabin with smoke gently wafting from its chimney, a deer carcass hung out to cure. Or maybe there was an Indian hunting party around the next bend, arrows poised in anticipation of prey that would fill their pots during the approaching winter.

This is the land of Hiawatha.

Most may maintain that Gitche Gumee, the shining big-sea water, is in reality Lake Superior. I preferred, on this day at least, to believe it was Lake Michigan, just ahead, around another couple of bends and just beyond the sand dunes.

The trees were beginning to change color, maples going from green to deep purples and golds. Canada geese waddled in twos and threes along the shore. The only sounds were those of nature, the leaves rustling in the breeze, the geese honking as they nibbled at the grass, water gently lapping at the sides of the canoe.

Then came the sound of a faraway motor on the open waters of Lake Michigan.

We rounded a bend, and suddenly the wind kicked up, a sign we were approaching the lake. The trees gave way to marsh, topped by dunes, and there, in the distance, appeared a broad expanse of the lake.

The two-hour journey back in time was over too soon.

It was a trip not to be missed — and not to be forgotten. ❖

Petr Klima, the movie

September 24, 1985

I f it ever becomes a movie, it won't play in Czechoslovakia.

Call it "Escape from Prague: The Petr Klima Story."

Scene One: Two perspiring teenagers in hockey uniforms sit side-by-side on a plank bench in an otherwise deserted locker room. On the wall behind them are hangers holding their street clothes, and above the hangers their names in Czech: "Petr Klima" and "Petr Svoboda."

One turns to the other and says quietly: "I have been thinking about leaving. About defecting. I believe I'm good enough to play in the National Hockey League."

The other shows no surprise. He puts his hand on his friend's shoulder and looks into his eyes. "I have thought of that, too. But it is not an easy decision, Petr. If we defect, we will never be able to see our homes again. Like you, though, I have dreamed of the freedom and the opportunity to play in the NHL."

They speak of it no more. They dress, shake hands and walk through the doors into the gray gloom of a Czechoslovak winter evening.

Scene Two: Halfway around the world, Nick Polano, assistant general manager of the Detroit Red Wings, is four rounds deep into the 1983 NHL draft and decides to gamble. He has heard of an 18-year-old Czech left wing who has pro potential. He has never talked to him, but he has heard through the grapevine the Czech might consider defecting.

When the Red Wings' turn comes in the fifth round, Polano speaks eight words: "The Red Wings select Petr Klima of Czechoslovakia."

Scene Three: It is the winter of 1984, Petr Svoboda has defected, but Petr Klima has not, and Svoboda is playing with the Montreal Canadiens. Klima has been drafted by the Czech army and is playing on the national hockey team. The team is in Vancouver for the Canada Cup when a Czech-speaking stranger approaches and says quietly: "Nick Polano of the Red Wings is here. He would like to talk to you. Can we meet?"

"Yes," Klima says. "But we must be careful. I am ready to defect, but I cannot do it until next year, after I am released by the army. If I leave now, I will be a traitor. I could be shot. We can talk tonight. I can get away, but we must not let them see us."

Later that night, they rendezvous in a hotel room. With the Czech-speaking stranger acting as interpreter and negotiator for Klima — who is aware what other Czechs are making in the NHL — the Red Wings and Klima agree on a contract.

"I will let you know when I'm ready to come out," Klima tells Polano. "Be ready to come meet me."

He opens the door a crack, looks down the hall in both directions, then slips out.

Scene Four: The phone on Polano's desk in Detroit rings. It is mid-afternoon, Aug. 15, 1985.

"He's in Rosenheim, West Germany, with the Czech team," the voice on the telephone says. "Come now."

"I'll be on a flight tonight," Polano says. "Set up a meeting for tomorrow."

Friday night in the train station in Nussdorf, near the West German-Austrian border, Polano and an interpreter meet with Klima.

"How will it work?" Klima wants to know. "What do I do?"

"We just walk out," he's told.

"I'm not sure. There are some things I must do. I will talk to you again tomorrow."

Scene Five: Polano sits with the interpreter in a locked car in an unlit parking lot on the outskirts of Nussdorf. They look at their watches.

"He should be here anytime," Polano says. And as if on cue, a black car pulls up beside his and Klima climbs out.

He has nothing with him. No passport and only the clothes on his back.

He gets into the backseat of Polano's car.

"We've talked enough," Klima says. "I am ready to go. But first I must stop by the hotel and pick up something."

"No," Polano says. "It's too dangerous. You might never get back out. What if they know you're planning to leave?"

"I must," Klima replies. "I will take care of it."

With German friends, Klima returns to the Czech team hotel and stops in the bar for a drink with a teammate. He says nothing of defecting and, after a few minutes, stands up.

"I'll be right back," he says, nodding toward the rest room.

But instead of going to the rest room, Klima slips out another door and goes to his room, where he stuffs pictures of his family and mementos of his homeland into a small bag, then slips quietly out a side door and into the night.

He has left Czechoslovakia for good.

Scene Six: Three weeks have passed. It is mid-September, and Polano, Red

Wings executive vice-president Jim Lites and Klima have crisscrossed
Germany, registering at hotels under assumed names in the fear Czechoslovak
agents are on their trail.

American immigration officials are trying to cut through red tape, but
Klima's papers have not been cleared. Polano worries that Klima is having
second thoughts, and as they look out the window of their room on the 40th
floor of Frankfort's Plaza Hotel, he asks Klima: "Are you having any thoughts
about going back?"

"Going back," Klima says, "would be like falling out of that window."

Friday, Sept. 20, Polano is called to the U.S. Embassy and handed an
envelope of documents.

"This is it," he's told. "Everything's in here. Tomorrow you all go to the
States."

Scene Seven: At 11 a.m. Monday, two dozen Detroit Red Wings are
gathered around coach Harry Neale in one corner of the ice at McMorran Arena
in downtown Port Huron when a solitary figure in a black practice jersey and
red shorts skates through a gate at the other end of the ice.

As he glides toward them, Petr Klima's new teammates salute him, banging
their hockey sticks on the ice in unison.

One part of his journey is complete. And another has begun.

*Klima played four seasons for the Red Wings before being traded to
Edmonton in 1989.* ❖

Personal best

Marilyn Stano never saw Ahmed Ismail.

Ismail won the ninth annual Free Press Marathon in
something just over two hours.

Stano finished last, five hours later.

Ismail has the stamina and the strength and the check for
$2,000.

But his heart can be no bigger than hers.

Marilyn Stano of St. Clair Shores is a 34-year-old nursing instructor at
Henry Ford Hospital. She is overweight. Thirty pounds overweight, by her

estimate. And then she tells you the rest of the story.

"I've lost 90 pounds since I started running six months ago.... That's the only reason I started running: to lose weight."

Marilyn Stano was the loneliest of the 2,788 runners who entered the race.

Most runners travel in packs, by twos or threes or fives. They chat with each other, encourage each other. They offer a helping hand when it's needed. But by the time she entered the Windsor Tunnel, just more than six miles into the race, Marilyn Stano ran alone — not at the back of the pack, but behind the pack. Far behind.

And it was, frankly, painful to watch her.

I'd had this idea about writing about the last-place finisher. I thought maybe it would be funny. It was not. It was uncomfortable and heartwarming at the same time.

She would run a little. Then she would walk a little.

At 10:37 in the morning, she was walking south on Woodward, just north of Grand Circus Park. Not another runner was in sight. C094, Scot Fredley, had passed 14 minutes earlier, leaving the street to me and a Detroit Police reservist manning the barricades.

Ismail had crossed the finish line 20 minutes earlier; Stano had covered about 11 miles.

And her only company was a Detroit police car with its red and blue lights going and a vulturous bus, poking along behind her, waiting to scoop up her weary carcass and offer her a seat with the others who had been overcome by the tortures of a 26-mile, 385-yard race against themselves.

Alone she lumbered on, through the cold shadows of downtown Detroit's empty skyscrapers.

Alone she ran out Michigan Avenue, all the way to I-94 and all the way back. And it was somewhere along that stretch that City of Detroit workers began catching up with her. It was somewhere out there that they began dismantling the barricades and picking up the bright pylons ahead of her. It was somewhere out there that she began to have to deal not only with the mental and physical trials of this race, but with traffic, too.

And it was while she was out there that I lost her.

I sat on a bus stop bench at Michigan and Cass, behind a dozen or so volunteers who stood on that corner and cheered the runners on with whistles and horns and cymbals, and I awaited her return.

At 12:09 p.m., 021I, Dianne Jaskolski, and 008E, Ann Bradley, ran past the cheering dozen.

"I wish I had that much energy," 021I said to her friend in labored words.

Fifteen minutes later, E327, Joseph Sanavage, jogged past the group.

"Thank you for waiting around," he said.

At 12:34, five runners came by in a group — 006E, I225, 036B, I295 and J040 — Lorraine Beaudette, Robert Mitchell, Jacqueline Zwick, Byron Siegel and Henry Caplan. Behind them was a bus. And a police car. And traffic.

And no Marilyn Stano.

She had become, I was sure, a casualty.

A dropout.

A good idea gone awry.

So I tried to forget Marilyn Stano. I got to the Belle Isle finish line in time to see a 79-year-old, Jim Ramsey, finish in something just over five hours. I got there in time to see Peggy Fanella get to the finish line with the help of a friend on a skateboard who kept her company while singing "Jingle Bells." I got there in time to visit with a 73-year-old, Stan Connelly, and Maggie Perron, a 56-year-old grandmother in her first marathon.

And I got there in time to talk to Tom (Turtle) Turley, who claims to be the most improved runner in the field because "it took me seven hours, three minutes and five seconds last year and I did it in 5:46:40 this time."

It was well after two o'clock. Ismail had been finished for four hours, and the workers were beginning to dismantle the clocks and ropes and barricades at the finish line when I began driving back downtown.

And it was there, on a sidewalk on Larned, that I saw a familiar figure walking alone.

Marilyn Stano, 6½ hours from the starting line and still two miles from the finish.

I parked and walked with her, half a mile, I suppose.

I told her I'd been watching and that I admired what she was doing and wondered why she didn't just quit.

"Oh, I've thought about all the reasons to do that," she admitted, keeping a slow but steady pace. "But I'm going to finish — and finish running — if it kills me. Six months ago, I said I'd finish this race, and I'm just stubborn enough to do it.

"I'm going to be sore, fool that I am, but I just want to feel what it's like to finish." And she was off, striding down Larned all alone.

At 11 minutes past three — seven hours, 11 minutes and 16 seconds after she started — Marilyn Stano finished her first marathon. ❖

Bobby Layne's wake

December 4, 1986

L UBBOCK, Texas — The card game had begun sometime the night before, and now it was almost one o'clock in the afternoon Bobby Layne would be buried.

Around the table, heaped high with several thousand dollars in crumpled bills, sat a handful of men who had been among his closest friends: a couple of old football players, a restaurant owner from San Antonio, two pals from Lubbock.

The night had passed. Breakfast time had gone by unnoticed. In three hours, Bobby Layne would be laid to rest.

They had come to Lubbock not so much to mourn Layne's death as to celebrate his life. To say, "This is what Bobby would want us to be doing three hours before his burial," would sound trite, but as they dealt another hand, not one of them doubted it was true.

At the same time, down in the lobby of the hotel where all the former Lions were staying, Gil Mains was recalling something that had happened in 1952, his rookie season with Detroit.

"We walked out of this place one night," Mains said, drawing his wallet from his hip pocket, "and Bobby pulled this wad of money out and was flipping through it when he saw a single. 'How the hell did that get in there?' he said, and threw it on the sidewalk.

"Hell, I was a poor rookie. I pounced on it."

A smile filled his face as he mimicked Layne, scornfully hurling a bill to the lobby floor. As with so many of the stories that have been told this week, you probably had to be there to get the full impact.

The men who came here to say good-bye to Bobby Layne were there: Dorne Dibble and Cloyce Box. Joe Schmidt and Jimmy David. Harley Sewell and Ernie Stautner. Yale Lary and Tobin Rote. Billy Kilmer and Charley Conerly. Harry Gilmer and Charlie Johnson. And hundreds more.

Their testimonials, given simply and sincerely in the 24 hours they were here, were eloquent tributes.

"I loved the ground that man walked on," said David, who played with Layne and later was an assistant coach with several NFL teams.

"Every time I came in here to scout Texas Tech, I'd have to allow myself

about three extra days because Bobby wouldn't let me leave. He'd load up the
pickup, and we'd go about 90 miles out into the country and hunt quail for
days.

"He was just a hell of a guy."

On his final day, Bobby Layne played to a full house, as he had so many
afternoons for the Lions in Tiger Stadium.

All the card games were over, the bar was closed, the stories came to a
temporary halt.

The 400 seats were filled in St. Paul's Church on the Plains by 4 p.m.
Wednesday, and the crowd spilled out onto the parched brown lawn. Inside, the
Rev. Harold O. Clinehens Jr. told the crowd: "If you came to hear a eulogy of
Bobby Layne, you are going to be disappointed. Bobby didn't want that, and
the family didn't want it. We are sad today, and not only are we sad, people all
over the country are sad with us... . We will miss Bobby Layne. We will miss
him a lot.

"We've lost a friend."

The church services lasted barely half an hour, a mere hyphen in the final
events of Bobby Layne's time on earth. And when the services were over —
and Layne was buried at the City of Lubbock Cemetery — there were some
tears shed. But not many.

Layne, who died at age 59, seldom had time for tears. Whatever joy he gave
football fans during his years as one of the game's premier quarterbacks, he
gave to these close friends a thousand times over.

It's presumptuous to judge a man by what little we know of him from afar.

Do you add up all the touchdowns and all the happiness he brought to
people? Do you subtract all the interceptions and the excesses of his life? Do
you count his friends and subtract his enemies?

I was taught it is not ours to judge, but in Bobby Layne's case, I cannot
resist.

I think you judge a man by what he leaves behind. And Bobby Layne left
happy memories and loving people. ❖

Clean and sober

June 27, 1987

His head was splitting and his mouth tasted like bile, stale and smoky. And all Mario Baillargeon could remember was his wife and baby girl had left him.

It didn't come to mind right away that he had skipped the past three nights at the harness track in Pompano, Fla., leaving horse owners to find someone to drive in his place.

In the first moments after he opened his eyes and painfully turned his body in the bed, he did not even know where he was.

"I was on a three- or four-day drunk, and I was a sick SOB, and I said to myself, 'This is enough,' " Baillargeon said, sitting in the shade at Hazel Park, where he is the leading driver for the 1987 harness season.

"Everybody was saying I was a bum. I was getting deeper and deeper in trouble."

So five months ago, he dragged himself from that bed and signed himself into an alcohol and drug rehabilitation clinic in Boca Raton, Fla.

"My wife had taken our baby and left me. I was throwing away my career," he said. "This is my last chance.

"You have to hit your bottom before you go for help."

But Mario Baillargeon still believed he could fool people. He believed he could fool himself, too.

"I didn't really go in to get cured," he admitted. "I went in just to get out of trouble. I figured my wife would come back and everything would be all right again and things would go back to being like they were. But after 10 days or so, I started to realize the books and films and lectures that were available there made sense."

Mario Baillargeon has been around harness racing since he quit school in Montreal at 15. He said he earned $100,000 in 1979, his second full season as a driver.

"By now," he said, "I should have $100,000 in the bank. I should have a couple of horses and a home, and I don't have any of that."

A month short of his 30th birthday, he has won more than $7.3 million driving sulkies, he said. "It is all gone. Gambling, cocaine, booze, women. You know, all gone.

"Now, in four or five months, I've got more money than I ever had."

Always, it seems, Mario Baillargeon could handle horses. Never, though, could he handle alcohol or the drugs that eventually began to accompany the alcohol.

"For the six or seven years before I went into the clinic," he said, "I never went straight home. I'd always stop at the bar with the guys."

For a long time it didn't seem to bother his work.

He averaged more than 1,300 starts, 200 wins and $800,000 in purses in his first three full seasons. In Montreal, he was the hot young driver — the one owners wanted behind their horses.

But in 1981, he came to the United States and things started to change. He drove in New York and Chicago and Detroit and on the West Coast. But he got fewer horses. He got fewer wins. And people started to talk about his habits away from the track.

He still had his friends, though. The buddies he drank with, the same ones he was starting to snort cocaine with.

"If I got a little drunk, I'd get a little coke, too. I never spent much on drugs... . People would give it to me. They'd ask if I had a winner for them, and maybe they'd give me a gram. If a guy won $2,000, he'd give you $500 worth of cocaine."

Baillargeon drove a couple of races after snorting cocaine and said Lefty Driesell's assertion that it can enhance performance is "shit."

"It scared the shit out of me," he said.

He married 2½ years ago, but neither the marriage nor his wife's pregnancy changed his lifestyle.

"She's in heaven now," Baillargeon said. "She can tell some bad stories. I'd be gone two or three days, and I would call her and ask her to come get me, and she would ask where I was, and I'd tell her I didn't know. I'd have to ask the bartender. Sometimes I wasn't even in the same city.

"At the end, I loved cocaine, but I loved the booze better. And when I did it, I was always around friends, or I thought I was with friends.

"When I went into rehab, only a couple of guys came to see me. I was hurt, but I learned.

"And when I came out, I realized I had to change my playground. I had to change my playmates. Obviously, the friends I had before were no good for me.

"One night, after racing, I would like to have beers with the guys. But after we finished, they'd go home. I know I wouldn't do that. If I have lunch and a beer today, I wouldn't show up at the track tonight."

Mario Baillargeon is having the best season a driver ever has had at Hazel

Park Harness Raceway. On April 28, he did something no driver had ever accomplished there: He drove seven winners.

He has heard what people say on his off-nights, though.

"One night I had only one winner, and I heard people say: 'Oh, he must be on dope tonight.' "

He was the eighth-leading harness driver in the nation 11 days ago. He had 167 winners in 695 drives. He was steady, reliable and good.

I was supposed to interview him that day — June 16. He didn't show up that morning. And he didn't show up that night for his rides.

He didn't show up the next night, either.

Or the next.

Or the next.

He was gone a week, a week in which his wife, Tammy, kept calling the track and saying her husband was sick.

Baillargeon knew what people were thinking, though.

"Probably half of them were sure I was drunk or coked up someplace, but what can I say? I know my reputation, and I'm trying to build it back up," he said.

"I'm allowed to get sick, too. I was sick a few days, and then I took the rest of the week off and stayed home with my wife, my mother-in-law and my baby."

And when he returned to Hazel Park, he drove four winners.

"I love what I'm doing now," he said. "I love it a lot more than I did when I was sick every night from the night before. I'm good at it. I know I'm good at it. And I can't do anything else."

He said he hasn't had a drink or used drugs since he walked out of the Boca Raton clinic in February.

He has been tempted, though.

"I feel strong," he said, "but not that strong. So I have my wife come pick me up at the track sometimes. I want her to. I don't want to take a chance."

Baillargeon's rehabilitation cost him $6,000. The best $6,000, he said, he ever spent.

"I think I would have been dead by now. It was that bad. I'm 29, and my liver is no good.

"I'm an alcoholic. I'm a drug addict. I always will be. But I don't use it.

"I know if I use it, I'll be dead, and I don't want to be dead now.

"I've got 10 more good years. I know it's all up to me. It's as simple as that.

"If I don't have any accidents — if I stay sober, I'll be OK." ❖

A day at the races

July 12, 1987

They always told me horse racing was the sport of kings, the place where crowned heads sit under parasols and while away their royal time, wagering a pound or a shilling on their favorite piece of horseflesh.

It's a lie.

At the 39th running of the Michigan Mile at Detroit Race Course, I did not see a king.

I saw Johnson. And I saw a guy who didn't want his name in the newspaper. But I didn't see any kings.

Not Billie Jean King or Larry King or Eric King.

In Detroit, horse racing is not the sport of kings but the sport of auto workers and carpet salesmen, cocktail waitresses and insurance agents.

I wanted to view the Michigan Mile through their eyes. So I spent the afternoon on the grandstand apron, where the asphalt is littered with failed dreams and crushed beer cups.

I hoped to find a bettor who would allow me to view the afternoon through his experiences. But it had to be someone who was enjoying himself, who was articulate and who wouldn't mind sharing his day with a half-million or so readers.

For eight races I searched. I listened to a middle-aged man complain all was not on the level in this sport. And I watched as a young woman picked up every discarded ticket that had not been ripped apart, hoping to find a thrown-away winner.

I saw no crimson or ermine, no tiaras or taffeta gowns.

I saw a lot of gold chains and some diamonds. I saw a lot of fishnet shirts and tank tops. A lot of cutoffs and jeans with holes in the knees.

In Detroit, horse racing is the sport of pipe fitters and pipe smokers, college kids and housewives.

I finally decided on approaching one man in a group of four and asking whether he would consent to be interviewed, and as he walked away from his friends I followed him.

"Whooo, if the right horse don't come in in this race, there's gonna be a lot of people not eating at my house," said the little man who suddenly appeared at my side.

"Uhhhh," I replied, as the man I was following disappeared into the crowd.

"Whatta you like in this race?" asked the man who had attached himself to my wrist, making sure to flash a handful of bills as he spoke.

"Uhhhh," I said.

"Lookee here. I've seen you around here before, and I'm going to give you the winner," he said, obviously confusing me with Dennis Weaver or someone else who bears at least a passing resemblance to me.

"Uhhhh," I replied, remaining consistent.

He pulled a wallet from his pocket and tugged slightly at a yellow card, just until the word "stable" showed on what appeared to be an identification card. This guy was an insider!

"Johnson's my name.

"C'mere," he said, tugging at my elbow as he led me toward a betting window. "Now you'll remember me when the race is over, right?

"How much money you got?"

I fished into my pocket and pulled out a five.

"Whooo boy, they about to whip you down, ain't they?" he said, shaming me into digging into my billfold for a 20.

"Bet $20 more," he said, noticing I had left some money in my wallet for dinner. "Bet it on the six horse."

The man behind the window didn't bat an eye. This was not the first time, apparently, he had seen this little man do his number.

I shoved the $20 under the window and put what was left of my money back in my pocket.

"Don't forget," the little man said. "I like to help, but don't forget me."

"What was your name?" I asked.

"Johnson," he said.

"Where'll you be after the race?"

"Right here."

"OK," I said, stuffing the winning ticket into my pocket. "OK."

I hustled off to find the man I hoped to watch the race with. I caught him as he walked away from another betting window.

I introduced myself and told him what I wanted: to talk to him about his day, to watch the Michigan Mile with him, to get the feeling of a single bettor as he watched his horse come thundering down the homestretch.

"You're serious," he said, looking at me in contemptible and uncomfortable disbelief. Then he started shaking his head violently.

I heard just a couple of words as he hurriedly walked away.

"I don't want my name in no damn newspaper," he said. I didn't hear the rest, but I figured I didn't need to.

So I watched the Michigan Mile by myself from the apron.

I watched the favorite, Waquoit, win by a record 7½ lengths. His number was 8. I watched Purple Mountain finish second. His number was 1. I watched Red Attack finish third. His number was 6. He was my horse. I tore up my ticket and walked to the spot where I'd last seen Johnson.

I waited awhile for him. I thought maybe he'd stop by to tell me what had gone wrong. Why Red Attack didn't win. He never came back.

In Detroit, horse racing is the sport of welfare mothers and good-timing fathers. It is the sport of those who hope to find a pot of gold at the end of a mile and an eighth. It is the sport of Johnson and not of kings.

But it's not a bad way to spend an afternoon, if you don't mind paying to meet interesting people. ❖

----- tennis

September 8, 1987

NEW YORK — There was a time when you could take the kids to a tennis match.

You could dress up a bit. Mom, perhaps in something frilly, and Dad in a white linen jacket, maybe with a flower in his lapel.

In hushed tones, they would critique the play.

They would "oooh" and "ahhh" at the power of Rod Laver, the grace of Margaret Court and the form of Arthur Ashe.

Politely, they would applaud. Not clap. Clapping is vulgar. It is done at football games and boxing matches. Applause is proper. It is done at the opera and poetry readings. And at tennis matches.

That was before John McEnroe. Before Hana Mandlikova, too, it turns out.

That was before tennis players began talking like stevedores or truck drivers. Or rodeo cowboys. That was before spectators at the U.S. Open had to wear helmets to protect against beanings. It was before players began using their rackets to beat up scoreboards. It was before four-letter words became the language of international tennis.

"——!" McEnroe shouted the other day, angered at a call.

"——!" he said again.

Then Mandlikova, a Czech, demonstrated how well she has mastered this language. "——!" she said, angered by a call. "——!" she said again.

New York is probably the most tolerant city in the world. Here they put up with sidewalks littered with yesterday's garbage and barges filled with last spring's garbage.

They endure muggings and graft and graffiti. And they probably would have continued to tolerate John McEnroe and Hana Mandlikova, too.

But tennis has seen enough.

Of McEnroe's weekend outburst, Ken Farrar, chief of supervisors of the Men's International Pro Tennis Council, said: "I can't conceive of a more vile, disgusting attack on a chair umpire.... Verbally, it ranks as one of the worst."

For yelling at a lineswoman, McEnroe was fined $500.

For verbal abuse of chair umpire Richard Ings, he was fined $5,000.

For obscene comments made to a CBS technician, he was fined $2,000.

Coming after a $350 fine for hitting a ball into the stands in a first-round match, McEnroe's fines have reached $7,850 for the U.S. Open, $35,800 for the year, and he is subject to an additional $10,000 fine and two-month suspension.

"That's John," Chris Evert said. "He's just a little dangerous when he's tense and in the heat of battle."

"Why," asked Pam Shriver, "does he keep doing this to himself?"

The ladies' words were still damp ink in the New York tabloids when one of their own — Mandlikova, the fourth-seeded woman in this tournament — began behaving so badly that Georgina Clark, supervisor of officials in the women's side of the draw, was summoned to her match.

"I was told the match was fragile," she said in the understated tongue of her native England.

The match was fragile if you consider fragile being a young sportswoman gesturing at a linesman and screaming: "——!" It was fragile if you consider fragile being the same young sportswoman slamming her racket into the scoreboard. It was fragile if you consider fragile being Mandlikova looking Clark in the eye and asking: "Why don't you default me?"

Clark stopped just short of that.

First Mandlikova was warned about her behavior. Then she was penalized a point. Then she was penalized a game. And, although it doesn't seem equitable, she was fined $500.

There was a time when you could take the kids to tennis matches and they learned about competition and poise and grace.

Take them to a match today, and chances are all they'll learn is: "——!" ❖

Fontes and Fon-tez

August 14, 1990

They used to joke about it, the way brothers might. The way good friends might.

They used to think about how great it would be to work together someday.

"We both used to say, 'If you get a head-coaching job, I'd be embarrassed if you call me and ask if I want to work with you. I'd just expect to show up and find a desk there with my name on it,' " the older brother said, standing in the end zone of the Silverdome.

And they would slap each other on the back and have a laugh and dream of the day.

In the end, it did not turn out quite that way.

In the end, the younger brother, Wayne Fontes, got the Lions' head-coaching job, and Len Fontes — his heart broken and their joint dream shattered — quit the game of football and took a desk job.

Something happened in Detroit to prevent them from realizing their dream last fall. Some say former general manager Russ Thomas told Wayne Fontes he would not have the Lions' coaching staff turned into a family affair.

But Wayne Fontes denies that, and Len will say only that "there was something on this end that didn't permit it."

So Wayne Fontes hired Billie Matthews — a running backs coach — to coach defensive backs. And Len Fontes, a defensive backfield coach with Super Bowl credentials, resigned his job with the New York Giants and took a job in marketing.

"Because of this Super Bowl ring," Len said, holding up the gaudy bauble won when the Giants defeated Denver in Super Bowl XXI, "my job was golf, lunch and dinner."

After 29 years as a football coach, it was easy work.

Football had always been Len Fontes' work and his love. But when his brother told him their dream was dead, something went out of him.

"I was 51 years old, and I knew I probably wouldn't make it to head coach myself," Len Fontes said. "The dream was going by the book, and I didn't want to be an assistant working for someone else any longer. So I kicked my feet and quit. I was getting out of the game forever."

Len Fontes is 11 months older than Wayne. He has had a career most people would envy, but he has had hardships, too.

When he was 23 — coaching his first team, in Logan, Ohio — their father died, and Len saw it as his duty to quit his job and move back to Canton, Ohio, to help his mother.

"The only job I could get was as phys ed instructor for a bunch of schools, kindergarten through sixth grade," he said. "I was the guy who went around to all the schools and blew the whistle. That was about it.

"My mother has lived with us ever since. I'll say something about 'my mother,' and Wayne will say: 'No, our mother.' "

Eventually — while Wayne was working his way from Visitation High in Bay City to the University of Dayton, to Iowa, Southern California and the Tampa Bay Buccaneers — Len caught on at Canton McKinley High, then Mansfield Madison, Dayton (the year after Wayne left), the Naval Academy and Miami (Fla.) before joining the Giants.

In 1986, when Wayne became the Lions' defensive coordinator, he thought he could, at last, make their dream come true. He asked his brother if he could get out of his contract with the Giants.

"Bill Parcells said no," Len said of the Giants' coach. "I told him it was a lifelong dream for us to coach together. But he wouldn't let me out of my contract."

So Len stayed with the Giants. And that winter, while the Lions won only five games, the Giants won the Super Bowl.

Three years later came the second disappointment.

Whatever the reason, Wayne did not — could not — offer his older brother a job. So Len Fontes left football and Wayne Fontes went about the business of trying to make the Lions a better football team.

Then, over the winter something happened. Maybe it had nothing to do with Russ Thomas. Maybe it had something to do with William Clay Ford. Or with the winning streak the Lions put together in the final five weeks of last season.

Or maybe it had something to do with Wayne Fontes' being hardheaded, refusing to believe no meant no.

Whatever obstacle had been there six months before was somehow resolved, and one day in February the telephone rang on Len Fontes' desk in New Jersey. And on that day he was not on the golf course.

Wayne Fontes, failing to honor the script they had dreamed of all those years, asked his brother: "Well, are you ready to come to work for me?"

But Len, cautious after the previous disappointments, replied: "Don't throw a tease at me. When you're 100 percent certain, when you've got everything straightened out, call me."

A day later, his phone rang again, and Wayne offered him the job of coaching the Lions' secondary, with Matthews becoming running backs coach.

"He said: 'It's a done deal. Would you like to come and work with me?' " Len Fontes recalled. "I told him: 'I'd love to.'

"And it's been even better than we ever thought it would be.

"It's great coaching for him. You can call all the meetings in the world, but I know without that what he wants. We're on the same page."

The Fontes family is close. Each summer the five brothers and their families gather for a joint vacation, highlighted by a three-day golf tournament. But there is at least one quirk about them, too.

Wayne and his brother Arnie, an executive with DuPont in California, pronounce their family name "Fonts." The rest of the family — including Wayne's wife, Evelyn — pronounce it "Fon-tez."

"He says Fonts is more masculine," Len said of his younger brother. "I tell him Fon-tez is more romantic."

Wayne Fontes explains that sometime during his undergraduate days at Michigan State, somebody yelled at him: "Fonts!"

"I didn't correct him, and I've been Fonts ever since, I guess," Wayne Fontes said.

Now the brothers — Fonts and Fon-tez — are one exhibition victory into their first season together, and if anything is better than winning, it is winning with your brother and best friend at your side.

"If there is such a thing as being better friends than brothers," Wayne Fontes said, "we're it."

And his big brother Len admits that when the dream finally came true, "I shed a tear, oh yeah. I had a tear in my eye. So did he."

He is emotional about the opportunity that finally put them in the same locker room. But he is practical, too.

This, a purely emotional man would say, is perfect. To Len Fontes, it is not perfect. Not quite.

"I could ask for more," he said.

"I'd like another big defensive end, another wide receiver."

The brothers Fontes had two seasons together; Len died of a heart attack in May 1992. ❖

Nick Zito

May 7, 1991

LOUISVILLE, Ky. — Sometimes you work until your fingers bleed and your muscles ache and your eyes blur.

Sometimes you work so long, so hard and so far away, your family is just an 8 x 10 on the nightstand.

And when all that work is rewarded — as trainer Nick Zito's was in the 117th Kentucky Derby — you find that it wasn't really worth it, that the prize was not worth the sacrifice.

Sometimes, after all those hours of labor, you look around and no one is standing beside you.

Sometimes you find you have sacrificed your family for your work.

But this time, Nick Zito turned around after Strike the Gold crossed the finish line first and found his wife, Jan, was there.

It was no cinch.

He told her last December he would not be home for Christmas. Or New Year's. He was off to Florida to train a horse that carried his dream. A horse that could win the Kentucky Derby.

Strike the Gold.

Sorry. The job comes first. The horse comes first. Bye. In mid-February, his wife and their children, 5-year-old Sarah and 7-year-old Allie, went to Florida for a five-week visit. They had become a family that visited, that did not live together. Before she arrived in Louisville for the Derby, they had last seen each other ... let's see ... sometime around the 20th of March, they think.

"It puts a strain on a marriage," Jan Zito said. "I knew when I married Nick Zito, if you wanted to be with him, you were going to have to go to the barn; he wasn't going to come to you." And that has been the way it has been.

He has gone his way, she hers. And, occasionally, their paths have crossed.

The Kentucky Derby drove a deep wedge into the relationship because of his intense belief in Strike the Gold and his refusal to let anything interfere with his preparation for the race.

"Last year, they came to the Derby (with Thirty Six Red) on emotion," she said. "This year, they felt they had the horse. He was paranoid. He felt if it didn't win, it would be because he'd missed something."

As the weeks went on, Zito's wife, in New York, heard nothing from him.

But all his employees around the track did. One morning he told a group of writers that he had great admiration for his jockey, Chris Antley, but "if he screws up, I'll just have to run him over with my truck."

Make of it what you will. It could have been the pressures of the upcoming race. It could have been the absence of his wife. It could have been a mixture of the two. Whatever it was, it was making Nick Zito a very tense man. Around the media he was charming, but in the barns he sometimes lost control.

He screamed at Antley and anyone else who was handy, and his wife heard about it when she arrived.

"The help was all ready to quit," she said. "They said he was going off the deep end. They told me if I come to the Preakness, they're going to give me part of their paychecks."

She smiled. It was a joke. Saturday was good for the Zitos. A day to joke and smile and bask in success that had been so difficult to come by.

For a little while, all the hard work was worthwhile. He had been proven right, and when he was, he looked around — at the peak of his career — and found his wife at his side. The next day, though, she flew back to New York.

More long separations? More strains on the marriage? More need to weigh the career against the family?

"No," he said. "We'll be at Pimlico for two weeks. Then in three weeks we'll be in New York (for the Belmont Stakes). "We'll be OK now."

I love happy endings. ❖

Football widow

October 24, 1991

Fifty-four thousand of us saw her husband die, saw him topple over on the cold Tiger Stadium grass and take his final breath as Dick Butkus waved frantically for somebody — anybody — to help.

It was 20 years ago today, and Sharon Hughes has lived with a nasty memory for all those years.

Chuck Hughes died the most visible death in the history of the NFL, taken in an instant when a blood clot lodged in an already clogged artery killed him with 62 seconds left in the Lions' 28-23 loss to the Chicago Bears.

He was a lean wide receiver from Texas, 6-feet, 180 pounds, with hands that were quicker than his feet. He had just run a pass pattern, but Greg Landry instead threw an incompletion to Charlie Sanders. Hughes turned toward the Lions' forming huddle, took a couple of steps, threw both hands to his chest and fell facefirst at the 25-yard line.

And Sharon Hughes gasped.

They had been married four years earlier, after he finished his eligibility at Texas Western, and lived off TV dinners until he was drafted by the Philadelphia Eagles. Times got better. Their son Shane was born in 1969, and Hughes was traded to the Lions before the 1970 season. They had their whole lives ahead of them.

But, like all marriages, there were bad times.

One of the worst was Saturday, Oct. 23, 1971.

They had been invited to an afternoon party, and he wanted to leave their apartment at noon, but she spent the morning visiting with a friend. They argued when she wasn't ready at the appointed time.

At the party, they argued whether Shane — then 23 months old — should chew gum. His father didn't allow it. Sharon had been allowing it for some time. Chuck told her to take the gum out of the child's mouth. She refused. A silly argument escalated until they were shouting at each other.

"I'll tell you one thing!" she finally screamed. "I'm going to get rid of you or Shane before the end of the week because I can't live with both of you. It just won't work." Sharon Hughes went home from the party. Chuck Hughes went to the team hotel with his teammates.

They never spoke again. And 24 hours later, he was dead.

Sharon Hughes didn't get to tell him good-bye.

She didn't get to tell him she loved him.

She didn't get to tell him she was sorry.

"For years, I beat myself up," she said from her home in San Antonio. "I always felt it was my fault. When you make a threat like that … I felt they should have arrested me for murder."

She cried away a lot of dark, lonely nights. And when a second marriage was dissolving and she felt most alone, she clung to the memories of her college sweetheart for solace.

"I was feeling so sad, I just wanted someone to love me," she said. "And I could always fall back on those memories. I was lying in bed one night, and I saw the curtains moving, and I knew he was there with me. The windows were closed, but it wasn't hot enough to have the air conditioning on. I know the difference between dreams and visitations.

"I know it sounds crazy. When I was 25, when he died, I had no idea little souls could touch back in with us on Earth. But they can."

Plainly, she is self-conscious talking about visits from her dead husband. But, just as plainly, she believes it happens.

"We didn't talk," she said. "He didn't call Saturday evening. He always called Sunday morning before games, but he didn't call that Sunday morning. We never did get to amend the problem. I think he feels bad we didn't make up." Now, she said, he "touches in quite often."

There was the night Shane Hughes rented his first tuxedo and walked into his mother's bedroom and asked: "Well, Mom, what do you think?"

"I was just thinking: 'I'd give anything if Chuck could see Shane in that tux,' " she said. "And just then the hall light flickered. Shane said: 'What was that?' and I told him, 'Well, I have to tell you, that's Chuck.' "

There have been other instances, too. She said porch lights have been mysteriously turned off and on, and a bathroom heater was once turned on without explanation.

"My girlfriends say: 'After 20 years, how can you still talk about Chuck?' But the relationship I have with Chuck still exists today. It's always been a warm feeling."

Four years ago, she composed a letter to her husband. She told him all the things she didn't tell him in 1971. She told him the things he had missed, the Little League games, the prom, that his son — now a college student — had inherited his father's high cholesterol level. She wrote that she doesn't cry as much as she used to and how much she still misses him.

The letter was therapy for her. Now she can do no more.

But, she admits, it does not make up for what was. And for what wasn't.

"It's too late," she said. "You never think it's gonna be. We never got to say 'I'm sorry.' You're young, and you say things that are mean, and you think there's always tomorrow to say you're sorry."

Twenty years ago, she learned no tomorrows are guaranteed. And when her son grew from childhood to adolescence to manhood, she missed no opportunity to show her love.

"I always made it a point to give Shane a hug and kiss him good night no matter what he'd been in that afternoon," she said.

Sharon Hughes never told her husband she was sorry they had argued over chewing gum. She never told him she did not mean it when she said she could not live with him and their son.

And the memory haunts her. You think there's always tomorrow.

There is, though, only the present. Only now to pick up the telephone, to call someone, to tell 'em it was silly. It didn't mean a thing. To say you're sorry.

Sharon Hughes never did that. And she has regretted it for 20 years. ❖